PILLARS OF THE REPUBLIC

Pillars OF THE Republic

COMMON SCHOOLS and AMERICAN SOCIETY

1780-1860

Carl F. Kaestle

Consulting Editor
ERIC FONER

HILL AND WANG · NEW YORK

Library of Congress Cataloging-in-Publication Data
Kaestle, Carl F.
Pillars of the republic.
(American century series)
Includes bibliographical references and index.
1. Public schools—United States—History—18th
century. 2. Public schools—United States—History—
19th century.   I. Foner, Eric.   II. Title.
LA215.K33   1983   371'.01'0973   82-21163

To Liz

Contents

Preface

DURING the three decades before the American Civil War, state governments in the North created common-school systems. They passed legislation for tax-supported elementary schools and appointed state school officers. Reform-minded legislators and educators urged higher local school expenditures, more schooling for children, and the beginnings of professional training for teachers. Their goal was an improved and unified school system. Although there has been a resurgence of interest in American educational history during the past twenty years, no one has subjected the rise of common-school systems to sustained analysis since the influential works of Ellwood Cubberley, Paul Monroe, and other early twentieth-century historians who associated public schooling with democracy, progress, and humanitarian reform. In the meantime, books about particular urban communities by so-called revisionist historians have opened up new questions and developed new theories about the purposes of common schooling in the pre–Civil War era, challenging the focus, the tone, and the values of the Cubberley generation. I was thus pleased when Arthur Wang asked me to undertake a reassessment of the origins of common-school systems.

This book is the culmination of a series of books and articles I have written about the history of schooling. It draws on much of my earlier research on England and the American Northeast, as well as upon new research I have undertaken on the Midwest and the South. There is much description in the book—of rural district schools, of urban charity schools, of the legislative battles waged by reformers, and of the institutions they worked to establish, such as teachers' institutes and graded schools. Thus the book is structured around many traditional categories in the institutional and political history of education, and it should serve as an introduction for readers new to the subject. It offers, however, a new interpretation of the origins of public schooling and of the nature of popular resistance to that reform. I emphasize, for example, that there was a substantial rise in school enrollments in the first fifty years of the nation's history, prior to the common-school reform movement; that unlike England, America witnessed virtually no opposition to popular education per se, only to a structure of state control and financing and to the attempt to gather all groups into a common system with a common curriculum; and that the tension between localist tradition and centralizing innovation was the main dynamic in the drama of school reform after 1830.

I argue that the eventual acceptance of state common-school systems was encouraged by Americans' commitment to republican government, by the dominance of native Protestant culture, and by the development of capitalism. I argue that in translating republican, Protestant, and capitalist values into public policy, leaders were guided by a particular ideology. The reform version of this ideology called for state-regulated common schools to integrate and assimilate a diverse population into the nation's political, economic, and cultural institutions. This ideology and various aspects of the reform program were opposed by independent-minded local-control advocates, many Southern slaveholders, members of non-English and non-Protestant groups who favored cultural distinctiveness and independent schooling, blacks who had been left out of the new common-school systems, and a smattering of full-fledged radicals who opposed the whole religious and economic underpinning of the predominant ideology. These groups did not make common cause with each other, did not have the same goals, and did not succeed in preventing the creation of state common-school systems. They did, however, achieve various concessions and adjustments, thus contributing to the shape and content of American common schooling as it existed by 1860.

This book is about schools, not about all education. Families, churches, apprenticeships, and other institutions continued to play important educational roles in the early republic. But this was also the period during which the school was emerging as the principal agent of cognitive and moral teaching and as an important instrument of public policy. This book attempts to explain that process. It looks beyond schools to the broader economic and cultural context, but only in order to explain changes in the organization and purposes of schooling. If one wants to understand state policy toward education, schools are the appropriate focus. Society educates in many ways; the state educates through schools.

The chapters of this book are organized around two chronological periods, the early national period (1780 to 1830) and the antebellum period (1830 to 1860). Within these periods chapters are organized on a topical basis. After a brief prologue about the educational ideas of the founding fathers, two chapters describe rural and urban schooling in the early national period and note some connections between education and social changes between 1780 and 1830. The next four chapters concentrate on the North in the antebellum period. The argument moves from social structure to ideology, then to the reformers' program, and then to popular reaction. Common-school developments in the midwestern states generally followed the same lines as those in the Northeast. This raises some interesting questions about the causes of successful common-school systematization, because the Midwest was less industrial and less urban than the Northeast. Most southern states, in contrast, did not adopt tax-supported, state-regulated common schools by the time of the Civil War. Historians have long characterized the South as a region with different educational attitudes and institutions. This is a half-truth. There was much common-school reform effort and support in the South. Nonetheless, the North-South contrast is important. I have therefore postponed discussion of the South, except for occasional references, until a final chapter on regional differences in common-school reform.

By "common school" I mean an elementary school intended to serve all the children in an area. An expensive independent school, obviously, would not be a "common school," but neither would a charity school open only to the poor. Some of the tuition schools of the early national period were quite inexpensive and enrolled children from a variety of family circumstances. I have called these "common pay schools." "Common school" was not synonymous with "free school." In both the North and the South, even after the creation of state common-school systems, parents were often required to pay part of the cost of their child's instruction in common schools. Conversely, a "free school" was not always a "common school," for the term "free school" was often applied to charity schools attended only by the children of the poor.

The history of common schooling is complicated not only by endless local variation but by the fact that each state was different, and by 1860 there were thirty-three states. In doing my research I adopted Lord Bacon's advice that some books are to be tasted, others to be swallowed, and some few to be chewed and digested. I did considerable archival work in some states; for others I concentrated on the published primary and secondary sources; and others I studied only incidentally as topical interests led me into the sources. I have not attempted to cover the states west of the Mississippi. Because state policies about common schooling had little impact on Native and Hispanic Americans in the pre–Civil War East, these groups play no part in my analysis.

I have included a few pages of some previously published articles in this book. These include a portion of " 'The Scylla of Brutal Ignorance and the Charybdis of a Literary Education': Elite Attitudes Toward Mass Education in Early Industrial England and America," in Lawrence Stone, ed., *School and Society* (Baltimore, 1976), reprinted by permission of the editor and the Johns Hopkins University Press; a portion of "Social Change, Discipline and the Common School in Early Nineteenth-Century America," in the *Journal of Interdisciplinary History* 9 (Summer 1978), reprinted by permission of *The Journal of Interdisciplinary History* and the MIT Press, Cambridge, Massachusetts; and a portion of "Ideology and American Educational History," in the *History of Education Quarterly* 22 (Summer 1982), reprinted by permission of the *History of Education Quarterly*.

The endnotes in this book serve three purposes. They give the source of direct quotations so that interested researchers can check the context of the remark and read more of the arguments of the historical actors from whom I have drawn my examples. The notes also provide suggestions for further reading on special topics. In the index I have included references to those endnotes that cite basic secondary works. Finally, the notes give credit where I have relied upon other historians' works for background. In order to reduce the distractions of scholarly apparatus, I have placed note references only at the ends of paragraphs. In the notes I have omitted references if the source is already obvious in the text, most often in the case of annual education reports of states or towns. After noting the most helpful reference works on a particular topic, I have not repeated their titles to document general narrative details, nor have I provided notes to document statistics readily available from the United States Census volumes or other common works. Readers who are willing to accept on faith that the quotations are accurate, and who have no plans to dig further on particular topics, may safely ignore the endnotes. None of them discusses events, terminology, or interpretations.

In writing this book, I have been fortunate to have financial support, excellent research assistants, and keen, critical colleagues. The book benefited from some technical and more narrowly focused earlier projects and from the grants that supported them. These include a research grant from the National Institute of Education (1973–76), a John Simon Guggenheim Fellowship (1977–78), a Romnes Faculty Fellowship (1978–83) and other support from the Research Committee of the Graduate School, University of Wisconsin, and a grant from the Royalty Fund of the Wisconsin Center for Education Research. My judgments, however, do not necessarily reflect the position of the National Institute of Education, and no one should infer any official endorsement by NIE or by any of the other funding agencies mentioned above.

My research assistants have included JoAnne Brown, Martha Coons, John Jenkins, Jacqueline Jones, William Reese, and Mark Van Pelt. I have relied upon their superb work for many details and insights. Others who have commented on various drafts of the chapters include: Bernard Bailyn, John Cooper, Jurgen Herbst, Daniel Rodgers, John Rury, David Tyack, and Maris Vinovskis. During my very rewarding sojourn in Australia in 1981 many scholars commented on seminar presentations based on chapters of this book. In particular I am indebted to Donald

DeBats and Paul Bourke of the American Studies discipline at
Flinders University, South Australia, as well as various members
of the Adelaide Social History Group, the Faculty of Education
at Melbourne University, and the Faculty of Education at Monash
University. Some have suggested problems that I was unable to
resolve or revisions that I was unwilling to make. Thus, to re-
state the ritual caveat, I urge readers not to blame my faults on
my friends. At the University of Wisconsin, the staffs of the
Department of Educational Policy Studies and the Department
of History have been unceasingly supportive; in particular I wish
to thank Mary Jo Gessler and especially Jean Kennedy, who has
typed some of the chapters more times than either of us cares to
remember.

From start to finish I have had patience, encouragement, and
expert editorial advice from Arthur Wang and Eric Foner. They
have been gracious about a project that got behind schedule, and
they have made the book better through meticulous stylistic
suggestions and substantive challenges to my ideas.

The constant support of my wife, Elizabeth MacKenzie Kaestle,
has soothed the frustrations that resulted from trying to think
seriously about the writing of this book while taking my turn as
chair of an academic department. I owe much of my sanity and
my happiness to her companionship.

C.F.K.

"American democracy is supported by a thousand pillars . . . I mean, and you must have anticipated me, our free schools. These are in truth the very bulwark of our Republic."

Andrew Lunt, *Anniversary Address*
before the Salem Charitable Mechanic Association
(Salem, 1835)

PILLARS OF THE REPUBLIC

1

Prologue: The Founding Fathers and Education

RUDIMENTARY learning was widespread in Revolutionary America. Conditions in the British colonies had fostered education. Migration drawn largely from the middling social ranks of England and the continent resulted in a disproportionately literate population. Protestants in general, and particularly the Calvinist groups that predominated in the northern colonies, stressed Bible reading and early education as preparation for salvation. The colonies' commercial development and broad male franchise reinforced the importance of literacy for adults. Americans of the revolutionary era valued elementary education. Figures on schooling and literacy suggest that a majority of white men in the new nation could read and write. Indicators of women's literacy were rising, and the availability of schools was increasing at the time of the Revolution.

Elementary education among white Americans was accomplished through parental initiative and informal, local control of institutions. In a few cases, New England colonial legislatures tried to ensure that towns would provide schools or that parents would not neglect their children's education, but these laws were weakly enforced. Elsewhere the central colonial governments played little role in education. Towns or neighborhoods often decided to provide schools, funded in a variety of ways. Attendance was voluntary and usually involved some charges to parents. Other local communities left schooling to the initiative of families, who formed groups to organize subscription schools, or sent their children to study with entrepreneurial private-venture teachers or inexpensive "dame" schools in their neighborhoods. Most children attended school at some time, but much education also came through the family, the church, and the workplace. Some poor children were instructed in church-affiliated charity schools; others did without schooling, remaining illiterate or picking up the three R's from parents or friends. Nowhere was schooling entirely tax supported or compulsory. The demand for education did not come principally from above, although political leaders and ministers sometimes argued the importance of schooling. The proliferation of private-venture schools in the cities and neighborhood district schools in rural areas was a response to popular demand. Provincial America's informal, unsystematic, local mode of schooling resulted in a relatively high level of elementary education and proved capable of expansion.[1]

Nonetheless, educational opportunity was uneven at the time of the Revolution, and training beyond the rudiments was not widespread. The South's literacy rate lagged behind the North's, while in all areas, women, blacks, Native Americans, and poor whites were to differing degrees excluded from the culture of the printed English word. In the large commercial seaports, poverty had increased in the years preceding the Revolution, as had factional politics and ideological splintering. In the turbulent revolutionary decades, urban dwellers witnessed crowd actions that sometimes went beyond the intentions of their leaders. These tendencies to fragmentation added to the anxieties of newly won independence and created an urgent quest for coherence, discipline, and public unity among the new nation's leaders.[2]

The nation's Founding Fathers knew from classical political theory that the most stable governments combined elements of monarchy, aristocracy, and democracy. But Americans had expelled monarchy, and revolutionary leaders stood firm against the creation of a formal American aristocracy. How, then, were they to escape the degeneration into anarchy that they believed was the inevitable fate of pure democracies? They pinned their hopes on the creation of a republic, a representative form of government in which the general will would be refined and articulated by the best men. Here again, though, classical theory and much contemporary opinion warned them that republican government would not work in a country as large as America, especially with its well-defined sections and heterogeneous population. The perception of a precarious national government was intensified by disorders like the Whiskey Rebellion in Pennsylvania and Shays' Rebellion in Massachusetts. Political theorists and policy makers were therefore concerned not only with protecting liberty, for which the Revolution had been fought, but also with maintaining order, without which all might be lost. Education could play an important role in reconciling freedom and order. A sound education would prepare men to vote intelligently and prepare women to train their sons properly. Moral training based on the Protestant Bible would produce virtuous, well-behaved citizens. Not just the three R's but "an acquaintance with ethics and with the general principles of law, commerce, money and government is necessary for the yeomanry of a republican state," said Noah Webster.[3]

Republicanism united concepts of virtue, balanced government, and liberty. By "virtue," republican essayists meant discipline, sacrifice, simplicity, and intelligence, and they called upon ministers, teachers, and parents to aid in the creation and maintenance of a virtuous citizenry. Virtue and intelligence did not necessarily depend upon deliberate instruction, however. Republican thought emphasized the natural virtue and intelligence of a landed yeomanry. The symbols of American rural virtue were prominent in political discussions of the revolutionary era. Two problems undermined that faith in natural virtue. America had increasing numbers of citizens who were not landed yeomen; the natural virtue of such citizens could not be assumed. Also, factional politics became magnified as independence thrust upon the colonies the necessity of political union. To foster the intelligence required of republican citizens, some of America's most eloquent political leaders looked to education—not just through the informal colonial modes of instruction but through schools organized and financed by the states.

Along with anxieties about the future of the republic these men shared a sense of opportunity, of responsibility to mankind, a sense that a real revolution had been made, that they could build a new society based on enlightened ideas about the perfectibility of men and institutions. Here was a chance for a real departure from corrupt Europe. This was the ideal of the American Revolution, and education had a critical role in it. The ideal demanded new efforts and new forms of organization. "We have only finished the first act of the great drama," wrote Benjamin Rush, the Philadelphia physician and statesman. "It remains yet to effect a revolution in our principles, opinions, and manners so as to accommodate them to the forms of government we have adopted." Noah Webster argued that for the new state governments to aid colleges and academies while they did nothing about free common schooling was a glaring contradiction in a country where "every citizen who is worth a few shillings" can vote. "The constitutions are republican and the laws of education are monarchical," he complained.[4]

In the preamble of his 1779 bill for free schools in Virginia, Thomas Jefferson laid out the basic logic of state-sponsored schools for republican citizenship. Citizens must choose leaders wisely, defeat ambition and corruption in politics, and protect liberty by keeping a vigilant eye on government. All citizens should have a chance not only to vote but to be elected. The government needs wise and honest laws, Jefferson argued, and thus it needs educated and virtuous lawmakers. In a republic, these men must be chosen "without regard to wealth, birth or other accidental condition." Because there are many people who cannot afford a good education, Jefferson argued, all should share the cost, in order to foster the best possible representative government.[5]

A thoroughly American curriculum would help unify the language and culture of the new nation and wean America away from a corrupt Europe. "For America in her infancy to adopt the maxims of the Old World," said Webster in his famous spelling book, "would be to stamp the wrinkles of old age upon the bloom of youth, and to plant the seed of decay in a vigorous constitution." Instead, he advised, "begin with the infant in his cradle . . . let the first word he lisps be 'Washington.' " "The national character is not yet formed," wrote Webster in 1790. Common schools are needed to instill in American children "an inviolable attachment to their own country." Benjamin Rush joined Webster in emphasizing the theme of national integration, urging the creation of a national university "where the youth of all the states may be melted (as it were) together into one mass of citizens."[6]

In an essay on common-school education written in 1786, Rush's anxieties got the best of him, leaving a memorable and somewhat chilling reminder of the harsh side of revolutionary educational thought:

> In the education of youth, let the authority of our masters be as absolute as possible. . . . By this mode of education we prepare our youth for the subordination of laws and thereby qualify them for becoming good citizens of the republic. I am satisfied that the most useful citizens have been formed from those youth who have never known or felt their own wills till they were one and twenty years of age.

Then, in a famous line, Rush declared, "I consider it as possible to convert men into republican machines. This must be done if we expect them to perform their parts properly in the great machine of the state." Although Rush's flamboyant language is unusual, many shared his desire to achieve political conformity and disciplined behavior through education.[7]

Other educational theorists, however, wrote about the positive, liberating values of republicanism. In a prize-winning essay on education written in 1797, Samuel Harrison Smith, a Washington newspaper editor, listed five reasons for the broad diffusion of knowledge in the United States.

1. An enlightened nation is always most tenacious of its rights.
2. It is not in the interest of such a society to perpetuate error.
3. In a republic the sources of happiness are open to all without injuring any.
4. If happiness be made at all to depend on the improvement of the mind and the collision of mind with mind, the happiness of an individual will greatly depend upon the general diffusion of knowledge. . . .
5. Under a republic . . . man feels as strong a bias to improvement as under a despotism he feels an impulse to ignorance and depression.[8]

Writers like Smith stressed the exercise of liberty and unfettered intelligence more than the need for social order. All republican educational theorists, however, emphasized the heavy responsibilities of citizenship and the importance of moral training for the survival of republican institutions. "The virtues of men are of more consequence to society than their abilities," said Webster. While they reconciled freedom and order in different ways, these writers were similarly preoccupied with those two philosophical poles. They produced many proposals for state-supported common schooling, which they believed would contribute to disciplined, republican liberty.[9]

But did these republican educational theorists have any impact on the actual schooling of children in the new republic? Some commentators lamented the conditions of American schools in the 1780s and 1790s and joined in the chorus for reform. Governor George Clinton warned the New York legislature in 1782 that the war had created a "chasm in education," and he urged the members to encourage schooling for citizenship and restraint. Robert Coram of Delaware thought that schools outside the large towns were "completely despicable, wretched, and contemptible" and that the teachers were "shamefully deficient." This conviction that there was a "chasm" in education prompted some prominent men in the early national period to argue for state laws requiring free local schools, or even to argue for systematic state aid to common schools, both ideas without precedent in America. Even the oft-cited Massachusetts school laws of the seventeenth century had insisted only that towns maintain schools, not that they had to be free. No one had imagined anything as comprehensive as the plans of the Revolutionary generation.[10]

Flush with the enthusiasm and the anxieties of new nationhood, Thomas Jefferson proposed for Virginia a three-tiered system of local education—free elementary schools, twenty regional academies with free tuition for selected boys, and support at William and Mary College for the best ten needy academy graduates. Jefferson also envisioned regional-level supervision and general oversight of a statewide curriculum by the faculty of the college. These features were unheard of before Jefferson's proposal of 1779. In Pennsylvania, Benjamin Rush introduced a similar plan in 1786, calling for a state-supported university in Philadelphia, four colleges around the state, and free schools in every town. By this plan, he said, "the whole state will be tied together by one system of education." Revered by historians as harbingers of later state systems, these proposals failed to win legislative approval and had little or no effect on schooling at the local level. The persistent Jefferson introduced his 1779 plan again in the 1790s and in 1817, but each time it failed. As his supporter Joseph Cabell told him, "neither the people nor the representatives would agree" to property taxes for a general system of common schools. In the 1780s Jefferson had attributed the defeat of his Virginia school bill to the people's economic anxieties and the state government's scant resources. But by 1817 he charged that the proposal was foiled by "ignorance, malice, egoism, fanaticism, religious, political and local perversities." Virginians did not adopt a statewide free school system until 1870. In the meantime, they settled for a policy of charity schools for the poor. Rush's plan met a similar fate in Pennsylvania, where opposition to free common schooling was still fierce in the 1830s.[11]

William Wirt, an English visitor, said that Jefferson's bill had failed in the 1780s because "the comprehensive views and generous patriotism which produced the bill, have not prevailed throughout the country." But there was more principle to the opposition than Wirt's statement implied. The very devotion to liberty that schooling was designed to protect also made local citizens skeptical of new forms of taxation by the state, and of new institutional regulation by the central government. Furthermore, it was not clear to members of hard-pressed state legislatures that the republic would collapse without new systems of common schooling, or that the existing mode of local and parental initiative was insufficient. Resistance to new taxes, devotion to local control and individual choice, and a faith in existing educational arrangements—these were the factors that foiled early plans for state systems of free common schooling. While the great ideas of the American Revolution had some impact on the popular mind and found much practical expression in new state and national political arrangements, many local institutions were largely unchanged. This was the case with schooling. The Revolution was not a social cataclysm, and Rush's vision of a state school system to make "republican machines" in Pennsylvania remained only a vision during his lifetime.

Farther to the North, however, republican enthusiasm for education bore some legislative fruit. Massachusetts in 1789, then New York and Connecticut in 1795, tried three quite different approaches to state encouragement of elementary schooling. The Massachusetts law, similar to its colonial precedents, required towns of fifty or more families to provide an elementary school for at least six months a year and required towns of two hundred or more families to provide a grammar school where classical languages would be taught. It is difficult, however, to gauge the educational impact of the 1789 law. Because most towns already provided partially free elementary schools, because the grammar-school provisions were widely unheeded and unenforced, because the law provided no state financial aid, and because the permissive clause authorizing the organization of school districts merely recognized an already common practice, the law probably had a very modest effect on popular schooling in Massachusetts.

New York's legislation, in contrast, provided substantial state aid to local schools. Since 1784 New York had had a general education board, called the Regents, who granted charters and financial assistance to incorporated colleges and academies. In 1795 Governor Clinton complained that this aid was "confined to the children of the opulent" and urged state aid to common schools. The legislature responded with a five-year law appropriating $50,000 a year to be divided among local common-school committees that agreed to match at least half of their state allotment with local funds. The state money came from land sales and interest on surplus capital. These funds proved insufficient by 1799 and necessitated a direct property tax. In 1800 the state's senate, unwilling to tax property for education, refused to renew the law.[12]

It is difficult to assess the local impact of this early educational legislation in New York. Its effects were certainly more tangible than those of the Massachusetts law. Substantial sums of money reached the local level; we cannot assume that these funds would have been raised in some other way if the state had not acted. In 1800, 58,000 children attended the state-assisted schools, about 37 percent of all children from birth to age nineteen in the counties that reported receiving funds (sixteen of twenty-three counties). This is quite an impressive enrollment rate. If we assumed, for example, that the usual school age was approximately four to thirteen, about 75 percent of all school-age children would have been enrolled for some period of the year in these counties in 1800. Unfortunately, there are no systematic enrollment rates from the years just preceding or just following the five years that New York's school aid law was in effect, so we cannot tell whether the state aid increased enrollments or not. The New York State law of 1795 was a more thoroughgoing effort at state encouragement of schooling than the Massachusetts law of 1789, but it was unusual for its time, its impact is uncertain, and it was in any case short-lived. In the minds of most New Yorkers, apparently, republican education did not require state intervention.[13]

The most unusual law was Connecticut's of 1795. The legislature voted to sell all of its land in the Western Reserve territory, which resulted in the receipt of $1,200,000, with which it created a permanent school fund. The interest of the fund was distributed to localities for teachers' salaries, with no strings attached and no matching requirement. The state collected a supplementary property tax of $2 per $1,000 of assessed value until 1820, when the interest from the school fund was sufficient to render the tax unnecessary. Local school areas, based on existing Congregational Church parish lines but with no clerical involvement, were called "school societies." They were free to raise additional funds by taxes or by tuition. Some societies merely paid the teachers' salaries with the state money for as many months as it lasted and then charged tuition for supplementary months. This practice, which avoided local school taxes, apparently increased in the 1820s and 1830s, leading to the charge by school reformers that the 1795 law had vitiated local initiative. Nonetheless, the interest distributed from the school fund was considerable, averaging $50,000 a year in the 1810s and rising to over $100,000 a year in the 1840s. From the 1790s until the 1820s some foreign visitors and some American commentators rated Connecticut's common schools as the best in the country. This may have been nothing more than a coincidence, however. Common schooling did not languish in other states for lack of support. Elsewhere in the Northeast, local taxes and tuition sufficed to meet local needs. Statements like George Clinton's, that there was a "chasm" in post-Revolutionary education, do not reveal very much about actual school conditions in the new republic. Rather than looking for legislative precedents of modern school systems in this period, we should ask what kind of schooling ordinary people sought in the new republic, and what the institutional results were.

2

Rural Schools in the Early Republic

MOST Americans in the early national period lived in dispersed farm communities or very small towns. The proportion of people living in places with fewer than 2,500 inhabitants was 95 percent in 1790, and it was still 91 percent in 1830. In the rural Northeast and the new Midwest, the characteristic school was the district school, organized and controlled by a small locality and financed by some combination of property taxes, fuel contributions, tuition payments, and state aid. The district system had become prevalent in the North during the second half of the eighteenth century, as population dispersed outward from towns, and outlying neighborhoods demanded control of their schools. In the South, more commonly, itinerant schoolmasters selected a location on their own initiative and set tuition rates for parents who chose to send their children, or they were engaged by a group of parents to teach a term in a neighborhood "old-field school," a log cabin built on useless fallow land. Often these schools were not very different in curriculum or clientele from district schools in the North, though a smaller proportion of southern white children attended schools. The terms "public" and "private" did not have their present connotations, and most schools did not fit neatly into either of our modern categories.

When one investigates the actual history of district education, the first image that crumbles is that of the "little red schoolhouse," high on a hill and surrounded by a meadow. Schoolhouses of this period were not red; they were log or unpainted clapboard. Nor

13

were they in idyllic locations. Cleared land was scarce, and schoolhouses were usually located on plots that were good for nothing else, often next to highways or on swampy ground. Referring to Connecticut in the early nineteenth century, Heman Humphrey wrote, "all the school-houses that I remember stood close by the travelled road, without any playgrounds or enclosures whatever." Parents in a district often quarreled vociferously over the location of the schoolhouse, each wanting it as close as possible to home. In a book called *Sketches of American Character* (1829), Sarah Hale parodied the selection of a district school site: "The only requisite was, to fix precisely on the centre of the district; and after measuring in every direction, the centre had been discovered exactly in the centre of a frog-pond. As near that pond as safety would permit, stood the schoolhouse." School officials of the 1840s bemoaned the poor location of schoolhouses, claiming that it demonstrated public indifference to education. Schoolhouses are "sometimes adjacent to a cooper's shop or between a blacksmith's shop and a sawmill," wrote Michigan's Superintendent of Public Instruction. Reform-minded school officials had a jaundiced view of district schools, but on this point they were unanimous. There may have been some sturdy, ample schoolhouses in spacious fields, but they were the exceptions.[1]

The number of children attending these schoolhouses varied widely from district to district. Although one usually associates large classes and overcrowding with urban schools, the rural district schools in the North were often too small to accommodate the increased number of students who attended in the winter months, when farmwork slackened. "Not unfrequently sixty or seventy scholars were daily shut up six hours, where there was hardly room for thirty," said Heman Humphrey. Descriptions of the interiors of district schoolhouses of the period 1780 to 1840 are remarkably similar. The usual plan included built-in desks around three walls, with benches on which the older children could face either their desks or the center of the room. In the center of the floor were benches for the younger children, generally close to the stove or fireplace. The teacher's desk, on a low platform, was positioned in front of the fourth wall or in the center, depending on the location of the stove. Into these one-room schoolhouses tumbled the children of rural republican America. They began at younger ages and enrolled in greater proportions than their urban contemporaries. By the age of four or five, and until the age of about fourteen, most rural children in the North and a substantial number of white children in the South attended school at some time during the year. This does not mean that they received more education than children in cities, for the sessions were short, usually two or three months each in winter and summer. Beginning at about age ten, children typically attended only the winter session, when farm work slackened. There was no standard age for beginning school, and teachers did not attempt to prevent the attendance of toddlers, often as young as three years old, although one teacher called them "trundle bed trash."[2]

Many reminiscences tell of children beginning school at surprisingly young ages. Warren Burton, author of *The District School As It Was,* entered a school at Wilton, New Hampshire, in 1804 at the age of three and a half and became an "abecedarian," as the beginners were called. Horace Greeley, the famous New York editor, also grew up in New Hampshire. He began school when he was two years and ten months old. Elizabeth Buffum, another memoir writer, was born in 1806 and grew up in Woonsocket, Rhode Island. "When I was two years old," she said, "I began to be taken to the Quaker meeting as well as to school. . . . When I was three years old I could read very well." Not all children were such prodigies, however. William Mowry of Rhode Island wrote that learning the whole alphabet "would take probably the entire summer term," and for some children "a whole year would pass before this task was successfuly accomplished."[3]

Parents who sent very young children to school seem to have done so through a desire to have them out from under foot as much as from eagerness to get them started on the three R's early. One memoir speaks of "the front seats for the little ones sent to school to relieve the mothers of their care at home," and another refers to a two-year-old "sent to school to relieve his mother from trouble, rather than learn." One can understand the desire of rural mothers with busy work schedules to be freed from the care of toddlers. Whatever the motives of the parents, the youngest children did very little intellectual training in district schools. William Mowry said that when he went to school, the abecedarians got about five minutes of instruction twice a day reciting the alphabet. The rest of the time, he said, "we had nothing to do but to look on and thus cultivate our powers of observation."[4]

Two features of district schools added to the burden of the toddlers' inactivity. The benches, according to an apparently inviolable tradition, were backless, and high enough so that most children's feet did not touch the floor. "A more complete rack of torture and machine for making cripples could hardly be invented," said Hiram Orcutt. Also, the benches for little children were always closest to the fire, so that in addition to boredom, cramped muscles, and demands for silence, they had to contend with waves of heat radiating from the stove. Heman Humphrey remembered that "many of the smaller children had to sit all day with their legs dangling between the bench and the floor. Poor little things! nodding, and trying to keep their balance on the slabs, without any backs to lean against." Drowsiness was a constant tendency. A dramatic anecdote is found in the memoir of John Burroughs, who grew up in the Catskill Mountains of New York: "One afternoon the oblivion of sleep came over me, and when I came to consciousness again I was in a neighbor's house on a couch, and the smell of camphor pervaded the room. I had fallen off the seat backward and hit my head on the protruding stones of the unplastered wall behind me and cut a hole in it, and I suppose for the moment effectively scattered my childish wits."[5]

After children had learned the alphabet, they began memorizing words of one syllable and practicing vowel exercises like "ab, eb, ib, ob, ub, ac, ec, ic, oc, uc, ad, ed, id, od, ud." They practiced writing on slates and eventually with quill pens in copybooks. Students also worked their way through elementary readers, spellers, and arithmetics. The textbooks of Englishman John Dilworth were the best sellers until Noah Webster's nationalistic texts displaced them during the early nineteenth century. Some district schools and old-field schools offered older children a smattering of grammar, geography, and other subjects, but generally students were occupied with reading, writing, and arithmetic. Elementary arithmetic usually stopped at the mysterious "rule of three," a formula for solving ratios. The Old and New Testaments were common reading books in the early nineteenth century, and some district schools even used catechisms.

Despite many similarities of architecture, curriculum, and local financing, rural schools also reflected the nation's diversity. Rural schools were tied to their communities; as those communities varied, so did their schools. In some areas, teachers taught in foreign languages. Schools included different religious exercises according to local majority preference. Academies that dotted the countryside sometimes had distinctive religious or ethnic affiliations.

Within a single district elementary school, diversity of another sort challenged teachers. Most teachers attempted to group children into "classes" based on the level of their primers, but this was often frustrated by the diversity of texts owned by parents. By jealously defended tradition, children studied from the texts their families sent with them to school. A historian of Wisconsin education concluded that "each child would bring to school whatever the family happened to have, often books that had been brought along by his parents when they came to Wisconsin. There were sometimes as many different textbooks in use in a school as there were children in attendance." This complication, together with the diversity of pupils' ages, especially in winter session, presented teachers with the pedagogical challenge of the district school: how to keep order and accomplish something in schoolrooms that typically had forty to fifty and sometimes sixty children, when there was no convenient way to group them. Theodore Dwight described the confusion that could result. In a school he visited in Connecticut in the 1830s "the teacher was mending pens for one class, which was sitting idle; hearing another spell; calling a covey of small boys to be quiet, who had nothing to do but make mischief; watching a big rogue who had been placed standing on a bench in the middle of the room for punishment; and, to many little ones, passionately answering questions of 'May I go out?' 'May I go home?' 'Shan't Johnny be still?' 'May I drink?' "[6]

In the face of these challenges, some teachers did well and some did poorly. There is no way to generalize about the success of teachers in the rural schools of the early republic. Yet memoirs do allow some generalizations about the ways in which teachers coped with large groups of children. Partly from necessity and partly from conviction, teachers made memorization the children's major task. Despite a certain amount of talk about the need for children to understand what they were learning, the routine portrayed in school memoirs seldom deviated: children studied at their desks in preparation for rote recitation in front of the teacher. "Repetition, drilling, line upon line, and precept upon precept, with here and there a little of the birch—constituted the entire system," recalled Samuel Goodrich. "We did an immense amount of memorizing," said Elizabeth Buffum. "At twelve years of age I had recited *Murray's Grammar* through perhaps over a dozen times without a word of explanation or application from the book or the teacher."[7]

Occasionally memoirs refer to teachers who used the older children to teach the younger children, a sensible procedure given the circumstances. In large cities this innovation, called the "monitorial" system, became quite popular in the 1820s, but in rural district schools, the use of older children as instructors seems to have been rare. With the teacher in full charge of all recitations, it is no wonder that silence was demanded from the pupils studying at their seats. "I believe it was generally understood," wrote William Alcott, "that I was a *smart* teacher, by which was meant that I kept the school very quiet; and this, in those days, was regarded by many, as the very summit of pedagogic excellence." One of Warren Burton's teachers, Mehitabel Holt, also succeeded by keeping order. "Her punishments were horrible, especially to us little ones. She dungeoned us in that windowless closet just for a whisper. She tied us to her chair-post for an hour . . . a twist of the ear, or a snap on the head from her thimbled finger, reminded us that sitting perfectly still was the most important virtue of a little boy in school."[8]

Mehitabel Holt may have been stricter than some, but she was not unusual in her use of corporal punishment. Most district and old-field schoolteachers as well as their urban counterparts used and defended physical punishments to keep order. Alcott, who had some qualms about whipping children, tried in his fourth year of teaching to restrict himself to boxing ears, striking hands, and shaking heads. After that experiment he decided that the rod was better, because it involved less risk of injury to the student: "I defend its use by parents and teachers who are reduced to the dreadful alternative of inflicting pain, or see a child go on to suffering or to ruin. And I know of no method of inflicting pain so excellent." Acceptance of corporal punishment was widespread. Eliphalet Nott, who grew up in Connecticut in the 1780s, said, "If I was not whipped more than three times a week, I considered myself for the time peculiarly fortunate." In 1819, six-year-old James Sims was sent to a boarding school in South Carolina where new boys were always flogged, usually "until the youngster vomitted or wet his breeches."[9]

Although the type and amount of physical punishment varied from teacher to teacher, harsh and frequent punishments seem to have been characteristic of early nineteenth-century schools. Nonetheless, there are three qualifications to this generally brutal picture. First, some teachers were simply compassionate, gentle individuals who kept school without hitting children. Second, although not all women teachers abstained from corporal punishment, they were less likely to beat their students than men, partly because of gentler feminine stereotypes and partly because the older boys were often stronger than they were. It was for this latter reason that female teachers were in many districts employed only during the summer sessions, when the older children were generally working. As more and more communities began to employ female teachers, fewer schoolchildren were beaten. Third, a campaign for discipline through moral persuasion, though resisted by many male teachers, struck a responsive chord in others. Eliphalet Nott vowed, "I would not be like other men in regard to their treatment of children. . . . I made up my mind to substitute in my school moral motives." He claimed that his successful experiment in moral suasion attracted sufficient notice to propel him into the principalship of the prominent Plainfield Academy. Nott made it sound easy, but for most teachers it was difficult. A writer in the *New York Teacher* in the 1850s complained, "I have taken 'moral suasion' as my motto, but find my scholars have become so accustomed to the rod that they do not know what school is without it." He said that he found a piece of consoling advice in the *Wisconsin Journal of Education:* "Govern from a sense of right and justice when you *can,* from a feeling of fear when you *must*."[10]

Most teachers of the early nineteenth century did not stay with it very long. Little training was required, the wages were low, and the short sessions required teachers to combine jobs. Teachers doubled as farm laborers, tavernkeepers, prospectors, and craftsmen. There are no systematic records of the teachers of district schools before the 1840s, but memoirs and local records indicate minimal formal qualifications and high turnover of both male and female teachers. Women were rarely employed in the rural South in the early national period and were still a minority in northern district schools, limited to summer terms in most districts and excluded in others altogether. For females, teaching was usually a brief interlude between their own schooling and marriage. Some teachers, of course, had more formal education than others. Some male teachers in the North were college students earning their tuition money on the side. The town records of Dedham, Massachusetts, for example, document a procession of Harvard students teaching their winter schools. Still, the small number of colleges supplied only a fraction of the teachers needed for district schools, most of which were quite remote from college towns. Local common-school graduates, or those with a bit of academy training, sufficed where college students never trod.

In the South and in Pennsylvania, itinerant schoolmasters were often portrayed as drunken, foreign, and ignorant. James Sims of South Carolina endured two cruel Irishmen, he said, before a school was begun in 1822 by "the first native American teacher that we had among us." A contemporary in North Fayette, Pennsylvania, recalled an Irish teacher who had his dram at the tavern before school opened, and a neighbor in Plum said that a master named Patrick Murty loved his grog. "But at a time," he added, "when each took his dram three times a day, and thought it did him good, this peculiarity in Patrick was but little noticed, and Master Murty was the wonder of the county. Many young men of the day came from a distance to him to learn the art of surveying lands." Equally appreciated was an Irish teacher before 1820 in Harrison township, Pennsylvania, recalled by a former student: "Of an afternoon, when scholars were getting dull and time was hanging heavy, he would take off his coat, roll up his sleeves, get out in the middle of the floor, and dance them as beautiful a jig as you ever saw in your life.[11]

Despite such appreciative memoirs, teachers of district schools had quite a bad reputation in the eyes of would-be reformers, who wished to require more rigorous examinations by local communities, closer supervision, higher pay, and, eventually, normal-school training. We must treat the complaints of reformers cautiously, but by the 1840s, reports of the ignorance of common-school teachers were widespread. New York's Superintendent of Common Schools said in 1843 that some district schools had not been inspected in twenty years and that some local communities had certified teachers who could not even add. Some teachers, he said, were not only ignorant but intemperate. According to Vermont's new Superintendent of Common Schools, one successful district-school teaching candidate believed that the Mississippi was the largest river in New England and that 1847 was the number of years that had elapsed since the Pilgrims landed at Plymouth Rock. A midwestern school crusader claimed in 1842 that "at least four-fifths of the teachers in the common schools in Illinois would not pass an examination in the rudiments of our English education, and most of them have taken to teaching because they hadn't anything in particular to do."[12]

In the eyes of state education officials and other reform-minded commentators, district and old-field schoolteachers were not serving educational needs very well. From the point of view of rural communities, however, it seems that these transient, low-paid, inexperienced teachers served local needs quite well. The chief goal of northern district-school committees and southern subscription-school organizers was to provide children with rudimentary instruction at low cost under firm community control. Local taxpayers showed little interest in enhancing the professional status of teachers or increasing the length of school sessions. The viability of the locally controlled district school from the time of the

Revolution at least until the 1830s is underscored by the modest impact of educational reforms at the state level prior to 1840. The notion of a state system of education—that is, of a central authority with coercive power to establish, finance, and regulate schools—did not gain much ground in the early national period. The simplest reason it did not, aside from a strong tradition of local control, was that most communities were satisfied with their district schools. The district school met the educational needs of rural people, broadly literate but not highly educated, whose communities still depended to a considerable extent upon family and church for the inculcation of moral values and upon work for occupational training. These communities controlled their schools in ways that would become impossible as regulation became more centralized and teachers more professional.

Parents had considerable power in early rural education. They directly controlled what textbooks their children would use; through the district school committee or old-field subscription groups, they controlled what subjects would be taught, who the teacher would be, and how long school would be in session. Through the system of boarding the teacher around the district, parents could monitor the teacher's personal life and give their opinions about how the school should be run. Unless the teacher's own parents or relatives lived in the district and provided lodging, the parents of the district school's students usually fed and lodged the teacher in rotation. There were, of course, benefits to this system. "On the whole I liked it," said Heman Humphrey of Connecticut. The cooking was not always the best, nor the sheets quite clean, he admitted, but "it was a good school for us. By going into all the families we learned a great deal." Hiram Orcutt, who taught and boarded around a district in Rockingham, Vermont, acknowledged the advantages of getting to know the parents but resented the lack of privacy for rest or study, and he complained of the "criticism of ignorant and meddlesome fathers and mothers." District residents wanted teachers who would rule the school with an iron hand and withstand the pranks and rowdiness of the boys, but they wanted teachers who would also be amenable to their suggestions and hear their complaints.[13]

District schools were tied to their neighborhoods in yet another way. The schoolhouse was the only public building in many rural districts, and it was the scene of meetings, exhibitions, and contests, often involving the districts' adults. In larger villages, lyceums featuring traveling lecturers were sometimes held in schoolhouses. More typical and widespread were various forms of school exhibitions and evening schools. Heman Humphrey recalled the spring exhibitions held for parents at the end of the winter session in Connecticut district schools: "The anticipation of them kept up an interest all winter, and stimulated both teachers and scholars to do their best in the way of preparation. As the time approached, we had evening schools for reading and rehearsing the dialogues." Periodic spelling bees, singing schools, and other activities also brought the neighborhood residents to the school. The spelling bee, or spelling school, was probably the most popular of district school gatherings. It was sometimes held for pupils only, sometimes for everyone in the district, and sometimes as a contest between pupils of different districts in a town. William Mowry recalled spelling bees in Rhode Island fondly: "Oftentimes 'pieces' would be spoken and, after school was over, games would be played. When the sleighing was good, the best part of the whole entertainment would be found by the youngsters in an extended sleigh-ride."[14]

From transient teachers, crowded rooms, and stifled toddlers to community spelling bees and delightful sleigh rides, the rural school of the early nineteenth century reflected the close local control, the broad parental participation, the parsimony, and the limited educational needs of rural communities in the early American republic. Rural district schools were much the same in 1830 as they had been in 1780. Yet the period from 1780 to 1830 was a time of considerable social change, change sometimes slighted by historians because of the more startling growth of urban population, transportation networks, immigration, and manufacturing after 1830. Nonetheless the earlier decades saw expansion of the white male franchise, the building of canals, a rapid increase of population in the large cities (though they were yet a small part of the whole), the geographical spread of small-scale manufacturing, continued commercial development, and rising nationalism in literature and diplomacy. What impact did these social changes have on rural education?

Capitalism affected the rural areas of the North as profoundly as it affected the cities. As transportation and communication expanded, many farmers turned from diverse, self-sufficient production to single, cash crops. As a result, rural people had more contact with markets, both as producers and as consumers. The shift was gradual in some communities, dramatic elsewhere; it was resisted by some rural people, welcomed by others. Some areas suffered. Farmers on the stony soil of New England struggled to match the productivity of newly accessible midwestern grainfields. Merchant capitalists, eyeing expanding markets for goods like shoes and straw hats, increased the scale of production by organizing networks of household piecework. On the fringes of incipient industrial centers, rural women and teenagers spent long hours stitching and weaving for cash before water power and ingenious machines displaced their labors. The world of cash was a world of literacy and numeracy. For better or for worse, rural communities were being knit into networks of exchange and communication. This could only foster education, especially in a nation with widespread political participation for white men and a clear field for new institutional development, a nation whose Protestant ministers competed for allegiance through print and pulpit while they recommended Bible study for salvation and moral guidance.[15]

These forces affected the North more than the South. Sketchy figures from Massachusetts and New York for the early national period suggest that total school enrollment rates were higher in rural than in urban communities and were rising during the late eighteenth and early nineteenth centuries. In Massachusetts towns, the increase in enrollment levels began in the second half of the eighteenth century, but the lack of systematic data makes it difficult to estimate the magnitude. Similarly, lack of information makes impossible any numerical comparisons of enrollments in the Midwest or the South prior to 1840. Estimated statewide enrollment levels for New York State were 37 percent of children under age twenty in 1800 rising to 60 percent by 1825, at about which time they levelled off. In both New York in 1800 and Massachusetts in 1826, enrollment levels were clearly related to community size, the smaller towns having the highest percentage of their children enrolled. This correlation was not lost upon contemporaries. A writer in the *New York Enquirer,* after seeing some New York State school returns for 1828, remarked that the "education among the young population between the ages of five and fifteen is twice as extensive in the country counties as in the city." The consequence for the city was clear. "It is the want of early education which produces nine-tenths of the misery, vice, distress and immorality we see around us." Rural district schools, then, account for rising common-school enrollment rates in the early national period. Long before the common-school reform movement and the creation of state free-school systems, beginning at least as early as the late eighteenth century, the proportion of children attending school each year was rising, particularly among girls and particularly in the Northeast.[16]

How specifically can we link the expansion of educational enrollments in these mundane, locally controlled district schools to the larger religious, political, and economic features of social change in the early republic? The long-standing Protestant commitment to literacy must have been a factor in support of schooling, and there were widespread revivals among the Calvinist churches in the 1740s and again around the turn of the century, coincident with the apparent expansion of district schooling. Nonetheless, direct links between religion and school enrollment are difficult to prove. Similarly, it is plausible that the heightened political interest of the Revolutionary era, with the subsequent drama of constitution making, boosted common schooling, but it is difficult to demonstrate the effect of these developments upon schooling in the hinterland, where the enrollment increases occurred.

As with religion and politics, the notion that economic development would have an effect on education seems plausible, but the facts are obscure. It seems logical that wider geographical horizons, more impersonal markets, more printed communication, and a gradually increasing proportion of wage-earning workers in the labor market would foster the development of schooling for literacy, morality, and a more mobile world. But explicit connections between economic development and education by contemporaries were infrequent and vague. Nowhere was the contribution of education to economic growth emphasized or spelled out in detail. Even in treatises on political economy written by Americans in the 1820s and 1830s, education was a minor theme. If education was an ingredient in expansive capitalism, the connection escaped capitalists in the early national period.

While the fundamental religious, political, and economic causes of expanded common schooling in this period are difficult to trace, some proximate causes are less elusive. The expansion of enrollments in the rural areas and small towns of the Northeast seems most directly explained by the increasing acceptance of the district system of control and by the increasing provision of schooling for females. In New England and the Middle Atlantic region, the district system of school control came about as population dispersed from town centers. Outlying neighborhoods resisted paying for schools that were distant from their homes and began to demand control of separate funds for their own schools. In many communities, this resulted first in the "moving" school, an arrangement whereby a single teacher taught brief sessions in several dispersed locations. Later these neighborhoods hired their own teachers, receiving their share of local funds from the town, supplementing them by subscription in the neighborhood, and in many cases gaining the power to staff and supervise their schools. These arrangements developed over a long period from the mid-eighteenth to the early nineteenth century, encountering resistance in some communities and none in others. The decentralized system received legislative sanction in various laws—Connecticut in 1760, Vermont in 1782, Massachusetts in 1789, and New York in 1814—but the practice existed before the laws.

In Rhode Island, for example, a law of 1799 directed that towns be divided into school districts, but the districts had been developing on a town-by-town basis from the mid-eighteenth century on, in response to population dispersal and neighborhood development. Barrington divided into three districts shortly after it became a separate town in 1770. In Middletown the east and west districts shared a moving schoolmaster in 1745, and in 1754 the two districts, called "squadrons," were given the power to manage their school affairs separately. In Pennsylvania, where no legislation touched upon district schools until well into the nineteenth century, the same sort of neighborhood system arose informally. Recalling conditions of the early nineteenth century, a Lancaster County resident said, "Whenever a neighborhood felt the need of a schoolhouse, one was erected at some point convenient to those who contributed towards its erection. The patrons selected trustees, whose duty it was to take charge of the school property and to select a teacher for the school." The staunchly defended American tradition of neighborhood schools had its origins in the period roughly from 1750 to 1835, which saw a proliferation of district schools and their legal recognition at the local and state level. Bridging our modern categories of "public" and "private" in their means of support and control, these schools brought formal education closer to people's homes and greatly increased the total amount of schooling.[17]

Rising enrollment rates during this period were also affected by the increasing acceptance and provision of education for girls. Even though Protestantism assigned the same arduous route to salvation for women as for men, and thus the same need for literacy, women's political rights were nil in the early colonial period, and institutional provisions for their education ranged from discriminatory to nonexistent. It is very difficult to characterize popular attitudes toward female education because of the great range of opinion on the issue, but it is clear that a view favorable to schooling for girls was becoming more popular in the late eighteenth and early nineteenth centuries, and this development must account for a substantial share of the rise in enrollment in the northeastern United States. The advocacy of girls' education was based on two general propositions: first, that although women's intellects were different from and perhaps inferior to men's, females nonetheless were as capable as males of attaining a common education, and second, that they needed a good common education, not in order to fill the same roles as men, but because as wives and mothers they needed sound intellectual and moral training. Benjamin Rush argued the special importance of the mother's role in the new republic. In his *Thoughts Upon Female Education,* published in 1787, he urged a practical and moral education for mothers. "The equal share that every citizen has in the liberty and the possible share he may have in the government of our country make it necessary that our ladies should be qualified to a certain degree, by a peculiar and suitable education, to concur in instructing their sons in the principles of liberty and government." In succeeding decades, DeWitt Clinton, Emma Willard, and others took up these arguments and promoted education for the crucial domestic role assigned to women.[18]

The two principal arguments—women's capacity for education and their important responsibilities in educating children—were cited frequently as reasons for increasing girls' access to schooling in the early national period. Many elementary schools in the North admitted girls for the first time in the late eighteenth century, although access was often limited and segregated. In 1766, Medford, Massachusetts, admitted girls to its schools in the afternoon, after the boys were dismissed. New London, Connecticut, in 1774 offered girls instruction from 5:00 to 7:00 a.m. in the summer. Boston established summer writing schools for girls in 1782, and Newburyport extended the girls' educational season to six months per year in 1804, still gathering the girls separately, from 6:00 to 8:00 in the morning. In 1827 an anonymous correspondent wrote to the *Salem Register* that Salem was one of the worst places in Massachusetts for the provision of female education. In small villages, the essayist declared, boys and girls were now admitted equally, and the importance of female education was "unanimously acknowledged." Acceptance of girls' schooling occurred more rapidly in small towns than in cities. It thus coincided with, and contributed to, rising rural enrollment rates. Increasing amounts of formal education for girls is reflected not only in increased enrollment rates but in literacy rates as well. Recent research suggests that there was a substantial rise in adult female literacy in the Northeast between 1780 and 1850, indicating substantially increased education in the period before 1830. Less is known about female schooling and enrollment levels in the middle and southern regions, although in Pennsylvania, Quakers and Moravians were active in expanded female education in the last half of the eighteenth century, and in the South, as in the North, there were an increasing number of female academies in this period.[19]

By the second and third decades of the nineteenth century,

several states were aiding local district schools by distributing interest from permanent state school funds. Sufficient information to assess the impact of state funding on enrollments in this early period does not exist. Although payments from the funds provided only a small part of total school costs, state assistance probably encouraged the upward trend in enrollment. New York State, having repealed its 1795 common-school assistance law in 1800, created a state school fund in 1805, the income of which was distributed to towns, beginning in 1815. Connecticut's fund, created in 1795, suffered from bad management in its early years, but by 1810 it was providing annual assistance to local schools. Delaware created a fund in 1796 that was distributing some interest by 1817. In several states, funds created in the early decades of the century did not distribute any income until the 1830s or later. In other states, such as Pennsylvania and Massachusetts, state school funds were not created until after 1830 and therefore had no influence upon enrollments in the early national period.[20]

District schools were closely tied to their communities. Inexpensive and under tight local control, they satisfied most white rural Americans' desires for elementary education. Enrollment rates increased during the late eighteenth and early nineteenth centuries as the district system spread and people increasingly accepted female education. These trends were reinforced, no doubt, by the value placed on educated citizenship in a Protestant republic, the value placed on literacy in a society characterized by more written communication, easier travel, and more complex economic networks, and by the value placed on discipline in a volatile society whose leaders were attempting to reconcile political liberty with mobility, ethnic diversity, and expansive capitalism.

3

Urban Education and the Expansion of Charity Schooling

W HILE enrollment increase was the dynamic feature of rural schooling in the early national period, changes in the organization and funding were the key developments in urban schooling. Rural schools were funded by a combination of local governmental and parental resources supporting a common neighborhood school. Urban schools, diverse in character, were funded in different ways, for different sorts of students. Many children in the cities of the 1780s and 1790s were taught in independent pay schools. Most schoolmasters charged quarterly fees within the means of perhaps three-fourths of the population. Analysis of enrollment lists for New York City in the 1790s reveals that these pay schools were patronized by a wide variety of families. The only underrepresented groups were day laborers, many of whom could not afford even the lowest tuition costs, and merchants and professionals, who may have patronized boarding schools or hired tutors. Even these groups sent substantial numbers of children to the common pay schools, though not as great a proportion as proprietors, clerical workers, skilled craftsmen, cartmen, and mariners. Complementing these numerous common pay schools were "dame" schools operated by women in their homes for small children, providing custodial care and rudimentary training at low fees. Boston took notice of these numerous schools in 1789 by passing a statute requiring their proprietors to be licensed.[1]

Children whose families could afford neither a common pay

school nor a dame school might receive some elementary education through apprenticeship or through a church charity school.
Apprenticeship for boys was very common until the early nineteenth century, and orphan records show that girls, too, were
sometimes apprenticed, usually as domestic servants. Apprentice
indentures required masters to provide a modicum of education
for their charges. Those who did not were sometimes brought to
court. Thus, if a poor boy became an apprentice, he might be
sent to school for a brief period each year until he could read
and write, or he might receive instruction with the master's
family. Beyond the rudiments, however, masters had no responsibility. Whether training in the three R's developed into an
adult reading capacity depended on circumstances and individual
initiative. Stephen Allen, the son of a penniless widow, became
a sailmaker's apprentice in revolutionary New York City. He
was unusual among his fellow apprentices for his devotion to
reading. "My education was very limited, having left school
before I was twelve years old. I could read and write indifferently,
and had learned a few of the rules in Arithmetic, but possessed
no knowledge of grammar and was wretchedly difficient [sic] in
my spelling." He was very fond of reading, however, and had
kept his schoolbooks, which included a New Testament and some
of Dilworth's texts. The young apprentice purchased cheap
secondhand books with the money he was occasionally allowed
to earn. He moved from his school literature to "old plays,
Novels, Songs, Poetry, History," and sometimes even to "books
of a pernicious tendency." The self-educated Allen became one
of the early working-class mayors of New York City.[2]

Some poor children did not become apprentices. For them the
means of elementary schooling in large towns was the church
charity school. New York had six such schools in 1796, and in
Philadelphia there were at least twelve by 1810, including schools
maintained by the Episcopal, Presbyterian, Lutheran, Reformed,
and Catholic churches for the children of their poor members.
These schools generally accepted only the children of the sponsoring congregation. They offered a curriculum of rudimentary intellectual skills, strongly laced with religious exercises and the
memorization of scripture. The goal was to produce adults who

would be minimally literate, who would have a chance at religious salvation, and who would act according to the morality the schools taught.

Denominational charity schools at the turn of the century reflected a longstanding English and American tradition, but they served a relatively small number of children. However, as apprenticeship declined and social problems increased in America's commercial cities, charity schooling increased and reached out to the churchless poor. While rural Americans ignored the appeals of republican theorists for school systems to save the nation, social leaders in the cities saw pressing and potentially dangerous problems arising among resourceless or alien groups in the population. Poverty spread in the large cities of the revolutionary and early national period. Newly established almshouses filled, and economic instability worried people in the middling ranks of society. Incipient slums and deteriorating sanitary conditions alarmed city leaders. As in England, education was one recourse. Thomas Eddy, a Quaker merchant and philanthropist active in charity education in New York, was warned by the Englishman Patrick Colquhoun in 1803 that in nations where education had been neglected, "the manners of the people have exhibited strong instances of a deficiency, manifested by extreme ignorance and immoral conduct, as it respects a considerable portion of the lower class of society." But American city dwellers were already aware of the brewing problems. As early as 1791, the *New York Daily Advertiser* advocated increased charity schooling, arguing that the situation of many poor children "exposes them to innumerable temptations to become not only useless, but hurtful members of the community." Poor people, the article continued, "seldom keep any government in their families," and their children thus "unavoidably contract habits of idleness and mischief and wickedness." Thus began the indictment of the urban poor. It was a view sympathetic to children and disdainful of adults, a view that would dominate the writings of social reformers throughout the nineteenth century.[3]

Both the theories and the institutional models to meet new urban social problems were at hand. The psychology of John Locke, which emphasized the malleability of children's minds, and Enlightenment ideas about the perfectibility of human character gave impetus to philanthropic efforts to educate the poor. As Thomas Eddy of New York remarked, "The great preventive of offences is doubtless an early attention to moral and religious instruction, and thus to fortify the infant mind with good principles. The observation made by John Locke is remarkably appropriate and excellent: 'I think I may say, that of all the men we meet with, nine parts of ten are what they are, good or evil, useful or not, by their education.' " Although American reformers like Eddy looked to England for theories and models, there were important differences between England and America in the way that the social elite responded to proposals for the education of the poor. Both were capitalist countries undergoing urbanization and a similar economic transformation; both had representative government and legally protected religious dissent. Yet in England there was an extended, passionate debate over the wisdom of educating the poor, and in the United States there was virtually no debate.[4]

The advocacy of mass schooling for social stability was a minority view in England at the beginning of the nineteenth century but finally prevailed against vigorous aristocratic opposition. It was the mainstream reform view in America during these years and was virtually unopposed. With no truly conservative opposition to placate, American urban reformers nonetheless repeated the social justification for mass education offered by their English counterparts. Both English and American advocates emphasized collective goals—such as the reduction of crime and disruption—rather than individualistic goals—such as intellectual growth or personal advancement. The English opposition to mass education, especially strong in Tory, High Church circles, rested on two basic arguments: that it would make the lower classes unfit for their necessary occupational roles and that it would subvert proper authority by disseminating seditious and atheistic ideas. The first argument was based on a static concept of the occupational structure. Because "every step in the scale of society is already full," feared John Weyland, "the temporal condition of the lower orders cannot be exalted, but at the expense of the higher." This alarm was trumpeted in a hundred variations from the pulpit, in the press, and before Parliament. The second general argument was that mass education would lead to disorder. English conservatives predicted a multitude of dire effects, centering on political sedition, vice, and religious dissent.[5]

The vigor of this conservative position put advocates of mass schooling on the defensive in early nineteenth-century England. Even educational promoters proclaimed that writing and arithmetic were more dangerous than reading and should be carefully limited. Again and again the school advocates insisted that reading moral tales and the Bible would make men content with their lot, not ambitious, and that education would increase social stability, not disruption. Most important, education would reduce crime. Prevention was better than punishment, and cheaper. Wherever schools were opened, prisons would be closed. Persuaded or not, the conservatives were forced into acquiescence. Unable to halt the successful educational efforts of Dissenters, and openly fearful of losing working-class members to Dissent, the English Church had no choice but to establish its own educational programs; and thus the Tory-High Church faction was propelled into the nineteenth-century industrial world, in which mass education was unavoidable.

When meritocracy raised its alien head in England, it typically brought on a storm of renewed protest and dire predictions from conservatives. Thus the dialogue continued, keeping English mass education to its characteristic aims: social stability and a productive citizenry. In America, this dialogue between advocates and opponents of mass schooling did not take place. The contrast was noted at the time. Benjamin Shaw, an English charity-school advocate, wrote in 1817, after a tour of America, "I am ashamed to reflect that in my native country, Great Britain, there are so many in opposition to the education of the poor, and to that system which is here an undisputed good." Philanthropists in American cities avidly adopted English arguments and English institutions for educating the poor. They established Sunday schools, weekday charity schools, and later, infant schools, all based explicitly on English models. While Thomas Eddy corresponded eagerly with Patrick Colquhoun about the education of the poor, his son-in-law visited Joseph Lancaster's famous

Borough Road School in London. Divie and Joanna Bethune's enthusiasm for Sunday schools and infant schools can be traced across the Atlantic. Quaker Roberts Vaux, while keeping in touch with English coreligionists, helped found Philadelphia's charity-school system on the English model. Similar institutions mirrored a similar social philosophy. The institutions were the tools of moral education, aimed especially at the increasingly volatile urban poor. Appropriate habits had to be instilled and the bonds between social classes reinforced. In the first quarter of the nineteenth century, the main thrust in American urban education was charity schooling, and its advocates' social values were very similar to those of their English counterparts. The important difference between America and England in the period 1800–1825, then, is not in the social uses of popular education, but in the widespread consensus among the American elite about its desirability. Unlike English Tory opponents of mass education, conservative Americans generally believed in schooling for social stability. They feared ignorance, not instruction. The more anxious they became about the security of their world, the more they favored mass education.[6]

Despite social values and institutional forms shared with the English, the Americans displayed a greater tolerance for individual mobility. Yet this cannot be explained by the assertion of an American egalitarian consensus, implying that American charity schooling was designed to implement equality of opportunity. On the contrary, mobility was quite incidental to the educational goals of those philanthropists and public officials who advocated education for the poor in America. Radical working-class spokesmen, from Thomas Paine in the 1780s to Stephen Simpson in the 1820s, placed more stress on schooling for advancement, and the early craft associations and workingmen's parties argued for equal opportunity through schooling, but they became critics of separate charity schooling, finding middle-class allies among the early advocates of publicly funded common schools. Whether it was provided in separate charity schools or later in public common schools, however, almost no one in America opposed widespread elementary education or spoke out against individual advancement through schooling. The argument that mass education would make workers unfit for their station and spread sedition and dissent among the lower orders was almost totally lacking. Referring to the few American writers who uttered Tory-sounding objections, Joseph Tuckerman, Boston's city missionary, said in the 1820s: "To those who would leave a certain number uneducated that they may thus be fitted and disposed for the lowest office of life, I could observe . . . that if every child in our country, and in the world, between the ages of four and fourteen, were in a school . . . and should receive as much instruction as could be given to them, it would be found that in the diversity God has made of human capacities . . . there is an ample provision for the whole number which is wanted for every service."[7]

There are several reasons for the absence of opposition to mass education in America. The most obvious is that there was no formal nobility and no powerful church hierarchy in America. Also, Americans did not fear a literate public; indeed, as English reformers warned them, they had great reason to try to maintain their high literacy rates in the face of increasing industrialization. The objects of charity education in America, then, seemed neither so numerous nor so dangerous as in England. Third, the relationship between general literacy and rebellion was perceived differently in America. After all, Americans had rebelled against England, and the very success of that rebellion, some pointed out, was due to the widespread and right-minded judgment of the country's yeomen. Perhaps most important, American mass schooling efforts became increasingly acculturative as immigration increased. Even before the 1830s, despite the fact that a majority of the working class was still native-born, the rhetoric and mission of the school movement in the coastal cities were heavily influenced by the fear of immigrant vice, infidelity, and crime.

The combination of these social, political, and cultural conditions accounts for the consensus among the American elite on the issue of mass education. Philanthropists and social leaders of the middling and upper classes in both England and America justified charity schooling on grounds of stability, with little pretense to providing equality of opportunity or intellectual enlightenment. But elite Americans moved more swiftly and with less conflict toward charity schooling for social stability because they lacked the complication of an established church, had fewer poor people, fewer illiterate people, and greater cultural diversity to cope with.

The expansion of charity education, then, was no radical departure from eighteenth-century modes of urban education, and in America it occasioned little debate. It did not necessitate new initiatives by local or state government. By creating a network of charity schools, philanthropists laid the basis for the free school systems of mid-nineteenth-century American cities, but this was not their intent in the early decades of the century. They used a familiar institution—the voluntary association—to extend free schooling to the children of needy families not served by the traditional denominational charity schools. They did so at a time when voluntary associations of all kinds were proliferating in American cities. In New York, Philadelphia, Boston, and dozens of smaller cities, voluntary associations for a variety of purposes mushroomed during the 1790s and early 1800s. The political activities of Republicans and Federalists, the common interests of artisan groups, and the outreach work of an invigorated Christianity prompted the birth of many social, educational, and benevolent organizations. The larger a town was, the greater the likelihood it would have sufficient numbers to support voluntary association as well as the social stratification, suffering, and disruption to make obvious the need for mutual assistance and charitable groups. Women became active in unprecedented numbers, often in societies to help resourceless and deserted women or children. Occupational groups like cartmen or cordwainers organized mutual aid societies. Voluntary associations, having been relatively insignificant before the Revolution, became important instruments for facing the increasing complexity of urban life in the new republic.

Among religious groups, the most prominent in extending charitable work beyond their own denomination were the Quakers. Successful in commerce, secure in their own religion, and newly dedicated to proving themselves part of a larger American community, the Quakers participated in voluntary benevolent associations out of all proportion to their numbers in New York, Philadelphia, Baltimore, and other coastal cities. Considering their vigorous eighteenth-century opposition to slavery, it is not surprising that members of the Society of Friends were the leaders of post-Revolutionary manumission societies and African free schools devoted to the protection and acculturation of freed blacks. Increasing manumission by northern slaveholders of the revolutionary era led to increased numbers of freed blacks in the cities, which caused some whites to worry about the behavior of these urban migrants. Quakers established a school for Negro boys in Philadelphia in 1770, which was supplemented in 1787 by a school for girls and by an evening school for adults in 1789. In New York the Quaker-dominated Manumission Society organized a school in 1787 for freed blacks "in hopes that by an early attention to their morals they may be kept from vicious courses and qualified for usefulness in life." A similar school was opened in Baltimore in 1792, and by 1810, African free schools were operating in Burlington, New Jersey, Providence, Rhode Island, and Wilmington, Delaware. In Boston a group of white merchants and ministers began supporting an already-existing African school in 1801. Blacks were not wholly dependent upon whites' charity for schooling, of course. A number of the parents of the Boston African school paid weekly tuition charges, and a report from New York in the 1820s estimated that there were 100 black students in private schools in addition to the 620 enrolled in the African Free School. Yet the African free schools in the large cities substantially increased elementary schooling for black children. They also helped to demonstrate to some whites the fallacy of the widespread belief in Negro inferiority. Benjamin Shaw visited the New York school in 1817 and wrote:

> I am fully satisfied—and every skeptical man who visits this school and examines the scholars will be convinced—that the Negro is as capable of mental improvement as any white man in the creation of God. An African prince was there in one corner attentively copying the alphabet; a young man—say a boy about fourteen—reciting passages from the best authors, suiting the actions to the words; another answering difficult questions in geography &c &c. In fact, let the enemies of these neglected children of men perform a pilgrimage to New York and at this shrine of education recant their principles and confess that the

poor despised African is as capable of every intellectual improvement as themselves.[8]

It is difficult to assess how much good this formal education did for the personal advancement of black youths. A rare surviving statement on this point by a graduate of the New York African Free School is bitterly negative:

> Am I arrived at the end of my education, just on the eve of setting out into the world, of commencing some honest pursuit, by which to earn a comfortable subsistence? What are my prospects? To what shall I turn my head? Shall I be a mechanic? No one will employ me; white boys won't work with me. Shall I be a merchant? No one will have me in his office; white clerks won't associate with me. Drudgery and servitude, then, are my prospective portion.

Most whites were not bothered by the discouraging prospects of educated black youths. In this venture, as in all charity schooling, the upward mobility of the students was incidental. The main thrust was moral education, and literacy was directed more to this purpose than to individual advancement. Whites did intend to "elevate" those blacks who were willing to be educated, but only in the sense that they would be morally fortified to escape vice, criminal activity, and poverty, all of which their benefactors attributed to ignorance. Again, reformers sounded the theme of saving children from their parents. The founders of New York's Manumission Society worried lest blacks "were permitted to inherit the vices their parents acquired in slavery or to learn similar ones themselves through a want of proper education." Unlike rural district schooling, urban charity schooling was designed to intervene between parents and children, to introduce children to a culture and morality that reformers believed was different from that of their parents. Of course, many parents among resourceless and alien groups shared the reformers' values of respectability, order, deference, and industry, but this did not impress white leaders as much as the cultural differences, the poverty, and the high arrest records of blacks and other urban newcomers. Education would help reduce crime and vice while it muted cultural differences.[9]

The same strategy applied to charity education for poor whites. In the 1790s and early 1800s, voluntary associations mobilized to rescue orphans from the streets and poor children from their parents. Some of these groups provided immediate relief—food, shelter, and clothes—as well as distributing Bibles and advice. Many groups established schools. In 1796 a Philadelphia Quaker, Anne Parish, began a school under the auspices of the Society for the Free Instruction of Female Children, and three years later, other philanthropists began the Philadelphia Society for the Establishment and Support of Charity Schools, which by 1812 had about 400 boys and girls in its schools. In the meantime, the Philadelphia Association for the Instruction of Poor Children opened the Adelphi Schools in 1807. In New York also there were diverse groups, formally independent of one another but often overlapping in function and membership. In addition to the Manumission Society and the church charity schools, a Female Association began in 1798, and in 1801 it opened a school for poor girls of churchless parents. In 1823 this association was educating 750 students.

One organization soon came to dominate charity education in New York City. Established in 1805 at the initiative of a group of Quakers including Thomas Eddy, the New York Free School Society entered the field determined to provide education for the children of the churchless poor on a large scale. In their request for incorporation they warned the state legislature that poor parents were "indifferent" and "intemperate" and that their children were "inheriting those vices which idleness and the bad example of their parents naturally produce." Because education had been neglected, they continued, hospitals and almshouses were full. Nor did they confine their indictment to the poor. It was, more broadly, the "laboring class" that was becoming "less industrious, less moral, and less careful to lay up the fruit of their earnings." The Free School Society soon attracted financial support and the backing of such influential figures as Governor DeWitt Clinton, who became one of its trustees.[10]

Only a few years earlier, an ambitious young English teacher, Joseph Lancaster, had devised an elaborate plan of instruction according to which older students drilled small groups of younger students. Like traditional pedagogy, the monitorial (or Lancasterian) system emphasized recitation, but now, due to the use of student monitors, children could be almost continually engaged in active, competitive groups. The constant stimulation of monitorial instruction would increase motivation; the highly regimented procedures would maintain order in huge schools as well as inculcate discipline. A child could proceed at his or her own rate in each subject. Constant testing would insure mastery, while prizes and competitive spirit would replace cruel corporal punishment as means of motivation. Last, but certainly not least, the Lancasterian system, properly implemented, would allow a single master to operate a school with as many as 500 children in attendance. Lancaster demonstrated this, to the amazement of visitors, at his famous Borough Road School near London. In 1818, Lancaster himself sailed for the United States, where he promoted his system in New York, Philadelphia, and Baltimore. Even before his arrival, urban educational reformers in the new nation had embraced his system as a panacea for charity education.[11]

Lancaster's ideas were not profound, but they were timely. His system was cheap, efficient, and easy to implement. In an age when the number of poor children was increasing and there was generally no state support for elementary schooling, the Lancasterian system gave voluntary societies the tool they needed to expand their activities. In an age when urban reformers worried about the moral education of the poor, the system promised to inculcate obedience, promptness, and industry. Furthermore, by training future teachers as monitors at model Lancasterian schools and by providing elaborate manuals that explained procedures and lesson plans, the Lancasterian system promised a virtual guarantee of teacher competence in an age when teachers' qualifications and reputations were low. Finally, Lancaster emphasized the need for nonsectarian moral instruction; he provided a catechism and lesson plans for this purpose, at a time when charity-school advocates were attempting to go beyond denominational boundaries to reach the churchless poor.

As a result, the Lancasterian system became the most widespread and successful educational reform in the Western world during the first thirty years of the nineteenth century. Because a large number of students was needed to make a Lancasterian school effective, the system was confined largely to cities, but the speed and breadth of its adoption in American cities was remarkable. The New York Free School Society adopted the system in 1805, and other New York charity schools soon followed suit, including the African Free School and several church charity schools. In Philadelphia, the Association of Friends for the Instruction of the Poor began a Lancasterian school in 1808, using a manual that their leader, Thomas Scattergood, had acquired from Lancaster. The schools of other Philadelphia voluntary societies soon converted to the monitorial system. In Albany, New York, a Lancasterian school began about 1810, and by 1814 it enrolled 400 children. DeWitt Clinton, Governor of New York and a Lancasterian enthusiast, sent manuals and advice to interested educators from other upstate towns. By 1825 there were Lancasterian schools in Poughkeepsie, Hudson, Troy, Schenectady, and Utica. In Connecticut, Governor Wolcott recommended the system, citing as a model the already popular New Haven Lancasterian school. Hartford and Guilford soon joined the Lancasterian craze. A report to the North Carolina legislature recommended the system in 1817 as the product of a new science of the human mind. In 1821 Governor Hiester of Pennsylvania recommended the Lancasterian system, as practiced throughout Philadelphia, to educators in the rest of the state. Lancasterian schools were soon established in Harrisburg, Pittsburgh, Erie, New Castle, and other Pennsylvania cities, including, appropriately, Lancaster. Baltimore began its school system on the Lancasterian plan in 1829, and Virginians reported Lancasterian schools in Alexandria, Richmond, Norfolk, and five other cities.[12]

The new cities of the West, including Pittsburgh, Detroit, Lexington, Louisville, and Cincinnati, adopted Lancaster's method as a way to provide cheap, efficient, elementary instruction. In the West, said *The American Register,* "the only real modern improvement in the matter of education, the Lancasterian method, has been adopted with avidity, and is pursued on a large scale." The Detroit *Gazette* called monitorial schooling "a branch of that wonderful providence which is to usher in the millennial day."

Although the Lancasterian system did not result in the millennium, one former student in Detroit remembered Lemuel Shattuck's monitorial school fondly. In a detailed memoir, he explained that each class was directed by a student from a higher class, who sat at the end of the row giving instructions and keeping order. Recitations were held in half-circles marked out in the wide aisles. Each student attempted to move to the head of the class three times, which meant promotion to the next class. Two senior monitors, high-school students, presided from a raised platform, receiving reports from the class monitors. They awarded prizes for achievement and exacted penalties for misbehavior. Shattuck supervised all, "quietly entering the room, passing around, giving instructions, sometimes carrying a small rattan, or raw-hide, but seldom used, except to tap a pupil on the shoulder when found playing or dozing." The Lancasterian school, wrote the author of the memoir, "allowed the pupils to advance according to their industry and application to their studies." They "were not held back by duller scholars," he said, as is "often the case under our present school system."[13]

Not all Lancasterian schools got such good grades from their students, however. A boy who attended a Lancasterian school in New York City in the 1820s remembered the rigid lock-step procedures that the monitors enforced: "The monitors then unanimously give the order, 'Hands behind!' On the instant every boy has his left palm enclosed in his right behind his back, in a sort of self hand-cuffed state, and woe be to him who is not paying attention when the order is given, or is tardy in obeying it." So went the lessons for each class at its desks, every move made to a command. If a new era was to emerge from such a pedagogy, it would certainly be a mechanical era. Indeed, Lancaster's methods did answer a new concern among educational spokesmen for moral education that would inculcate not only the traditional values of hard work and obedience but would stress precision, standardization, and elaborate routine. Moreover, these values would be taught not just by precept and example, but would be reinforced by every activity in the schoolroom. These ideas, which became commonplace maxims of urban education after 1850, were fresh and appealing at the opening of the century. Lancaster's system best embodied these ideas, which helps account for its popularity. With its claims of economy, efficiency, nonsectarian moral training, and teacher-proof procedures, the system greatly facilitated the spread of charity schooling in cities of the early national period. There was more to charity schooling than Joseph Lancaster's monitorial system, however. Other institutions on English models appeared. Among these were the Sunday school and the infant school.[14]

Sunday schools began at the same time and in much the same way as nondenominational weekday charity schools. Early Sunday schools welcomed children of all religious denominations, were initiated by lay people, had only weak support among the clergy, and seldom met in churches. According to tradition, Robert Raikes, a printer and philanthropist in Gloucester, England, established the first Sunday schools. Raikes was distressed by the ragged, unsupervised children of factory workers playing noisily on Sundays in the working-class area of Gloucester. Some went to school or worked on weekdays, but all were idle on Sundays. Raikes paid some dame-school women in 1780 to teach free those children who were willing to come to school on Sundays. The idea of Sunday instruction for the children of the poor caught on, and Raikes expanded and publicized his activities. By 1785 there was a Sunday School Society in London, and by 1790 the idea had crossed the Atlantic. The two main goals of Philadelphia's new First Day School Society were to give rudimentary instruction to the "offspring of indigent parents," and to keep the Sabbath from being "employed to the worst of purposes, the depravity of morals and manners." By 1800 there were more than 2,000 children in Philadelphia's Sunday schools, and similar schools had been established for black children in New York and for factory workers' children in Pawtucket, Rhode Island.[15]

Sunday-school enthusiasts in America soon organized societies to coordinate these scattered but numerous schools, along the lines of Philadelphia's interdenominational First Day School Society and similar English groups. In 1815, Eleazar Lord, a New York merchant who had spent some time observing charitable work in Philadelphia, convinced his associate Divie Bethune that New York needed a society like Philadelphia's, and the next year they created the New York Sunday School Union Society. In the meantime, Bethune's wife Joanna founded the Female Union for Promoting Sabbath Schools, which established schools for children of both sexes and for female adults.

Until about 1830, American Sunday schools maintained their original charity-school characteristics. They were initiated, managed, and financed by lay people gathered into sex-segregated societies. The classes themselves were also taught by lay people and were segregated by sex and race. Sunday schools placed emphasis on rudimentary intellectual skills as well as on morals and nonsectarian religion. Sunday-school enthusiasts in some denominations, such as the Methodists and the Episcopalians, dissented from the interdenominational character of the movement and formed their own associations, although some individual churches of these denominations stayed in the pan-Protestant organizations. When they were pressured to join the Episcopal Sunday School Society, the Sunday-school organizers from St. George's Church in New York replied, "We embarked on board the Union Ship, and unless she is shipwrecked we shall continue to sail under her flag." In 1817 this "union" movement culminated in the establishment of the Sunday and Adult School Union, a national organization, which became the American Sunday School Union in 1824. Sunday schools flourished in Charleston, Richmond, and elsewhere in the South. In Delaware the state legislature granted a per pupil subsidy to Sunday Schools throughout the state. By 1827 a newspaper in Springfield, Massachusetts, estimated that 200,000 children attended Sunday schools in America. Sunday schools were not limited to cities. Indeed, the highly organized Union Sunday School movement was one means by which a standardized, interdenominational Protestantism was exported to the countryside.[16]

Typically these early Sunday schools met both in the morning and afternoon. School activities included prayer, hymn singing, learning the alphabet from cards, and, for the older children, reading, memorizing, and reciting the Bible. Early Sunday schools placed heavy emphasis on memorization of passages from the Bible. Some schools paid out a form of currency for verses memorized, as well as for good behavior and good attendance;

the currency was redeemable in Bibles or other appropriate prizes. Some schools made marathon memorization into an outright contest. Ella Gilbert Ives recalled her frustration when "night after night in the dimly lighted schoolroom, I toiled over the gospel of John, only to see the reward swept from me by a boy nearly twice my age. His name was Homer, and he committed the entire gospel, while I stopped at the difficult fifteenth chapter." It seems incredible, but Sunday schools often reported children who had memorized hundreds of hymns or several books of the Bible.[17]

By the mid-1820s the American Sunday School Union began discouraging marathon memorization, suggesting instead uniform, selected Biblical passages that teachers would explain and children would memorize. Their plans were widely adopted, but the reform did not fundamentally alter the role of memorization or the exclusive reliance on the Bible as a text. Of course, memorization was not unique to Sunday schools; it was the mainstay of pedagogy in this period. Memorization of the Bible served several purposes. The process itself was good for the mind, people thought. Memorization helped children develop habits of discipline and industry. The content was also important. By memorizing the Bible, children would learn the substance of Christianity: its traditions, its precepts, and its examples of proper moral behavior. In addition, many children must have learned to read better by preparing to recite the difficult and often elegant prose of the Bible.

From Robert Raikes down through the early years of the American Sunday School Union, Protestant Sunday-school workers looked upon illiterate, churchless, street children as waifs who needed help and sympathy, who needed to be rescued from their parents' ignorance and immorality, and who at the same time were offending God by profaning the Sabbath. Sunday schools thus attacked vice and sin by keeping children off the streets on Sunday while teaching them literacy and morality. Protestant Sabbatarians were antagonistic toward people who took Sunday as a day of recreation, and their sensitivity on this matter helped create and sustain Sunday schools. Protestant emphasis on the Bible as a text underscored their faith that Christian scripture provided the basis for morality and respectability. In this regard Sunday schools were not very different from other charity schools. To become acculturated in an American charity school of the early nineteenth century was, to a large extent, to accept the King James Bible as one's primer.

One of the central goals of charity-school workers was to rescue children from an allegedly harmful family environment. Some reformers believed their success depended upon getting started when children were very young. This impulse to reach disadvantaged and potentially disruptive children while they were still impressionable and relatively "unspoiled" spawned the infant-school movement. As with Sunday Schools, the inspiration and the institution were English. Although children as young as two years old had gone to dame schools and district schools in America long before reformers devised the infant school, Americans regarded the infant schools fashioned in England in the second decade of the nineteenth century as distinctly new. They were aimed at the children of the poor and, more specifically, at the very young children of working mothers. More important, they tried to implement new pedagogical ideas. Robert Owen established the first such school in 1816 at New Lanark, his famous factory town in Scotland. Designed as part of an educational program to better the workers' lot and create a model industrial community, Owen's infant school also served the more immediate purpose of relieving working mothers of their infants during the day. The infant school at New Lanark employed female teachers and provided a relaxed mixture of play and rudimentary instruction. Owen's infant school dramatized his strong faith that educational environment could determine character. Among his rules for infant schools were: no scolding, no punishment, continual kindness, and encouragement of questions. Answers were always to be rational, instruction to emphasize the examination of actual objects, and the schedule to include plenty of exercise, music, and dance when children got restless. This seems radically different from Lancaster's regimented monitorial system, but both men were atempting to devise new pedagogies that harmonized with children's natural inclinations, rather than forcing them to sit still and quiet for long periods. Indeed, some infant-school workers used aspects of the monitorial system in their schools.[18]

Although other charity-school workers soon branded Owen as irreligious for his lack of attention to the Bible, and as a visionary for his utopian dream of a better industrial world, he was nonetheless like them in believing that the central purpose of workers' education was to shape individual character for a stable society. Owen's infant-school idea was picked up by Samuel Wilderspin, who opened an infant school in a London slum in 1820. His school placed more emphasis on moral training and less on rational development. It was thus more congenial to the main thrust of charity schooling. Wilderspin's book, *On the Importance of Educating the Infant Children of the Poor,* which appeared in 1821, soon became influential in England and America. Arriving home from a European tour, John Griscom of New York labelled Owen a "visionary schemer" and called for infant schools with more religious emphasis. In 1827 Joanna Bethune entered the field for just that purpose. Encouraged by Governor DeWitt Clinton, she organized the Infant School Society of New York, which began establishing schools for children from eighteen months to six years of age. An infant school opened in Philadelphia in the same year, due to the efforts of Reverend Maskell Carll, an admirer of Wilderspin. Three different infant-school societies cropped up in different parts of Philadelphia, and by 1830 the city had nine infant schools. Soon infant schools were reported in Boston, Worcester, Salem, and Charlestown, Massachusetts, in Hartford and New Haven, Connecticut, in Providence, Rhode Island, in Charleston, South Carolina, and in many other cities. To reach children as soon as they could walk, educators thought, was to break through the generational transmission of poor character and to rescue infants from the newly alarming and vicious environment of early American cities.[19]

But the motives of infant-school advocates were diverse. While all agreed that social morality was built upon individual character, and that infant schools could elevate the character of poor children, they had different views of the world and became involved in infant-school work for different reasons. Three religious purposes could be served through support of infant schools:

saving children's souls through religious education, saving one's own soul through good works, or preparing for the millennium, which some people expected imminently. Joanna Bethune unites the first two motives. In her diary, Mrs. Bethune prayed: "I thank Thee for the honor of being at the commencement of both Sabbath and infant schools. . . . Thou knowest that I love Thee, and love to feed Thy lambs." Evangelical urban charity work united selfless service with a desire to be well regarded by God and fellow men. There was, however, a more profound religious motivation than rectitude and the salvation of individual children. The Protestant belief that Christ would come again to rule the earth for a thousand years was widespread in the nineteenth century, and many believed that benevolent works might hasten the millennium. Sylvester Graham, a Philadelphia minister, preached in 1829 that "the latter-day glory may be at hand," and urged that "the Bible be stereotyped upon the pages of the youthful heart, by Infant and Sunday-School instruction." The Infant School Society of the City of Boston declared in 1834 that "a ray of millennial light has shone on us, and reveals a way in which poverty, with all its attendant evils—moral, physical, and intellectual, may be banished from the world."[20]

Among the worldly purposes of infant schooling, public morality through character training was central, but advocates of infant schools like Governor Clinton of New York also emphasized that education would be the bulwark of republican government by reducing "fraud, intrigue, corruption, and violence." In this regard, charity education was just an extension to the urban poor of the same purpose rural people had long argued for district schools. Education would produce intelligent citizens who would not be misled by demagogues and radicals. Then there was the range of social benefits most often associated with moral education: reduced crime, poverty, and intemperance.

In addition to the religious and social purposes of infant schools, the reform appealed to some people on purely pedagogical grounds. For educators like Bronson Alcott and William Russell of Boston, it mattered little whether the pupils were poor or not. Infant schools were a pedagogical advance, a way to adapt schooling to the true nature of early childhood. For Alcott and Russell, and also for Owen, the real breakthrough was not merely in offering instruction to the poor, but in recognizing that young children needed kindness more than discipline, curiosity more than authority, and real objects more than words. Russell, editor of the *American Journal of Education,* wrote that Boston's public primary schools would improve if they adopted infant-school methods, and Sarah Hale asked in her popular *Ladies' Magazine,* "Why should a plan which promises so many advantages, independent of merely relieving the mother from her charge, be confined to children of the indigent?" Boston school officials disagreed, claiming that infant-school pupils adjusted poorly to later school discipline.[21]

In Boston and elsewhere, the infant-school movement caused lively debate about appropriate methods of early childhood education. It spawned a few private middle-class infant schools, but it originated and had its major impact in the urban charity-school effort of the early national period. This effort emphasized personal morality and stigmatized the parents of poor children as vicious and indolent; it thus appears in retrospect self-serving and unjust. Yet charity-school workers—from merchant patrons to adolescent Sunday-school teachers—were not simply rationalizing self-interest by blaming the victims of an inequitable economic system. If they were partly the creators, they were also the captives of religious theories that emphasized individual responsibility and economic theories that demanded an unregulated marketplace. Even as sympathetic a commentator as Mathew Carey, who strove to reform factory conditions in Philadelphia, saw charity schooling as a way to ameliorate unavoidable low wages. "Unhappily, such is the constitution of society that a considerable portion of mankind, even in prosperous times, and in the most favoured countries, are doomed to pass their lives in indigence, from which no care, no industry, no sobriety, can extricate them." Carey argued that "although any changes for the better for these ill-fated classes, in regard to wages, may be hopeless, much of the distress and suffering of the poor may be mitigated by inculcating on them habits of order and regularity and cleanliness, with economical modes of employing their slender pittance so far as regards the kinds of food they consume, and modes of cookery, and in various other ways." Urban missionaries, according to Carey, should teach good habits, spread religious instruction without proselytizing, fight intemperance, urge parents to send children to infant and charity schools, and distribute relief funds to the most needy.[22]

It was an age of outreach to the poor in American cities. For motives of religious enthusiasm, benevolence, social control, and the desire to acculturate poor and alien groups, many wealthy and middle-class urban dwellers gave time and money to voluntary associations to relieve and elevate the poor. Educational institutions, such as African free schools, monitorial charity schools, Sunday schools, and infant schools, were their most visible and—according to their social philosophy—their most fruitful ventures. Of course, many poor children were untouched by the charity-school movement. Nor can we assess with any confidence the effect such schools had upon the children who did attend. Still, charity schools taught large numbers of poor children to read, which may have enriched their lives even if it did not enhance their economic opportunities. More important to the patrons of charity schools, the children were exposed to the Protestant Bible and the discipline of the schoolroom. These, they believed, provided the moral principles and behavioral expectations appropriate for children in nineteenth-century America.

Schooling for children of urban families who could afford tuition charges continued in its traditional mode in the period from 1780 to 1830. Parents sought schooling from an array of independent pay schools and academies. The most affluent families hired private tutors or patronized select boarding schools, while private-venture day schools served those in the middling ranks—extending from clerks and proprietors, through skilled laborers, to many low-income workers who strove to avoid the pauper stigma of charity schools. From the most modest to the most fashionable, these schools operated in an open market, according to supply and demand. The words "private" and "public" do not apply accurately to the charity and pay sectors of schooling, however. In some states, such as New York, academies received regular legislative grants, and their admirers considered them "public" institutions, in the sense that they provided the public with education and attempted to prepare children for responsible public life. Theodore Dwight, for example, declared in 1834 that Massachusetts' academies were part of "the great machinery of public education." Some educators of the early nineteenth century, however, began to use the word "public" in a sense closer to its twentieth-century meaning, referring to the town-supported free schools of cities like Boston and Salem or the charity-school systems of Philadelphia and New York. Conversely, such commentators began to refer to independent pay schools as "private." Still, by 1830 the terms did not yet have their modern connotations. The New York Free School Society renamed itself the Public School Society in 1825 and invited non-indigent children to attend. This was a crucial step in the transition from a charity-school system to a common public-school system. Despite the name change and new admissions policy, however, the Society was until 1853 run by a self-perpetuating board of trustees and supported by private benevolence in addition to public grants, and the pauper stigma took many decades to wear off.[23]

Although the independent pay schools of large cities served more children than the charity schools in the period from the Revolution until at least 1830, it is more difficult to make generalizations about them because they left fewer records and differed so much in curriculum, cost, organization, and philosophy. Still, some examples may be given and some generalizations ventured. Edward Everett Hale, son of a Boston newspaper editor, described his schooling and youthful activities in an autobiographical book, *A New England Boyhood*. Born in 1822, Hale was sent from age two to six to Miss Whitney's school, "very much on the go-as-you-please principle, and where there was no strain put upon the pupil." When he was six, he was sent to a "man's" school to learn Latin, geometry, and "other queer smattering bits of knowledge." From there, at age nine, he entered Boston Latin School, a prestigious college-preparatory school within the city's system. "But," said Hale, "there was no public school of any lower grade, to which my father would have sent me, any more than he would have sent me to jail." Of the schools operated by the city, all he heard was about whipping, poor teaching, and "constant low conflict with men of a very low type." At age thirteen, Hale completed the Latin School preparation and entered Harvard. Later he studied divinity privately and became a prominent Unitarian minister, as well as an essayist and writer of fiction, including the well-known short story, "The Man Without a Country."

Hale's reminiscence of his early years demonstrates how various aspects of his family and neighborhood life complemented the education he received in schools. "My father was one of the best teachers I know," said Hale. Among other things, his father introduced him early and painlessly to Latin, so that the boy missed "the agony with which some boys remember their first studies of *amo, amas, amat.*" Edward's school had a lending library, and he thought that checking books out was fun, but the family had more and better books at home. The boy also had subscriptions to magazines, such as the *Juvenile Miscellany* and *Boy's Own Book.* His home amusements included reading, drawing, and chemistry experiments. He and his brother were entered in swimming school in summer and in gymnastics class, a new German fad, in winter. Considering his family connections, his talented parents, his access to elite institutions, and his idyllic, happy childhood, Hale was perhaps not typical even among the middling and upper classes. But his was the kind of boyhood that was possible among the more privileged, and it stands in striking contrast to those of children in the growing ranks of the poor and the near-poor.[24]

Other diaries and reminiscences reveal similar patterns of opportunity for boys of well-to-do urban families in the days before public common schools. The sons of Robert Livingston of New York attended the prestigious Round Hill boarding school in Northampton in the 1820s. At a time when inexpensive pay schools were charging three or four dollars per quarter, Livingston was paying $120 per quarter for each of two boys' room, board, and tuition at Round Hill. In return he got the assurance of a superior classical education for his sons, with personal progress reports from Joseph Cogswell, the headmaster. The curriculum for Livingston's son Eugene included Latin, French, Spanish, algebra, mechanics, English grammar, and composition.

Cogswell wrote that Eugene was "a little too distrustful of his own powers. . . . I am fully persuaded that the same faithful prosecution of his studies will give him a highly cultivated mind and a familiar acquaintance with the various subjects of enquiry, which every gentleman should understand."[25]

Girls from privileged families also attended boarding or independent day schools, where they learned composition, grammar, modern languages, and other accomplishments deemed appropriate for women. Some of the curriculum in pay schools for girls was identical to those for men. However, girls less often studied Latin and Greek, which were part of the male-segregated, collegiate tradition. Also, the course of study for girls often added polite accomplishments like music and needlepoint. Governor Trumbull of Connecticut sent his teenaged daughters Harriet and Maria to stay in New York City with the fashionable widow Kitty Duer during the winter of 1801. From the Duer library, Maria chose William Guthrie's *Universal Geography* and David Hume's *History of England*. They attended church twice on Sundays, and sometimes studied the sermons. Halfway through their six-month sojourn, however, Maria reported to her mother that she had only "got partly thro' the second volume of Hume's History of England." "We don't find much time to read," she said, "as we go four times to dancing school, three to drawing and Harriet takes a music lesson three times a week—we sometimes don't get our dinner at home more than once or twice in a fortnight." Maria also expressed some shock that New Yorkers were "so dissipated—and they swear—and get tipsey." Such were the risks of finishing a wealthy daughter's education in the big city.[26]

Working people of middling occupational status also supported independent schools in large cities. A prominent example was the General Society of Mechanics and Tradesmen in New York, which opened a school for boys in 1820 and one for girls in 1826. By the late 1830s these schools enrolled 500 pupils, of whom generally 50 to 60 were free pupils, the children of indigent or deceased members. The Society also supported a lending library of 10,000 volumes and evening lectures for apprentices and others. These activities exemplified artisan culture, an attempt to unite manual labor, learning, and respectability. When one of the members offered a free course of evening lectures on English grammar for apprentices, the Society's officers thanked him for "exhibiting to the world the novel and interesting spectacle of literature mingling with labor, and of a master mechanic and apprentices devoting their leisure evenings to literary improvement." For some members' children, the Society's education program was not a means to enrich a life spent in manual labor, but a way to rise in the occupational hierarchy. Scholarships were endowed at Columbia College on behalf of Society members' children, and in 1840 the College's preparatory grammar school set aside six free places for pupils from the Mechanics' Society school so that the college scholarships could be better utilized. A year later, Mrs. Wheaton, principal of the girls' school, reported that forty of the Society's female graduates were teaching in the city's public and private schools. Members of such societies were probably skilled craftsmen and small-scale proprietors, with few from the lower ranks of day laborers or mariners. The initiation fee of the New York group, for example, was $10 in 1792 and $30 by 1832. These were not insignificant amounts, and there were further charges for schooling and library privileges. Families who could not afford this kind of artisan culture were left with the charity schools, or with the cheaper pay schools, or with no formal schooling at all.[27]

Although the intellectual rudiments and moral slogans were virtually the same in charity and pay schools, there was a fundamental difference in the cultural process going on in charity schools, on the one hand, and artisan and elite pay schools on the other. Charity schooling was an explicit attempt to intervene between the parents and children of a supposedly alien culture. Charity schools were thus antagonistic to the child's family and peer influences. The school competed with the other educational experiences of the child. In schools created and patronized by the middling and upper ranks, the cultural message was more in harmony with the family's goals, and we may presume that this was also true of the independent pay schools patronized by workers lower in the social scale. Such independent schools complemented and extended the educational role of the family.

While the independent pay schools flourished in a hundred varieties for those who could afford them, the growing charity-school movement expressed the anxieties of the social elite about public morality and cultural harmony. Urban schooling in the early national period represented the diversity and turbulence of urban life. There was, then, a great contrast between rural community schooling and urban specialized schooling. All such dichotomies in social history run the risk of oversimplification, yet this one persists even when we examine smaller inland cities and their immediate rural neighbors. Schenectady, for example, was a small upstate New York city. It had a population of 3,900 in 1820, which grew to 8,900 by 1850. Yet its educational development was very much like that of New York or Philadelphia. The tradition of independent pay schools continued to account for a majority of Schenectady's schools throughout the early national period. Hopeful schoolmasters advertised daytime and evening lessons in the three R's, surveying, dancing, and music. Union College operated a preparatory grammar school, which in 1818 added a girls' department and an English curriculum for boys who were not planning on college. Philanthropic citizens tried to meet the schooling needs of the less affluent by creating a Lancaster School Society and a Sunday School Society in 1816, an Infant School Society in 1829, and an African School in the 1830s. The Sunday schools aimed to give rudimentary instruction to poor children, particularly those who worked. One Sunday school of the 1830s was held in a factory and attracted fifty to sixty children. The monitorial day schools received grants from the city, but they also charged low tuition fees (25 cents per quarter in 1816). These schools thrived until the 1850s, when Schenectady officials somewhat reluctantly converted them into free public schools.

Across the Mohawk River, little Glenville counted 2,500 inhabitants in 1820, when it became a separate rural township. Glenville had no independent or charity schools. The town operated district schools supported by local taxes, by state school funds, and tuition charges to parents. The contrast, then, between urban and rural school in the early national period seems quite generally applicable. Two quite different modes of schooling served the rural and urban communities of the new republic.[28]

The dynamic aspect of rural district schooling was the expansion of enrollments. The dynamic aspect of urban schooling was the shift from diverse independent pay schools to consolidated free-school organizations. Although charity schools served fewer students than pay schools in American cities of the early national period, charity schooling was the innovative sector in urban education. Here began the pedagogical, organizational, and financial reforms that exended public schooling, and with it Anglo-American Protestant culture, to growing numbers of poor people. As charity schooling expanded during this period, independent pay schooling was on the wane, becoming progressively more elite and expensive. But the charity-school movement was more than just a proliferation of separate benevolent societies working with different indigent children for a common purpose. It began that way, but by the 1820s, in New York, Philadelphia, and elsewhere, a single monitorial school organization became dominant, controlling the bulk of charity schools and attaining favored status for financial assistance from the city and state. In many cities, the charity schools literally became the public common schools.

Urban educational leaders consolidated various charity schools under one organization, obtained increased governmental aid, developed procedures for supervision, and attempted to expand the schools' clientele beyond the poor to include all children. The example *par excellence* is New York City. The New York Free School Society began expanding as soon as it was created. Incorporated in 1805 to serve children of churchless indigent parents, the Society changed its charter in 1808 to include the churchgoing poor as well. Gaining a reputation for excellence and efficiency, largely through its enthusiastic use of the Lancasterian system, the Society gradually consolidated most of the city's charity schooling under its aegis. In 1816 the Brick Presbyterian Church discontinued its charity school, sent the children to the Free School Society, and gave up its share of public money to the Society. The Almshouse school in 1823 and St. Michael's Episcopal charity school in 1826 followed suit. In 1825, the Free School Society convinced the city's Common Council that no public funds should be distributed to denominational schools, thus ending aid to such expanding competitors as the Bethel Baptist Church. Having garnered most of the public money, the Free School Society changed its name to the Public School Society and invited all children to attend its schools, "where the rich and the poor may meet together, where the wall of partition, which now seems to be raised between them, may be removed." The renamed Society began charging tuition for those who could afford it; in 1832, instruction became free for all students. In that year the Infant School Society gave over its operation to the Public School Society, and in 1834 the Manumission Society transferred its seven schools for blacks to the same burgeoning system.

By 1835 the Society was by far the largest school organization in New York City, with fifteen upper departments and numerous primaries. Of course, the common-school ideal had remained largely a dream in the early national period, and the pauper stigma stuck to the Society's schools. However, the expansion of the Society's system, and its change of policy, must have increased the socioeconomic mix among the students to some degree. The process of systematization involved more than just consolidation. The trustees of the Public School Society attempted to standardize procedures and content, introduced supervision, carried on teacher training, and articulated more clearly the different levels in their system. They spoke enthusiastically about the efficiency of a large, rule-governed organization and dreamed of completing the "perfect system."[29]

The process was similar in Philadelphia. Philanthropists established a variety of charity-school societies in the 1790s and early 1800s to serve poor children whose parents were willing to declare their indigence. In 1818 the Pennsylvania legislature created a Board of Controllers for Philadelphia's charity schools, and this board took over the work of most of the voluntary societies. The law provided for school construction, the creation of a model school for teacher training, and free textbooks for the city's indigent students. This consolidation, plus wholehearted faith in the Lancasterian system, paved the way for rule making, standardization, and supervision. In 1836 the state passed a law opening the charity schools to all children, and in the same year the city's Board of Controllers adopted Philadelphia's infant schools and turned them into primary departments. "The stigma of poverty," wrote the Board's President, "has been erased from our statute-book." By 1836, then, Philadelphia's charity schools, like New York's, had been consolidated, had gained a virtual monopoly of public education money, and aspired to be the common schools of all children in the city.[30]

Smaller cities like Baltimore and Schenectady did not undergo elaborate bureaucratic development, but their Lancasterian school societies nonetheless received government aid and provided the nucleus of later public school systems. Even in Massachusetts, with its tradition of town-supported schools, the development of urban school systems was not wholly dissimilar. Public primary schools had been established in Boston in 1818 for parents who could not afford to pay to have their children learn to read. The town's schools had previously required reading ability as a qualification for entrance. The public primaries, then, were designed for low-income parents. Edward E. Hale's statement that his father would no sooner have sent him to a Boston public school than to jail suggests that even the next higher level of schools, the writing schools, failed to attract the affluent. In 1826 about one-third of Boston's school children were in independent pay schools. In Salem an even more thriving pay-school sector persisted, with a consequent segregation of children by their parents' income level. In 1806 the Reverend William Bentley, a school-committee member, commented that the free schools "are admirably supported, but the many private schools draw away all the children of the best families." Later enrollment figures suggest that the separation continued well into the nineteenth century. In 1837, 56 percent of Salem's schoolchildren were in private schools. Soon, however, a trend toward more inclusive public schools began. The mayor commented in 1843 that "the expenditure for public schools . . . will probably be increased until the result which seems inevitable should be reached, and all or by far the largest part of the children of this city shall be included within the Public Schools." By 1875, 82 percent of Salem's schoolchildren were in public schools.[31]

In New England cities, as well as in the cities of the Middle Atlantic and southern states, the only free schools of the early national period were charity schools or town schools, generally attended by children of low-income families. By the 1820s many supporters of these schools for the poor were striving to make them into common public schools. They thus competed with the independent pay schools, which gradually became more expensive and exclusive. Whether it began with charity schools explicitly for the poor or public schools shunned by the affluent, the transition of urban free schools into consolidated systems with a monopoly on public funds started in the 1820s and was supported by two major arguments: that a single agency was more efficient and that children of different classes should go to the same schools.

Curiously, however, the expansion and consolidation of charity schooling did not result in a larger total percentage of urban children going to school, at least not in the few cities for which adequate information has survived. The absolute numbers going to charity and public schools was increasing, both because of the rapid increase of population and the shift from independent schools to the emerging public systems. Also, the regularity of children's attendance as well as the annual length of school sessions may have been increasing. But the percentage of children who were enrolled in public and private schools combined seems to have remained roughly constant in large cities, at least in the Northeast. In New York City the proportion of those under twenty enrolled in school hovered around 26 percent (plus or minus 5 percent) from the 1790s to mid-century. In Salem, with a stronger town-school tradition and less severe urban problems, the level was higher—42 percent—but it remained remarkably stable throughout the period 1820 to 1875. The failure of urban enrollment rates to grow despite increased free school facilities is not too surprising considering the rapid increase of population in these cities, the increasing stratification of wealth, and increasing foreign immigration, which resulted in an ever-increasing number of families who did not see extended schooling as an advantage or who could not afford to forgo the income of their children. It may have been the case that almost all children in the cities of the early republic went to school for a few years at the prime common-school ages (approximately ages seven to twelve). Studies of United States Census data demonstrate that this was the case for the years after 1850. And it is almost certainly true that the expanding charity-school systems of the urban Northeast (and, to a lesser extent, elsewhere) helped to maintain this possibility for low-income city dwellers. Yet it is important to emphasize the stability of combined public and private enrollment rates over the first half of the nineteenth century, lest we underestimate the vitality of independent schooling at the beginning of the century and assume that government support expanded the participation rates in urban schooling. The charity-school sector of urban education in the early national period was nonetheless a dynamic force. Urban charity-school workers tried out new organizational schemes, expanded the capacity of their schools, and absorbed a growing share of urban schoolchildren.[32]

When men like Jefferson and Rush had proposed state free-school systems in the Revolutionary era, a predominantly rural population had persisted in its attachment to local control and parental initiative. Traditional modes of education proved responsive to social changes occurring in the countryside, and enrollment levels in rural schooling increased. In the cities, the proportion of children enrolled seems to have remained roughly constant. New organizations, arising from the charity-school effort, tried to accommodate the exploding number of urban people and laid the groundwork for more systematic state intervention during the antebellum period. Republican theorists had earlier argued in vain that state free schooling systems were essential to produce intelligent, disciplined citizens and to unify a diverse population. After 1830 more Americans came to share this view.

4

Social Change and Education in the American Northeast, 1830–1860

THE cultural, political, and economic evolution of the United States in the early national period had fostered the development of elementary schools, not as a result of state policy, but as a result of local custom. By 1830 schools were available to most white Americans in the North. Enrollment rates were lower in the South, but comparisons are made difficult by lack of detailed information about the unregulated schooling typical of this period. In the North, rural district school enrollment became almost universal, and throughout the nation, charity schooling for the urban poor was advocated with little opposition and with increasing organizational vigor. Locally controlled, voluntary elementary schooling was a common feature of life in most American communities by 1830. Most states, both North and South, had little legislation on elementary schooling and offered little or no financial assistance to localities. In many communities, school sessions were brief, facilities were crude, and teachers were only a few steps ahead of their pupils. Uniformity was provided only by the strong Protestant religious content of most schools, by the popularity of certain textbooks, and by informal traditions of school architecture. America had schools, but, except in large cities, America did not have school systems.

There had long been Americans who dreamed of state school

systems—Jefferson in Virginia, Rush in Pennsylvania, Gideon Hawley in New York, James Carter in Massachusetts—but by and large they had failed to persuade their legislative colleagues that state-level organization and regulation of common schooling were necessary. After 1830 a new generation of educational reformers appeared, and the tide began to turn. To ask whether change resulted from the heroic efforts of great men and women or was a functional adjustment of institutions to larger patterns of social change would be to create a false dichotomy. The individual achievements are real; processes of educational change can be hastened, retarded, or altered by the actions of forceful individuals. But we will understand better what was possible and what was probable by looking first at the material context, that is, the objective indices of social and economic change, and then at the ideological context, the dominant set of values used by the reformers to make sense of human relationships in the changing material context.

The United States economy expanded rapidly in the 1830s. Cotton was the key, and an interregional transportation revolution provided the means. Along new canals and railways, southern cotton and western foodstuffs came to the Northeast, the manufacturer and exporter of America's raw materials. All regions were affected by economic development, but the Northeast was on the cutting edge of change. After a depression from 1837 to the early 1840s, expansion resumed. By the late 1840s the Northeast had become unmistakably a manufacturing region, with steadily increasing productivity and commodity output. The rate of urbanization peaked in New England in the 1840s and in the Middle Atlantic states in the 1850s. Foreign trade and foreign immigration boomed throughout the period. When we consider national population statistics, which include frontier and agricultural regions, the trends appear more moderate than in the Northeast, but still impressive. The acceleration of social change in the 1830s and 1840s is still clearly evident. While the total population of the country grew at a steady rate of about 35 percent per decade from 1830 to 1860, the proportion of people living in communities of more than 2,500 people rose from less than one in ten to about one in five. The great majority of American workers were still farmers, but increased factory production and cheaper transportation influenced both agricultural and urban life, increasing the specialization of crops and the decline of household manufactures. Technological change came to the countryside, too, most notably in the form of horse-drawn iron ploughs. Meanwhile, the population in large cities, the number of workers in textile industries, and the number of immigrants arriving in America burgeoned. Cheap immigrant labor fed the expansion of industry. Comparing 1840 with 1850, the total population increased 35 percent while the number of immigrants entering the country increased 240 percent. The tremendous material success of American capitalism in this period is indicated by the increasing capacity of ships arriving in the nation's ports, which doubled in the 1830s, again in the 1840s, and again in the 1850s.[1]

Productivity spelled affluence for many, and average real wages rose, but the rewards were uneven. Strains were put on human relations not only by the exploitative nature of wage labor and the widening inequality of wealth, but also by the development of larger, impersonal markets, by very rapid population growth in the cities, and by the arrival of so many non-English people. Educators of the antebellum period continued to stress the traditional goals of American schooling—intelligent citizenship, industrious habits, and upright behavior. Indeed, the confident, expansive aspects of native, Protestant culture continued to buoy their optimism about America's future. But at the same time, educators' concerns about crime, poverty, cultural alienation, and political instability took on a new urgency. The fact that state intervention in education succeeded in this period while earlier it had failed, and the fact that it coincided with accelerating urbanization, industrialization, and immigration, suggests that there were causal connections between educational reform and social change in the years from 1830 to 1860. Plausible as such connections may seem, they are very difficult to sort out and to establish conclusively. No single term quite does justice to the complexity of social development. Instead we must look at interrelated changes in the economic, demographic, cultural, and political characteristics of American society to assess the impact each may have had on emerging systems of public education.

The economy of the antebellum Northeast was characterized by expansive capitalism, with larger-scale commercial networks, a gradual shift of people from self-employment to wage labor, and increasing class and income stratification. Most regions were not very industrialized until the late nineteenth century. However, in New England, where only one in a hundred workers had worked in establishments of twenty or more employees in 1816, the ratio was one in seven by 1840. Larger work forces in manufacturing meant that workplace and home, which had often been in the same place, were separated for more and more workers. The effects of these economic developments on common schooling may be seen in both a positive and a negative light, for they had both liberating and exploitative educational consequences. Capitalism in the broad sense, over the long run, was associated with increasing literacy and learning. Trade and finance put a premium on long-distance communication, placed central reliance on money and credit, and fostered the creation of urban entrepôts that could serve as centers of learning and publication as well as of commercial activity. Commerce encouraged knowledge of the written word and of basic arithmetic. There was a reciprocal relationship between literacy and publication. The more widespread the printed word, the more schooling was encouraged; the more literacy increased, the more market there was for newspapers, almanacs, periodicals, and books. By 1835, Richard Cobden claimed that there was six times as much newspaper reading in the United States as in England, and in 1853, Per Siljeström, a Swedish visitor, wrote that "in no country in the world is the taste for reading so diffused among the people as in America." Between 1840 and 1860 the dollar value of books produced in the United States more than tripled, while the number of daily newspapers rose from 138 to 387. While long-standing traditions of literacy and technological innovations in publication supported the expansion of print in nineteenth-century America, economic growth also played a role, by fostering communication networks, material affluence, and urbanization.[2]

Capitalism in the countryside of the Northeast meant larger markets, anxiety about agricultural productivity in a competitive situation, population drain from economically declining areas, small-town boosterism, and small-scale manufacturing. These changes tended to break down traditional rural insularity and resistance to state regulation and higher expenditures for education, making the hinterland more hospitable to common-school reformers' efforts in 1860 than it had been in 1830. At the beginning of the antebellum period, rural enrollments were higher, largely because seasonal agricultural work was compatible with a high rate of winter school enrollment. By the eve of the Civil War, rural towns in the Northeast were also increasing expenditures and length of school sessions, becoming more like their urban neighbors. Despite rural-urban differences, in the long run commerce, capital accumulation, communication, and schooling expanded throughout the Northeast.

In addition to these long-range trends, there were other, more dramatic economic developments in the antebellum Northeast: an increasing number of wage-earning workers and the establishment of America's first large factories. If we look at the male work force, the majority was still either self-employed or could hope to be during their careers. Only a minority of manufacturing workers worked in large enterprises. Still, the shift in the relationship of industrial wage-earners to the means of production heralded the creation of an American proletariat. Some historians have argued that this was the focal point of the relationship between industrial capitalism and common schooling. They have not emphasized the intellectual skills that schools taught, nor literacy as an economic asset. Their argument instead links the creation of industrial wage labor to educators' increasing interest in moral training and discipline.[3]

Schoolteachers have always been concerned with discipline and moral character, yet there seems to have been a quantum shift in the purposes, methods, and importance of school discipline in antebellum America. In the eighteenth century, teachers had ruled by virtue of their ascribed position, backed by the threat and frequent exercise of the rod. They commonly said they taught "morals," but the moral education of ordinary children in schools was not a mission of the state and was not a matter of public debate. By 1840, in contrast, the authority of teachers and the advisability of corporal punishment were widely discussed. Although a breakdown of family discipline had often been alleged in previous periods, it was not seen as a reason for enhanced school authority. Antebellum school reports emphasized discipline for orderly procedure in schools as well as for the production of model citizens. Advocates of new pedagogical schemes like the monitorial system and the graded school emphasized that more regimented procedures in schools would themselves shape appropriate character. They thus made the "silent" curriculum of antebellum school reform explicit. School committees urged skeptical teachers to use moral persuasion instead of corporal punishment, but when necessary they defended corporal punishment against parental challenges and harangued parents about the necessity of supporting teachers' efforts to shape children into industrious, frugal, temperate, subordinate, trustworthy, brave, clean, and reverent adults.

There were four significantly new developments in moral discipline in the nineteenth century: first, moral discipline, like other educational goals, became increasingly associated with schooling; second, the state, through local school committees and fledgling state education agencies, strenuously asserted the authority of teachers over children, in competition with parents; third, after centuries of virtually unrelieved schoolroom recitations and birch-enforced authority, the pedagogies of Joseph Lancaster and Johann Pestalozzi, which aimed at internalized discipline through proper motivation, challenged traditional practice; fourth, accompanying these developments, public discussion of the relationship between personal morality and social order greatly increased, spurred by the social strains of the period and witnessed in the proliferation of new periodicals and government agency reports.

There is much evidence to support the view that school discipline was intended to inculcate habits leading to future work discipline. However, there is also much evidence to suggest that work discipline was not the central purpose of school discipline and is not a sufficient explanation of it. Emphasis on the productive setting overlooks other adult activities shaped by schooling. Local school committees and other writers on education placed more emphasis on the prevention of crime and on the training of intelligent and acquiescent citizens than they did on behavior in the workplace. Although these goals are entirely compatible with work discipline, they are not unique to capitalism. Also, focusing on the socialization of premodern workers into the regimented world of the factory overlooks the strong emphasis on the same virtues in rural schools. Furthermore, the emphasis on capitalist exploitation of workers understates the pervasiveness of the virtues promoted by school discipline. Promptness and industry were urged as the route to success not just for the manual worker but for the businessman and manager as well. Work discipline was not aimed uniquely at laborers. However, in general it did not pay off for them. Despite the claims of manufacturers that educated men rose to be foremen, and despite the hard-earned savings set aside by some factory laborers, workers' frugality and industry were also widely rewarded by subsistence wages and discrimination. Still, many school people and social reformers believed that discipline would lead to self-help as well as stability, that imposed discipline would benefit the individual as well as the society. Their sincerity in this belief is not contradicted by the fact that it was a naïve and inhumane view of the matter. The character-training movement was much more than self-interested bourgeois hypocrisy, though there may have been some of that too. It was a widely accepted solution to many of the troubling problems of the transition to industrial capitalism in a culturally diverse political democracy. Work discipline was only one aspect of school discipline; to establish that schools served this purpose is not to demonstrate that the need for work discipline caused schools to exist, or was their essence, or exhausted their many functions.

Finally, the emphasis on school discipline to influence adult behavior overlooks the purposes of discipline in childhood. There were two compelling reasons for training children to be obedient, punctual, deferential, and task-oriented. The first is simply that discipline was needed for the orderly operation of a school. Local school committees ritualistically announced that good government in the classroom was the prerequisite and the *sine qua non* of learning. The pressures for silence and regimentation in classrooms with sizes ranging from thirty to eighty children per teacher are obvious, quite apart from the demands of the outside world.

As schools became more graded and students more classified, the informal, chaotic, individualized instructional world of eighteenth-century classrooms gradually gave way to a well-defined, lock-step curriculum. Schools thus became in some respects like factories, but not necessarily because they were mimicking factories, or preparing children to work in factories. Rather, both the workplace and the schools, as well as other nineteenth-century institutions, were partaking of the same ethos of efficiency, manipulation, and mastery.

The second reason for encouraging childhood discipline is that most parents wanted children to behave in a deferential and obedient manner. Despite tensions between parents and teachers, we may presume that many parents supported the general school goal of character formation, for the sake of their immediate parent-child relationship as well as for their child's future. This basis for consensus on virtues to be instilled would presumably have existed prior to the nineteenth century and thus does not explain the rise of emphatic interest in character formation by schools. The nineteenth-century surge is explained rather by a shift of educational responsibility from the family to the school, a shift that was accelerating in the period from the Revolution to the Civil War.

Different aspects of economic development affected schooling in different ways. By fostering commerce, geographical mobility, and communication, capitalism encouraged schooling for literacy, mathematics, and other intellectual skills. By creating more wage labor, capitalism contributed to the demand for work discipline, although other factors also account for school discipline. By creating more tightly coordinated productive hierarchies, such as in factories, industrialization promoted the values of punctuality, subordination, and regimentation that came also to characterize schools, although the pervasiveness of the factory *per se* as a model must be doubted in these years when most manufacturing was still small-scale. Finally, to the extent that the beginnings of industrial capitalism exacerbated or highlighted class tensions (and surely it did so to some degree), it reinforced the stress on social harmony in the common-school curriculum. American leaders were worried about urban disorder and cultural cacaphony, but they were bolstered by their belief in American political liberties and by some complacent theories of political economy, and they looked to free common schools to provide a common language, common social mores, equal opportunity for elementary education, and popular acceptance of the conditions of American economic life. Capitalism thus had many effects on common schooling, in some regards resulting in instruction that enhanced individuals' opportunities and enriched their lives, in other regards resulting in instruction that attempted to bind people to a social order in which injustice outweighed opportunity.

Capitalism and industrialization were closely related to the development of cities, and urbanization played an important role in both causing and facilitating educational reform in the antebellum Northeast. Urbanization can be measured by such summary statistics as the number of cities of a certain size, or the percentage of the whole population living in cities of various sizes. By any of these measures, the American Northeast was undergoing dramatic urbanization in the antebellum period. The population of the region as a whole was urbanizing, while the population size of the great coastal cities shot up into the hundreds of thousands and some sizable manufacturing cities in the interior were created almost overnight. As we have seen, American urban dwellers of the early national period developed modes of schooling distinctly different from those of their rural contemporaries. Those of affluent and middling ranks supported an entrepreneurial system of independent tuition schools for their own children and charity schools run by benevolent societies for the children of the poor.

Population density in large cities increased tensions and made social problems more visible. This lent urgency to the idea that schools could inculcate morality in the hope of maintaining social order. In cities the prevention of crime and poverty became the leading moral mission of public schools. Density of population also made practical the large, economical charity schools begun early in the nineteenth century. The density and scale of urban population allowed, even demanded, new ways of organizing common schooling. Systems of graded schools with standardized curricula and supervisory personnel became features of urban education. In New York, Philadelphia, and Boston, large numbers of children could be classified, instructed, and promoted according to system-wide rules. Not all urban educators thought that these developments were good, but most revelled in antebellum innovations like supervision and graded schools that would serve the goals of efficiency and uniformity.

The moral and cultural mission of urban schools reinforced this new bureaucratic ethos. Cultural conformity and educational uniformity went hand in hand; a set of moral values centering on hard work and subordination was well conveyed in busy, highly organized schools. In the early years of the republic, Noah Webster had written textbooks to encourage standard American pronunciation, hoping to mold the different sections into a unified nation. In the antebellum period, educators faced the much greater cultural diversity of new European immigrants, some of whom did not speak English at all. Immigration resulted in a national population whose diversity was unmatched in Western history. The presence of so many culturally alien people in antebellum America greatly reinforced the use of emerging public school systems to teach children a common English language and a common Protestant morality, much as earlier charity schools had been directed at those qualities of blacks or poor whites that educational reformers saw as undesirable or threatening. Immigrant groups in city and country attempted to recreate European institutions and maintain their cultures. When they tried to do this through daily schooling, it meant that they had to muster enough financial resources to support private schools or that they had to attempt to gain a cultural foothold in the public schools of their community. Both strategies were difficult. Selective migration, language problems, and a discriminatory job market meant that many immigrants were poor. And public school officials, with broad popular support, were generally unyielding to demands that the immigrants' language or customs be accommodated in the classroom. Religious differences made compromise within the public schools even more difficult. Antebellum immigration greatly swelled the ranks of the Roman Catholic Church in America. Protestants, heir to centuries of English enmity toward Catholicism, staunchly rejected religious pluralism for public schools.

Finally, immigrant groups were themselves split on issues of assimilation and cultural pride. Within most groups, especially in the second generation, there were "modernists" who thought it desirable to learn English and to Americanize. Nonetheless, champions of immigrant cultural integrity succeeded to some degree both in creating distinctive independent schools and in getting public schools to respond to their demands.

American-born Protestants reacted in various ways to the cultural and economic problems of immigration. Residential segregation, job discrimination, and occasional violence operated to differing degrees in different communities. But throughout American history, many people have looked to public education to resolve cultural conflict. While the schools have often abused different cultures, demanding cultural conversion without yielding equal opportunity, it was nonetheless a peaceful and seemingly democratic solution, accepted by some immigrants as well as by native-born Americans. Thus education for assimilation became one of the central preoccupations of nineteenth-century school officials. Too often educators equated Anglo-American Protestant traditions and values with something mislabeled American culture and then insisted that newcomers take it or leave it. However, the same problem that generated this crude answer also eventually produced some sophisticated thought about cultural pluralism and an ideal of the culturally tolerant common school.

In addition to these economic, demographic, and cultural factors, political developments affected education in the antebellum period. Enfranchisement was a long, gradual process, and white male suffrage was nearly complete in many states before the 1830s. However, the development of political parties and a wider exercise of the franchise in the antebellum period made citizenship education a continuing issue. If the republic was to have universal white male suffrage, it needed universal white education. Public schools could teach patriotism, encourage participation in civic affairs, and teach girls how to teach future sons the same lessons. America's rising nationalism in the antebellum period generated a spirit of international competition that also affected education. Urban educational reformers had long taken arguments and institutional models from England, but in the 1830s and 1840s, educators' attention shifted to the Continent, and particularly to Prussia, where universal compulsory education made its debut and pedagogical innovations impressed visitors from many nations. Neither the government nor the schools of Prussia were democratic, nor did Americans of this time in general approve of compulsory attendance. Yet many American observers admired Prussia's centralized system of schools. Teachers were trained and certified by the state. American visitors marvelled at the warmth and enthusiasm they saw in Prussian classrooms. Critics at home warned of the Prussianization of American schools, but common-school reformers argued that America need not become autocratic to adopt the best elements of state-regulated schooling. More important, they argued, America could not ignore such efficient systems of education and hope to compete politically or economically with nations like Prussia.[4]

The expanded activity of various states in encouraging and organizing education was not an isolated governmental initiative. Changes in the extent of state regulation also occurred in such areas as transportation, banking, welfare, and the treatment of deviants. Attacks on special corporate privileges and a rising humanitarian faith in institutional reform led to a surge of governmental activity in regulating and establishing institutions. Midwestern and Eastern states began investing heavily in transportation, first in canals, later in railroads. Spurred by regional competition, the revolution in transportation nonetheless helped integrate the nation and, incidentally, habituate people to state intervention in economic and social affairs. The spirit of intervention was expressed by Governor William Seward of New York in 1840 when he declared that if a nation "may employ its revenues and credit in carrying on war, in suppressing sedition, and in punishing crimes," it certainly could also employ the same resources "to avert the calamities of war, provide for the public security, prevent sedition, improve the public morals and increase the general happiness." Nothing was more central to this job than the common school. Americans, long persuaded of the value of schooling and concerned by the many social changes of the antebellum period, assented to the increasing involvement of state governments in education, not unanimously, but decisively. Economic, demographic, cultural, and political trends influenced their choices. Decisions about the shape and the content of public schooling were also influenced by the prevailing system of beliefs that helped Americans to understand and respond to social change.[5]

5

The Ideology of Antebellum Common-School Reform

As the pace of social change quickened in the American North during the 1830s, so did educators' advocacy of free common schooling dedicated to moral education and good citizenship. It was an era of social reform, and common-school reformers were in the forefront. They were confident that improved public education could alleviate a host of worrisome problems and secure the nation's destiny. Educational leaders came to the common-school cause with different values and different purposes in mind. Horace Mann and Henry Barnard, among the best known common-school crusaders, agreed on most educational matters but differed on social issues like slavery, and they saw the effects of industrialization differently. Further variety is evident in the religious views of educational reformers. As a boy, Horace Mann rebelled against his Congregational minister's harsh Calvinism, with its belief in infant depravity and predestination. Mann became a Unitarian, and some of his later foes in Massachusetts school work accused him of being irreligious. In contrast, Calvin Stowe of Ohio, John Pierce of Michigan, and other common-school reformers were staunch Congregationalists. Despite this range of theological and social views, there was a great deal of common ground among public-school leaders. They were characteristically Anglo-American in background, Protestant in religion, and drawn from the middling ranks of American society. They shared views on human nature, nationhood, and the political economy. These social beliefs provided the ideological context for the creation of state school systems.

"Ideology" is used here to mean a set of apparently compatible propositions about human nature and society that help an individual to interpret complex human problems and take action that the individual believes is in his or her best interest and the best interests of the society as a whole. Ideology is the aspect of culture that attempts to justify and defend a set of social relations and institutions. All people display ideological thinking at some times, to varying degrees. Its manifestations range from organized statements in print to the workaday, unuttered social beliefs implicit in individuals' actions. Although dissenting groups articulate ideological expressions in print, much of the world of print is dominated by the ideology of the dominant social group. It is difficult to discern the ideologies of ordinary people. The sources are largely limited to things written by people in the upper portion of the social scale. Much of the evidence is indirect and fragmentary. Also, individual behavior is not predictable from group ideologies. As John Plamenatz writes, "In a large and complex community, most people belong to several groups whose membership is not the same, so that any one person shares different ideologies with different people." Still, although there is an irreducible element of unpredictability about ideology in the individual case, the concept can be helpful by placing individuals' beliefs in the context of large belief systems.[1]

In enumerating the beliefs that constituted the ideology of antebellum school reformers, I shall first state the key social beliefs that were shared in a general way across many different political, regional, and social groups of native Protestant Americans, and then discuss some variants within that broadly based ideology. The ideology centered on republicanism, Protestantism, and capitalism, three sources of social belief that were intertwined and mutually supporting. Native Protestant ideology can best be summarized by enumerating ten strands or major propositions: the sacredness and fragility of the republican polity (including ideas about individualism, liberty, and virtue); the importance of individual character in fostering social morality; the central role of personal industry in defining rectitude and merit; the delineation of a highly respected but limited domestic role for women; the importance for character building of familial and social environment (within certain racial and ethnic limitations); the sanctity and social virtues of property; the equality and abundance of economic opportunity in the United States; the superiority of American Protestant culture; the grandeur of America's destiny; and the necessity of a determined public effort to unify America's polyglot population, chiefly through education.

The most forceful and influential variant of this ideology, a strain which I call "cosmopolitan," advocated government action to improve the economy, shape the morals, and unify the culture of mid-nineteenth-century America. In the antebellum period, this version of native Protestant ideology found its most effective political expression in the Whig Party, though it included many Democrats of the sort that Marvin Meyers has called "progressive." From their beliefs in Protestantism, republicanism, and capitalism, cosmopolitan spokesmen justified government intervention at a time of rapid change, to regulate morals, develop institutions, and create a more homogeneous population. Their version of native Protestant ideology, then, was centralist, assimilationist and moralistic. It was not "cosmopolitan" in the twentieth-century sense of secular or pluralistic. The uncertainty of native Protestants was not about the superiority of their moral values and cultural preferences. It was about whether they would prevail. Their ideology was part of a culture that was insistently didactic, and it became more assertive as new and threatening groups appeared on the American scene. Their cosmopolitan perspective envisioned an integrated economy, more centralized public direction, improved communication, and a common moral and political culture based on Anglo-American Protestantism, republicanism, and capitalism.[2]

The growing complexity of the economy and concern about training an increasingly diverse population for citizenship inclined many people to policies that they believed would help create discipline, unity, and social order. Nor were these incompatible with liberty and opportunity as cosmopolitan reformers understood those concepts. Still, there was substantial opposition to centralization and state regulation. The clearest opposing variant within the native Protestant perspective might be called localist. Finding political expression chiefly through the Democratic Party, localists resisted government intervention in institutional and personal life.

Native Protestant localists shared many ideological perspectives with native Protestant cosmopolitans, but they believed that cosmopolitan reformers had wrongly interpreted the ideology's very first proposition. The sacredness and fragility of republican government required local control and participation in institutions, above all else. A thoroughgoing delineation of variants of native Protestant ideology in nineteenth-century America would also identify a Southern slaveholding variant and possibly—though the evidence is still shrouded—one or more working-class variants.

Arguments about the relationship between ideology and class cannot be conclusive at our present state of knowledge. Did the social beliefs shared by Horace Mann, Henry Barnard, John Pierce, and William Seward constitute a class ideology? The fact that most writers on educational and moral reform were themselves middle-class does not necessarily make it a middle-class ideology. But there is some sense in calling the reformers' ideology "middle-class." Protestant revivalism and reform activities had a bourgeois character. Religion, reform, and education provided pious activities and sometimes careers for young middle-class males and females. The adoption of such values and participation in such activities may have played a role in the redefinition of the middle-class family and in the embourgeoisement of some middle-level workers such as clerks, foremen, and teachers. Furthermore, many of the details of this ideology seem middle-class, such as the presumption of a middle-class home in the prescriptive domestic literature, or the derogatory attitudes toward poor workers and immigrants in schoolbooks, newspaper commentary, and sermons. That the social outlook of the reformers favored the native middle class and was articulated largely by people of middle-class backgrounds is clear; but it is also true that there was substantial agreement across class lines about Protestant native social beliefs and about cosmopolitan school reform ideas—not just about the words, but about their meanings.[3]

Leaving dissent to a later discussion, we return to the social outlook that lay behind many antebellum discussions of education. Despite the shadings of class culture, and despite disputes between Whigs and Democrats about how to organize education and regulate morals, this set of social beliefs was widely embraced by native

Protestants of both parties and of varying economic circumstances. Democrats had no monopoly on republican values, nor were Whigs the sole defenders of property and capitalism. Blue-collar workers, like white-collar workers, appear to have responded positively to promises of stability, opportunity, political participation, and national superiority. A closer look at the central propositions of native Protestant ideology suggests the process by which culture and material life were translated into educational policy. While this ideology provided the rationale for organizing state systems of schools, it also provided many of the values the schools taught to children. The homilies of native Protestant belief became both the justification and the message of common schools.

Americans of the 1830s and the 1840s inherited from the revolutionary generation an anxious sense of the fragility of republican government. European history did not augur well for the survival of republics, and developments in America suggested the dangers of cultural diversity and regional loyalties. Born of English radicalism and devoted to concepts of personal liberty and equality, republican ideas nevertheless had a deeply conservative side. In the 1790s, Americans fretted about the dangers of faction and mobocracy; politicians worried lest the American experience fit conventional cyclical theories about the downfall of empires. Political leaders in the new nation argued that upon the American experiment hung the fate of freedom and progress. The survival of the American republic depended upon the morality of its people—not in armies or constitutions or inspired leadership—but in the virtue of the propertied, industrious, and intelligent American yeoman. One embodiment of "virtue" in republican thought was the yeoman, independent in means and judgment but willing to sacrifice for the common good; another embodiment was the citizen, Benjamin Rush's "republican machine," who was intelligent and free but subordinated himself to the common good as articulated by virtuous leaders. Both of these images stressed the dangers to republicanism in the absence of virtue, and both provided themes for American schoolbooks. The insecurity of republican government justified a stress on self-sacrifice and subordination in the educational thought of the Founding Fathers.[4]

By the 1830s, the fall of the American republic seemed less

likely. Economic progress, diplomatic stability, and new religious currents gave rise to a general atmosphere of optimism about human nature and the moral potential of properly constructed institutions. At the same time, there were new forces to fear, particularly in the American Northeast—manufacturing, foreign immigration, the decline of landholding, the fragmentation of Protestant religion, and the growth of cities. In the face of these problems, American republicanism, with its focus on self-sacrifice and subordination, seemed ever more relevant. With growing democracy, the price of participation would be proper attitudes; with growing diversity of culture and ideas, the price of respectability would be acquiescence in the social outlook of native Protestant leaders. Political education consisted of stressing common beliefs and glorifying the exercise of intelligence in a republic, while urging respect for laws and downplaying the very issues upon which citizens might exercise their intelligence. No less than the Founding Fathers, we may presume, political commentators at midcentury believed that the republic depended upon the widespread exercise of intelligent free speech. But they also perceived in their day numerous threats to stability, much evidence of turbulence and excess, and many centrifugal forces in American life. Therefore they too stressed order as much as liberty. The responsibilities of republican citizenship were stern and weighty. These responsibilities required not only independent judgment but discipline. In schoolbooks and popular essays the image of the republican citizen is of a man who is constructive, on occasion critical, but always cautious and respectful. School textbooks lauded liberty but left it vague, while excoriating Anne Hutchinson and Shays' Rebellion along with the French Revolution. In his famous *Twelfth Report* (1848), Horace Mann argued that schools should allow no controversial issues to be taught. Both the precariousness and the preciousness of the republic were underscored by the diverse immigration into America. John Pierce, Michigan's common-school leader, said in his 1837 report that unrestricted immigration made the American republic "the boldest experiment upon the stability of government ever made in the annals of time."

Republican beliefs such as these were nearly universal among public commentators in antebellum America. They were entirely compatible with the other central tenets of native Protestant ideology, and they had clear educational implications: schooling should stress unity, obedience, restraint, self-sacrifice, and the careful exercise of intelligence. The survival of the republic depended upon the virtue of its citizens. This republican belief was reinforced by a second major strand in the ideology: the proposition that social morality consisted of the moral character of all the individuals in the society. The nation was born in revolution and had weathered decades of anxiety that the system would collapse because of the insufficient virtue of its citizens. Emphasis was on whether individuals would ruin the system, not the reverse. The morality of the social system as a system was beyond question; the moral quality of the society was therefore to be improved by improving the moral quality of individuals. The implications for educators were reiterated again and again. Michigan's John Pierce put the argument succinctly: "Generally speaking, the child uneducated in knowledge and virtue is educated in the school of depravity. And what is true of the individual is true of communities." Early urban missionaries in the Northeast constantly stressed the correlation of poor character, vice, and poverty. The Reverend Elia Cornelius told the Salem Society for the Moral and Religious Instruction of the Poor in 1824 that poverty results from "vicious habits" nine times out of ten and that "the moral and religious improvement of the poor is the surest and best means of relieving their wants." Twenty-five years later, a relief worker in New York, echoing fellow reformers elsewhere, declared that the destitution and misery of the poor "are owing to moral causes, and will admit only of moral remedies. Condition must consequently be improved, by improving character."[5]

The emphasis on individual character, however, was not aimed solely at the poor, the inebriate, and the criminal. Because social morality depended upon every individual's character, all needed moral education. The criminal and the poor were just the most visible signs of the connection between character and career. A local school official in Vermont said that teachers stamped characters on children, "molding them for the places they are to fill, whether in a senate or a prison, a pulpit or a scaffold." In emphasizing individual morality, the schools were mirroring a general trait of native Protestant culture. From the moral philosophy texts of the colleges, to the evangelical religion spreading through all regions of the country, to treatises on political economy, the hope of the future was pinned on individual conversion and regeneration. The role of the schools was clear. In a popular teachers' manual of the 1830s, Orville Taylor declared, "It is our duty to make men moral." In the 1830s, Frederick Packard, a textbook writer, linked republican government and moral training: "Ever since the world began, the depraved passions of men have required some kind of restraint. . . . As ours is emphatically (at least we think so) the freest country of all the earth, we are more exposed than any other country to have our liberty used as a cloak for licentiousness."[6]

Alongside the related virtues of self-control, self-sacrifice, and restraint stood industry. The necessity of hard work was a central message of schoolbooks and children's fiction in antebellum America. In Cobb's *Juvenile Reader No. 2* (1833), the "Diligent Scholar . . . goes home as quickly as he can, he has so much to tell his parents and to do for them." As a result, "if he is to go into a store or be an apprentice, many people who have heard of his good character will wish to have him." Grammar books featured aphorisms on industry, such as, "It often requires deep digging to obtain pure water," "The path of fame is altogether an uphill road," and "Idleness is the nest in which mischief lays its eggs." Although such admonitions go back to Franklin's Poor Richard and earlier to the Puritan stress on work, the connection between industry and career success became a more frequent and explicit theme in the 1840s, when the problems of poverty, cultural diversity, and urban life began to appear more intractable and troubling than social commentators had imagined in the more optimistic days of the 1830s. "The idle boy is almost invariably poor and miserable," said Wilson's *Third Reader* (1860), while "the industrious boy is happy and prosperous." Joseph Burleigh's *The Thinker, A Moral Reader* (1855) was uncompromising: "Remember that all the ignorance, degradation, and misery in the world, is the result of indolence and vice." The industry theme was a two-edged sword. It aimed at creating an industrious populace, which would render a permanent poor class impossible in America, but it also helped to explain the poverty that did exist.

Hard-working people in temporary poverty caused by personal calamity deserved charity; but those unworthy individuals whose chronic poverty was caused by indolence deserved their plight. Their children, of course, had to be rescued and taught that industry was a central trait of the virtuous individual.[7]

The most elaborate tale of work socialization appears in a very popular children's book of the period, Jacob Abbott's *Rollo at Work; or, the Way to Be Industrious.* Rollo, who was five years old, decided that he would like to learn how to work, and his father agreed to teach him. One has to learn to work steadily, said Rollo's father, "without stopping to rest, or to contrive new ways of doing it, or to see other people, or to talk." Rollo tried this out on a nail-sorting task, but he didn't do very well, which brought a rebuke from his father. Rollo "felt guilty and ashamed." That evening his father took him on his lap and said: "You see it is very necessary that you should have the power of confining yourself steadily and patiently to a single employment, even if it does not amuse you. *I* have to do that, and all people have to do it, and you must learn to do it, or you will grow up indolent and useless." Two days later Rollo was assigned to pick up stones in the road and pile them behind the barn. But he was "not quite faithful. His father observed him playing several times." For this, Rollo was given bread and water for dinner, on the back steps, while the family enjoyed beefsteak and apple pie. Crying over his bread and water, Rollo "determined that he would never be unfaithful in his work again." The bread-and-water punishment was the turning point. Rollo learned to work, even to enjoy it. "In fact, in the course of a month, Rollo became quite a faithful and efficient little workman." In the subsequent Rollo books, Jacob Abbott allowed his hero to have quite an adventuresome and happy childhood, not just yard chores with no talking. The *Rollo at Work* book is just a lengthy version of the standard textbook message on industry. Often found side by side with more cheerful and expansive visions of life, and even frivolous concessions to childhood, these stern stories about work were supported by the larger ideological context. They derived from a conviction that social order and social morality depended upon individual character and that the chief badge of character was work.[8]

For women, work socialization was a very different process from that of men, and the definition of woman's proper roles was a central element in the ideology of the antebellum generation. It had a profound impact on education. Female work socialization did not offer careers, influence, public recognition, authority, or wealth. Instead, domestic tranquility, a good husband, and the special care of children rewarded the industry and virtue of a young woman. Of course, male and female roles in the home had been differentiated to some degree throughout history, due to the child-bearing and nursing role of women, due to differences in aspects of physical strength, and due to the subordination of women by men. In the nineteenth century, however, the middle-class literature on motherhood and domesticity became a veritable crusade. It became as sentimental as it was insistent, and it brought to the center of American Protestant ideology various concepts about women that had previously been absent or incidental.

Women had three central roles in the middle-class home. As wives they were to create an evening sanctuary from the busy, corrupt, daytime world their husbands inhabited. As homemakers they were to manage a frugal and healthy household, according to the latest knowledge of domestic science. As mothers they were to nurture and instruct children to make a virtuous new generation for a perilous society. The concepts of the home as sanctuary and the wife as domestic scientist were substantially new, and the emphasis placed on childrearing became more emphatic after 1830, with the role assigned more strictly and consistently to women.

The doctrine that these were the crucial roles for women had both liberating and constraining implications for education. On the one hand, the strong emphasis on mother as the teacher of young children, and the importance of that training for the moral and political future of the nation, encouraged the view that women should be well educated, at least in the common-school subjects and perhaps beyond. On the other hand, the concept of strict spheres of activity placed limits on the extent and nature of appropriate female education. As the home became more clearly demarcated from the social life outside its doors, the roles of men and women became more strongly and explicitly differentiated. Writers frequently called the home a "haven" or a "refuge" and stressed the separate "sphere" of women's activities.

School texts taught young girls about the three domestic roles. Angell's *Select Reader* (1833) discussed how wives could soften the violent impulses that men develop in "the busy theatre of a contentious world." In "The Wife," a piece reprinted in several school readers, Washington Irving wrote that a wife is like "the vine, which has long twined its graceful foliage about the oak and been lifted by it into the sunshine." Yet when the oak is struck by lightning, the vine will "cling round it with its caressing tendrils, and bind up its shattered boughs." "So it is beautifully ordered by Providence," explained Irving, "that woman, who is the mere dependent and ornament of man in his happier hours, should be his stay and solace when smitten with sudden calamity."[9]

Of course, there was much work to be done in the domestic circle between male calamities. "Every woman should be a good house-keeper," declared Horace Mann. "A well-ordered house is worthy the dignity of being compared with a well-ordered state." Writers of the 1830s and 1840s complained that declining respect for housework was a big problem in America. Domestic science arose in this period of social reform as a response to the housewife problem. The person most responsible for compiling and popular-izing scientific knowledge for the housewife was Catharine Beecher. In her *Treatise on Domestic Economy* (1841), Beecher argued the necessity of the subordination of women, the separation of male and female roles, and a domestic emphasis in female educa-tion. She then went on to provide details on anatomy, diet, exer-cise, manners, household budgets, childrearing, leisure, house con-struction, cleaning, washing, sewing, gardening, and other areas of female concern. This and other works on domestic economy tried to promote the dignity, complexity, and importance of house-work, while they disseminated practical suggestions on household management, health, and other matters important in the woman's sphere.[10]

Despite all the emphasis on comforting one's husband and man-aging one's housework, the most insistent theme in the domestic literature was on childrearing, and this strong emphasis on the educational responsibility of mothers is also reflected in the school textbooks of the antebellum period. The education of young chil-dren fell to the mother, not just because more fathers were now away from home all day, but because women had an emotional, biological, and spiritual propensity for children. In *The Powers and Duties of Women,* Horace Mann said that "the true mother continues to be one with the child for years after its birth. Her consciousness embraces and interpenetrates its consciousness. . . . Her soul is an atmosphere around its soul; and if that atmosphere be pure, then, indeed, the child breathes the air of heaven before it is contaminated with the foul vapors of earth." For this protective and nurturant role, mothers were ideally suited.

The fact that the domestic ideal was widespread does not tell us whether young women in general accepted the roles prescribed for them. Ideas in marriage manuals, magazines, and schoolbooks cannot be mistaken as evidence of the beliefs of those who read them. They are, rather, evidence that a very broad range of writers supported the ideals in print and that young women in antebellum society encountered these ideals to the degree that they read magazines and domestic manuals or went to common schools. While the women's magazines and advice literature may have been read mostly by people in the middling and upper ranks of society, the common schools enrolled a very high percentage of children from families of all occupational groups, at least for a few years of their lives. Public schooling thus was a crucial didactic instrument of American Victorian culture.

Emphasis on woman's proper sphere affected not only the textbook messages girls received but also the structure of the curriculum. While antebellum views of women furthered the expansion of educational opportunities for girls, which had begun in the late eighteenth and early nineteenth centuries, they also encouraged a different emphasis for girls than boys. This was usually justified not because women had inferior capacity to learn but because they were necessarily destined to a different function. Horace Mann declared that the "female had every right to a full and complete mental development which belongs to the other sex. As compared with man, I believe she would reward all labors and expenditures for her thorough education with quite as ample returns of beauty, utility, and power." However, the type of education might differ because "God had created the race male and female, on the principle of a division of labor." Catharine Beecher also advocated more domestic education for girls. "A little girl may begin, at five or six years of age, to assist her mother; and, if properly trained, by the time she is ten, she can render essential aid." Between ten and fifteen, continued Beecher, girls should concentrate on staying healthy and learning domestic skills. "During this period, though some attention ought to be paid to intellectual culture, it ought to be made altogether secondary in importance." Stephen Simpson, leader of the Philadelphia Workingmen's Party in the 1830s, warned against too much public education for girls. "Their duties are not public—nature claims all their energies as the mother and the nurse of our kind. . . . We want no race of fabled Amazons." The Salem, Massachusetts, School Committee, recommending sewing classes for girls in the 1840s, commented, "It is a matter of complaint in our city, and seemingly just, that the girls have too much intellectual and too little home education. . . . Boys need, strictly speaking, a more intellectual education than girls, since the latter are destined for the duties of the home, while the main province of the former, as men, is ever abroad, in the complications of business, requiring that rigid analysis and calculation happily spared to the wife and mother." No one could have summarized the prevalent midcentury view of female education any better.[11]

The role of the female in providing a proper environment for her children's moral development and her husband's domestic repose reflected an increasing concern for environment among antebellum reformers and social commentators. This is most obvious in the literature of childhood development. By the end of the eighteenth century, there was a range of American views on early childhood, ranging from the persisting Calvinist view that children inherited the original sin of Adam and were thus innately depraved, to the Enlightenment view, stemming from Locke's psychology, that the mind begins as a clean slate and children are morally neutral at birth, to the more romantic view of Pestalozzi, influenced by Rousseau, that children were not only innocent but naturally good and that educational strategies should shield the child from the dangers of a corrupt world. The emphasis was on protecting and molding the child, not breaking the will. It was part of a long-range transition in the central focus of childrearing: from soul to character to personality. In the century roughly from

1750 to 1850, the balance gradually shifted toward character training and toward a softer, protective, environmental view of development. This view portrayed children as innocent and vulnerable, but also as malleable and capable of great moral and intellectual accomplishment.[12]

However, almost all commentators believed that there were racial, ethnic, and sexual limitations on human potential, whatever the environment. As the century progressed, the strains of ethnic relations and the apparent intractability of urban social problems reinforced traditional stereotypes. Although the doctrine of infant depravity had lost some ground, there remained a range of opinion on the heritability of character. In his popular *Seven Lectures to Young Men* (1844), Henry Ward Beecher said that "the children of a sturdy thief, if taken from him at birth and reared by honest men would, doubtless, have to contend against a strongly dishonest inclination." Elsewhere he argued, "You can make a great deal more of a potato if you cultivate it than if you do not cultivate it; but no cultivation in this world will ever make an apple out of a potato."[13]

The environmental thrust of childrearing literature of the antebellum period must therefore be understood within a context of group prejudices. Olney's *Practical System of Modern Geography,* in its twenty-first edition by 1836, provides examples of national stereotyping. "The Irish in general," wrote Olney, "are quick of apprehension, active, brave and hospitable; but passionate, ignorant, vain, and superstitious." The Italians are "affable and polite" and excel in the arts, "but they are effeminate, superstitious, slavish, and revengeful." Another text said that South American Creoles were "naturally indolent, and altogether averse to serious thought and deep reflection." Negroes, said an 1851 geography, are "destitute of intelligence." Environmentalism did not overturn racism, a pervasive aspect of white American culture, north and south. Natural philosophers of the antebellum period forged theories about the separate creation of the races, speculated that blacks and whites were of different species, and fretted that an increase in the black population would cause the downfall of the republic. While a few northern abolitionists joined with blacks who pressed for integrated schools, most common-school reformers shied from the issue. Horace Mann feared that if he took sides in the Boston integration issue he might "never get another cent" for school improvement. In a speech to blacks in Ohio in 1852, Mann said that "in intellect, the blacks are inferior to the whites, while in sentiment and affections, the whites are inferior to the blacks."[14]

The Victorian faith in environment and human potential, then, was still fettered in racial and national stereotypes. As with the domestic values for women, racism affected not only the messages children received in schools but the structure of schooling as well. Both gender and racial stereotypes contradicted the value placed on equality and perfectibility in native Protestant ideology, and both kept the schools from being truly "common." Still, the environmental emphasis in character formation was substantial, and it had several corollaries in the reform thought and institutional practices of the antebellum decades. In childrearing, this theme underlay the discovery of early childhood and the intense discussion of moral training by mothers; in schooling, the environmental analysis supported the new "soft" pedagogy, an effort to get children to internalize discipline rather than having authority imposed, to have teachers rule by "moral suasion" rather than by coercion; in incarcerative institutions like prisons and asylums, the new "moral treatment" was an effort to reform and cure deviants through a highly structured environment rather than by physical coercion; in urban affairs, new sensitivity to the degenerating physical environment led to efforts at reform of water supply, ventilation of tenements, and sanitation. The common thread in these efforts was the desire to create environments conducive to proper character development while at the same time convincing people of the legitimacy of the institutions and the solicitousness of those in charge.[15]

Property holding, like the family, had been a traditional prop to social stability in America. Leaders of the revolutionary generation had argued that property holding was a natural right and that incursions upon it by the state justified resistance. By property holding, however, they meant something more than home ownership. In an agrarian society, property holding meant access to a portion of the natural resources represented in land, a place on which to work and on which to enjoy the fruits of one's labor.

While there had been from the start a substantial number of propertyless people in British America, the proportion increased in the nineteenth century. This posed two somewhat distinct problems: to persuade people of the sanctity of property in order to protect owners from assaults on their property, and to provide general moral education for a growing class of unpropertied persons who would not benefit from the natural virtue assumed to arise automatically from having a stake in society.

These concerns were united in the homilies of the period. Property was to be respected because it taught virtue. Everyone should be taught to desire property and to respect property. "Security of property is the great incentive to industry," said Taylor's *District School*. Even rude frontiersmen, said Timothy Dwight, can "become sober, industrious citizens, merely by the acquisition of property." "The love of property," he continued, "seems indispensible to the existence of sound morals. . . . The secure possession of property demands, every moment, the hedge of law, and reconciles a man, originally lawless, to the restraints of government." Redistribution of land equally, argued a popular school text, would do "a hundred times more harm than good." Francis Wayland, perhaps the most influential political economist of the antebellum period, said that private property was responsible for "all progress in civilization." Theodore Sedgwick, another leading theorist, reminded readers that Christianity forbade the destruction of property and said that the uninhibited pursuit of property "explains the unexampled prosperity, riches and happiness" of the North. The key proposition was "that the labourers here are permitted to work for their own benefit, to work for profit."[16]

Antebellum Americans held varying opinions about property and the resulting class structure, reflecting different ideological leanings and different economic realities of the antebellum North. The Whigs and their Republican successors saw a land of small proprietors and small landholders, a land still full of opportunity and mobility. Northern Democrats and more radical critics saw a growing industrial proletariat and a growing capitalist class, and they emphasized the antagonism between those with property and those without. Nonetheless, even radicals felt compelled to deny that they were assaulting the sanctity of property. "Our object is as remote from that as the existing system of extortion is from justice," wrote Stephen Simpson in his *Workingmen's Manual*. School texts reinforced the sanctity and virtues of property and the folly of common ownership or redistribution of wealth.

In this pro-capitalist native Protestant ideology, the availability of property and education combined to produce a system of fair opportunity. This perspective transcended party. To be sure, some urban labor spokesmen attacked this aspect of the ideology; but the assertion of widespread opportunity through property and education crops up in the writings of men from different parties and occupational groups. It seems that educational reformers struck a strong chord in American culture when they articulated the opportunity theme. Michigan's superintendent of common schools, John Pierce, wrote that "by means of the public schools the poor boy of today, without the protection of father or mother, may be the man of learning and influence of tomorrow; and he may accumulate and die the possessor of tens of thousands; he may even reach the highest station in the republic." An open education system made the arbitrary redistribution of wealth unnecessary.[17]

Many educators and political economists believed that the availability of land and education in America not only provided men with an equal chance but would in fact maintain a greater equality of condition than in other countries. This was as important as equality of opportunity. Republican thought stressed that citizens should be on a more equal footing in a republic than in highly stratified, aristocratic societies. Congratulating his fellow Vermonters for creating a state school system, Horace Eaton wrote in 1846, "Experience proves that as a society advances in age, there is ever a tendency to wide disparities of rank and condition. And what means can be devised that shall be so effectual in guaranteeing against them as the general diffusion of knowledge? Here is an equalizing power—a levelling engine." A complete system of universal schooling, claimed Horace Mann in his 1848 report, would "obliterate factitious distinctions in society."[18]

Several qualifications should be noted with regard to educators' pronouncements about equality of opportunity. First, and most important, the fair chance was open mainly to white, native males. Even the most ringing statements about the equality of all men were not taken to include women or black people, and non-English immigrants faced various forms of discrimination. Samuel Goodrich, author of the popular Peter Parley stories, explained eq"ality this way in a civics textbook: "Equality does not mean that a woman shall be equal to a man, but that all women, all children, all citizens, shall enjoy the same relative rights, privileges and immunities." Second, even for white males, occupational mobility through education was neither a central theme nor a central purpose of the antebellum public school reform movement. The overriding emphasis for all schoolchildren, and especially for children of the poor and the working class, was on morality, not mobility. Finally, educators frequently lapsed into an explicit expectation that most children would inherit their parents' station in life. *The Progressive Reader* (1834) counselled children that "everything ought to suit the station in which we live, or are likely to live. . . . Make yourself contented and cheerful in your station, which you see is so much happier than that of many children." A Michigan education report of the 1840s lauded America's lack of hereditary privilege and abundance of opportunity but on the same page advised parents to educate children "in a manner suitable to their station and calling."[19]

The theorists' rosy view of the American political economy found its support in English laissez-faire writings, in the democratic politics of antebellum America, and in the generally rising productivity of American industry and agriculture in the antebellum period. It was, however, a view of prosperity and opportunity that increasingly forced one to wear blinders in the 1840s and 1850s. Opportunity for advancement was almost nonexistent for blacks, almost irrelevant for women, and beyond the reach of many in an increasingly immigrant, urban work force. Although the American political economists created a description that was partial and quickly became dated, they provided many of the homilies of native Protestant ideology. And while its proponents were committed to the status quo of capitalism as they understood it, it was a status quo that they believed was freer and fairer than any the world had yet known.

Two remaining concepts—the superiority of Protestantism and the special destiny of America—rounded out native Protestant ideology and had a strong impact on education. Seen through a twentieth-century lens of pluralism and cultural relativism, these beliefs may seem brash and chauvinistic, but their validity was crystal clear to nineteenth-century Protestant writers, who expressed them fervently, without apology. English Protestants had considered themselves the defenders of the faith ever since their split with Rome, and the American Puritans, in turn, believed that they had salvaged what was best in English Protestantism. Other Protestant groups shared this sense of purification and mission in the New World. In some sects this impulse took the form of utopian separatism, but the larger American Protestant groups translated their sense of Protestant superiority and mission into an ethnocentric faith in American mainstream culture and institutions. They associated Protestant Christianity with republicanism, with economic progress, and with virtue. "The principles of democracy," argued Catharine Beecher, "are identical with the principles of Christianity." The religion of New England, according to an early school geography, is the "best in the world, perhaps, for a republican government." Protestant writers made it clear that when they said "Christian," they meant Protestant. Textbooks characterized Protestant Christian nations as "more powerful," "more advanced in knowledge," and "most distinguished for justice and kindness." The tendency of the Roman Catholic religion, in contrast, "was toward degeneracy and ruin," as the case of Rome demonstrated. In a sermon of 1851, Thomas King, a popular Boston minister, charged that the Catholic church was "the ally of tyranny, the opponent of material prosperity, the foe of thrift, the enemy of the railroad, the caucus, and the school." Despite this celebration of America as a Christian nation, and Protestant commentators' equation of Christianity with Protestantism, it was possible for non-Protestants to subscribe to many elements of American Victorian ideology. Protestants had no monopoly on the adulation of property, hard work, or female domesticity. Nonetheless, Catholics or Jews who embraced such beliefs must have felt marginal. The superiority of Protestant culture was not merely one of a miscellaneous list of beliefs; it was an integral part of the ideology, supporting and being supported by other social beliefs.[20]

These beliefs culminated in yet another aspect of the ideological context: the unique destiny of America. Several beliefs contributed to this historical proposition—the superiority of Protestantism, the existence of a providential guiding hand in history, the im-provability of human nature, the westward progress of civilization, and the supportive relationship between material and moral prog-ress. These beliefs combined to suggest to Americans that their nation was destined to reach the peak of human civilization and, with God's help, to overcome all obstacles to material preeminence and spiritual elevation. Some dissenters argued that workers reaped little from so-called material progress, that the Panic of 1837 and subsequent hard times revealed the weaknesses of the financial system, and that materialism and human progress were not the same thing. But most sermonizers, essayists, and textbook writers ignored these discordant notes and trumpeted the main theme. Americans, said a history text of the 1850s, "are to work out, not alone our destiny, but that of the whole world. . . . The inferior races shall be educated and made fellow laborers in the great work of human progress."[21]

The notion of divinely guided progress was rooted in a long-standing Western tradition, and within the Christian church a substantial body of doctrinal debate centered upon the perfection of the world through the second coming of Christ. These beliefs were called millenarian, because of the conviction that Christ would reign one thousand years upon earth before the raising of the dead and the final, eternal judgment day. Many Protestants believed that individuals could work toward the second coming by moral reform and spreading the gospel. When this view is combined with faith in material production and innovation, we can see how the different strands of Protestant American thought about progress reinforced each other. Thomas King's sermon in honor of railroads provides a dramatic illustration:

> Providence had another and higher use for those iron tracks and flying trains. After the mercantile heart had devised and secured them, God took them for his own purposes; he uses them to quicken the activity of men; to multiply cities and vil-lages, studded with churches, dotted with schools, and filled with happy homes and budding souls; to increase wealth which shall partially be devoted to his service. . . . The beneficent genius of

the age keeps his special and invisible express, laden with packages of providential blessings, upon every train that runs through our communities.[22]

The image of God's providential Protestant express promoting commerce, westward expansion, schools, and churches is a fulsome metaphor for native Protestant ideology. Its core—the beliefs that related an emerging view of human nature to a developing government and economy—was basically this: human beings are born malleable and potentially good but need much careful guidance; all men are equal in some formal ways, but some groups are more able, wise, and refined than others; and therefore it is important that in education, economics, and politics, institutions be shaped to maintain the values and leadership of cultivated, native, Protestant Americans. Running through their ideas about institutions and social relations, from the family to the state, was a twofold prescription: self-discipline for those who already adhered to the belief system, and assimilation for those outside the consensus. For both of these goals education was critical. The pervasiveness of a semiofficial, nationalistic, nervous ideology that stressed self-discipline for insiders and cultural conversion for outsiders helps to explain the similarity and the success of school reform in different antebellum Northern states. The need for common schooling was itself a central tenet of the native Protestant ideology.

Although the reformers' specific proposals about centralized supervision, tax support, teacher training, and consolidated school districts met considerable resistance, the educational reform cause benefited in general from widespread consensus about the importance of common schooling. Essayists, state superintendents, and local school committees continually coupled their specific reform proposals with a repetition of the unassailable social functions of common schooling. The rhetorical effect was to imply that if one was against centralization, supervision, new schoolhouses, teacher training, or graded schools, one must also be against morality, good order, intelligent citizenship, economic prosperity, fair opportunity, and a common American culture. The claim that state intervention was imperative gained further plausibility from the fast-paced urbanization, immigration, and industrialization of the period, with the accompanying stresses on the family, the Protestant churches, and the workplace. To many Americans, an expanded educational role for the state seemed justified and urgently needed, simply to accomplish traditional goals of morality and literacy.

Morality was the most important goal of common education, and it promised many benefits. Among those most often cited were good work habits, deference to adults, restraint from vicious and debilitating habits, a reduction of crime, and the protection of property. Orville Taylor's popular *District School* emphasized that teachers had a heavy responsibility to parents and to the future of society in shaping the character of "pliable, susceptible" children. "Society expects that teachers will make children and youth social, honorable, and benevolent members." In another widely read teacher's manual, Alonzo Potter urged teachers to "inspire the young with deep reverence for parents and for old age" and give them training "which will lead them, without surrendering their own independence, to have due respect for the recorded wisdom and experience of the past." Schools needed to introduce American boys to a "humanizing culture," said Potter, lest as adults, "in the absence of higher sources of exhilaration, they rush to the gaming table, and, above all, to the intoxicating cup." In Germany, where the fine arts were cultivated, he claimed that "drunkenness is almost unknown." Horace Mann advocated vocal music on the same grounds. Music had a "harmonizing, pacificating tendency" that could be "applied in the management and discipline of children in school." Music promotes "peace, hope, affection, generosity, charity, and devotion." In Prussia, that fount of good educational ideas, vocal music pervaded schools, families, and social occasions. "It saves the people from boisterous and riotous passions."[23]

Throughout discussions of education, of course, there was a strong emphasis on obedience, discipline, and order, for the good of the school, for the good of the parents, and for the good of the children when they grew up. "If there is any place on the surface of the earth where order is the first, and last, and highest law, that place is the schoolroom," said Charles Northend, author of *The Teacher and the Parent* (1853). The "spirit of obedience and subordination" children learned would "also tend to prepare them for higher spheres of usefulness and happiness." Some educators, however, qualified the theme of subordination to authority. Although schools should develop "the highest respect for textbooks and established maxims," said an Illinois report, they should also "fully awaken the idea of bold and independent thinking and manly research." Support for plain old-fashioned obedience was widespread, but many of the leading antebellum reformers urged authority mixed with affection, discipline more internal than imposed, morality more by example than precept, and lessons emphasizing understanding more than rote memorization. These pedagogical aspects of the reform were widely discussed in journals, teachers' institutes, and education reports. Classroom memoirs suggest that some budding young professionals tried hard to implement these concepts, while many other teachers relied on traditional authority and the threat of corporal punishment. Teachers tending in either direction, though, could subscribe to the proposition that the central purpose of common schooling was moral education, and that moral education would reduce vicious behavior and crime.[24]

To maintain law through moral education was part of the republican experiment. Moral education thus overlapped citizenship education. Future citizens—and the women who as mothers and teachers would train them—not only needed to know some United States geography, history, and law but also needed to be impressed with the moral responsibility of protecting American institutions. In conservative hands this doctrine extended to the denigration of labor organizations and the denunciation of foreign culture in America; but in its general form it elicited broad support as an important and almost self-evident purpose of common schooling. Ignoring the fact that the majority of Americans could not vote, Pennsylvania's superintendent stated in 1842 the democratic principle that animated citizenship education: "The foundations of our political institutions rest upon man's capacity for self-government; not the capacity of one, of a hundred, of a thousand, but of *all*. . . . Enlightened public opinion will be a wall of fire around our free institutions, and preserve them inviolate forever."

Twenty years later, the superintendent of public instruction in Illinois reiterated the main purpose of public schooling: "The chief end is to make GOOD CITIZENS. Not to make precocious scholars . . . not to impart the secret of acquiring wealth . . . not to qualify directly for professional success . . . but simply to make good citizens." Moral education in common schools would produce virtuous citizens.

But morality is more than a list of rules for conduct supported by the argument that society demands good order and fairness. Morality must arise from a larger tradition. For most nineteenth-century Americans this source was Christianity. If the chief purpose of public common schooling was moral education, and if morality had to be grounded in religion, there had to be some way to have religion in the schools. With the proliferation of Protestant denominations and the immigration of Roman Catholics, religion became a problem for those who argued that all children should attend the same tax-supported common schools. The common-school reformers' solution was to advocate Bible reading and prayers common to most Protestants, while cautioning against the discussion of any controversial doctrines like those of the Trinity or transubstantiation. There was some dissent among Protestants against this policy, but most eventually accepted it. Outside of Protestant ranks, Jews generally (though not unanimously) acquiesced in the common-school idea, following a policy of accommodation toward public schools while arranging Jewish religious education outside of school hours. Catholics, of course, were the largest group to dissent on religious grounds from the antebellum reform program of consolidated, Protestant-oriented common schools.

The growing antagonism between Protestants and Catholics in this period may have helped persuade Protestants to close ranks on the issue of religion in the public schools. Education officials, legislators, and essayists agreed on the propriety of Christian Bible reading in the schools. Predominantly Protestant themselves, they endorsed the notion that there was a common core of scripture and belief among Christians, and they had no qualms about supporting a common-school policy that was openly Christian, avowedly nonsectarian, and implicitly Protestant. What sort of religious instruction actually went on in schools is difficult to discover, and fragmentary evidence suggests great local variety. But the pan-Protestant policy of a generalized Christianity for common schools became educators' standard answer to the problem. In addition to using the New Testament as a text, the superintendent of Brooklyn's schools believed that these Christian doctrines could be taught without controversy: "That there is one God; that we are His creatures, dependent on Him for our mercies, and accountable to Him for our conduct; that we are sinners and need a Savior; and that One 'mighty to save' has been provided." "These," he said, "are truths freely admitted and incidentally taught throughout our public schools." An Illinois superintendent said that moral education should be based on those "original, immutable, and indestructible maxims of moral rectitude," on which people of all faiths agreed.[25]

Just as morality had to be based upon some common religious tradition, common-school promoters believed that republican government had to be based upon a common culture. With increasing foreign immigration, it became clear that white Americans did not share a common culture and that schools would have to deal with the problem. But the idea that common schools could homogenize culture preceded the problem of immigrant assimilation and was part of a larger national impulse. Rush and Washington had worried that political fragmentation and regional diversity would endanger the republic. Noah Webster had designed his textbooks to promote a consistent American language and a common knowledge of geography across regional boundaries. The purpose of his spelling book, he wrote, was "to destroy the provincial prejudices that originate in the trifling differences of dialect and produce reciprocal ridicule, to promote the interest of literature and the harmony of the United States." This nationalizing function of common schools persisted into the antebellum period, apart from the problem of foreign immigration. Recommending Webster's dictionaries for all schools, the Illinois superintendent said in 1855: "Great care should be taken to eradicate provincialism and to procure that purity and uniformity of language so much to be desired. It will operate as a bond of national brotherhood." With increasing immigration in the 1840s, the homogenizing function of common schools took on particular urgency, especially in the cities. "When foreigners are in the habit of congregating together, they retain their national customs, prejudices and feelings," said New York City school authorities in 1843. Because of this, they "are not as good members of society as they would otherwise be." In 1850 the New York county superintendent said that the assimilation of immigrants "is a necessary Americanizing process" devoted to "perpetuating and making stable the government of our free country."[26]

Intellectual education did not receive as high a priority as moral education in discussions of the purposes of common schools. Far more emphasis was placed on character, discipline, virtue, and good habits than on literacy, arithmetic skills, analytical ability, or knowledge of the world. Despite the emphasis on morality, however, a great deal of time in classrooms was devoted to instruction in the three R's, with a smattering of grammar, geography, and history. Because educators were expected to speak about the public benefits of education, they generally related intellectual education to such collective benefits as intelligent citizenship and increased productivity. Writers like Orville Taylor, Alonzo Potter, and Francis Wayland, along with Mann, Barnard, and other state leaders, agreed that intellectual education would make industrial workers and farmers happier and cleverer, that education would spawn innovation and boost America's competitive position in the world, that intelligent citizens who understood something of history and political economy would reject demagogues and elect men of broad vision, and that literacy would provide people with an entrée to healthy, refined leisure activities. Incidentally but sincerely they acknowledged that education could enhance one's enjoyment of life and one's economic fate. The themes of self-improvement and personal advancement were stronger among Democrats and spokesmen for workingmen's groups than among the prominent educational reformers and the generally Whiggish theorists they relied upon. Statements about the purposes of common schooling therefore varied in emphasis. Nonetheless, all writers on education stressed social responsibilities and morality as paramount goals of common schooling, and none saw the different purposes of education as contradictory. With a republican government, Protestant morality, and an expansive economy, full literacy and the personal advancement of able individuals were wholly compatible with social progress and harmony. People in different classes, with different political perspectives or different educational philosophies, could agree on a list of purposes for common schooling: moral education to produce obedient children, reduce crime, and discourage vice; citizenship training to protect republican government; literacy for effective economic and political participation; and cultural education for assimilation and unity. Common-school advocates might emphasize the protection of property when speaking to taxpayers and self-improvement when talking to manual workers, but common themes transcended: workers valued respectability, hard work, obedient children, and the protection of their own property and lives; elite capitalists accepted the idea of a meritocracy and saw no threat from popular education. The appeal of common schools in different directions helps explain the prominent role of public education in native Protestant ideology.

The coherence of native Protestant ideology gave it much persuasive force. If you assented to one or more of the propositions, it followed that you should be for any one of the others; thus, if you believed in Christianity and the republic, it followed that you should believe in the subordination of women. Conversely, if you assaulted one of the beliefs, you could be portrayed as assaulting the entire belief system, because the beliefs were interdependent; thus, if you attacked the unequal distribution of property, you could be portrayed, according to the ideology, as opposing the whole system. This rhetorical strategy—generalizing opponents' specific proposals into an assault on the social system—can be seen in educational arguments. When some people proposed removing the Bible from classrooms in Wisconsin in 1858, the state superintendent replied that "Christianity is everywhere incorporated in the law of the land." To remove the Bible from the schools would endanger "all we now hold dear and sacred: our homes, our country, Christianity and the Bible." Historians have previously noted many overlapping articles of native Protestant social thought, but it is worth noting here again the tight web of cross-references and logical connections made by antebellum social commentators. They demonstrate the coherence of the ideology and help explain its potency. There were logical tensions and contradictions in the ideology—for example between racism and a belief in human perfectibility, or between domesticity and equal opportunity—but rhetorically each proposition was taken to be mutually reinforcing and completely compatible with the others. This is one aspect of ideology as simplification. While a culture as a whole may embody many paradoxes and contradictions, articulated ideology is a particular reflection of culture, a didactic and programmatic set of propositions used to defend institutions or reform; as such, articulated ideology tends to mute contradictions and stress coherence.

Here, then, is a series of propositions linking various tenets of native Protestant ideology, paraphrased from sermons, domestic manuals, political economy texts, education reports, and other social commentary: republican government depends upon individual character; flaws of individual character are responsible for poverty; the development of proper character for the republic depends upon the domestic teaching role of women; Christianity supports domestic female subordination; Christianity supports private property; private property is a spur to industry and incentive; private property is thus responsible for material progress and prosperity; property rights are central to the republican cause; the principles of Protestant Christianity are the same as the principles of democratic republican government; individual freedom in economic life reinforces political freedom; proper environment is a key to education and social reform; millennial Protestant Christianity supports moral reform and social progress. Common schools were related to this network of beliefs in many ways. They trained children to be good citizens, they developed moral character and work habits, they drew people into a common culture based on native Protestant ideology, they spread literacy, and they offered opportunities for individual advancement. When asked if he supported the system of common schools, George Hillard wrote in 1850: "I cannot conceive of the permanence of our institutions without a system of popular instruction. When, therefore, I am asked if I approve of the system, it is as if I were asked whether I approve of laws and magistrates, of marriage, and of property."[27]

Most of the middle-class reformers who had a formative influence on public schooling in the antebellum period were native-born Anglo-American Protestants. They believed earnestly in this ideology as a whole. Assent to the propositions of native Protestant ideology, of course, did not predict which way a person or a group would lean on important issues like centralization, assimilation, or moral regulation. This is demonstrated at the group level by the heated debates among native Protestants over central versus local control, generalized Christianity in the schools versus distinctive religious doctrines, and other matters. At the individual level, the complexity of ideology is dramatized by the differing social philosophies and politics of men like Horace Mann of Massachusetts, John Pierce of Michigan, William Seward of New York, and Henry Barnard of Connecticut, all of whom supported the creation of strong state-regulated common-school systems. Despite their differences, the cosmopolitan variant of native Protestant ideology that these men display became the dominant public philosophy in the American North by midcentury. It called for government action to provide schooling that would be more common, more equal, more dedicated to public policy, and therefore more effective in creating cultural and political values centering on Protestantism, republicanism, and capitalism. "The national education is at once a cause and an effect of the national character," said Henry Barnard. With their cosmopolitan, native, Protestant ideology as a guide to the national character, he and like-minded contemporaries set out on a vigorous program of common-school development.[28]

6

The Common-School Reform Program

AT a banquet in Gettysburg in 1826, a young councilman named Thaddeus Stevens raised his glass and toasted: "Education. May the film be removed from the eyes of Pennsylvania and she learn to dread ignorance more than taxation." In the next decade, as Stevens rose in Pennsylvania politics, he and others worked to fulfill that hope. Spurred by examples from Europe, where "the hitherto pent up sluices of knowledge" were being thrown open, Pennsylvania legislative leaders embarked upon the development of state-sponsored schools. In 1838, despite evidence that many Pennsylvanians still opposed taxation for education, the Superintendent of Common Schools declared optimistically that the state's policy was now to make education "as general and as unbought as liberty." During the late 1830s the same question was decided more or less in the affirmative in other northern states. Calvin Stowe, in his widely reprinted *Report on Elementary Public Instruction in Europe,* told the Ohio legislature that "the whole world seems to be awake and combining in one simultaneous effort for the spread of education, and sad indeed will be the condition of that community which lags behind in this universal march." In 1840, Governor William Seward of New York, riding a crest of Whig victories, told the legislature that "the improvability of our race is without limit" and that a reform of the educational system had been too long "postponed, omitted, and forgotten." He proceeded to introduce legislation to establish a state superintendent of instruction, county superintendents to carry out the state's programs, state-aided district libraries, improved education for black children, and other changes.[1]

These free-school advocates, as well as Mann of Massachusetts, Pierce of Michigan, and others, were born in the Northeast around the turn of the century. They were from families of modest resources, and they rose in the world through education and hard work. They believed firmly in the major tenets of native Protestant ideology. Along with kindred workers throughout antebellum America, these men were the "fathers" of public common schooling. They aimed at more schooling for each child, more state involvement, more uniformity, and a more pervasive public purpose for schooling.

As members of a self-conscious reform movement, common-school leaders in the various states communicated frequently, sought the support of other public figures, imitated the latest educational innovations of fellow reformers elsewhere, and devised means for the popular dissemination of their ideas. Like other antebellum reformers, common-school advocates called their efforts a "crusade." They built upon the strong tradition of school-going in America, and they justified their pleas for more organization and expenditure with appeals to the central propositions of their ideology. The program of common-school reform was remarkably similar across the country. Although the innovations and the leading spokesmen were often associated with New England, the Middle Atlantic and midwestern school advocates simultaneously developed similar programs, often with an eye on Europe rather than on New England. In the South there were many voices for common-school reform, pleading the same causes— free schooling, improved facilities, better classification, longer school years, better teacher training, and other improvements. In the 1840s, southerners consulted Horace Mann, Henry Barnard, and other northern educational leaders, while they also produced their own reports on European education, staged their own education conventions, and fought for common-school funding in their legislatures. Advocates and opponents existed in all regions. On balance, the systematization of state-sponsored common schooling prevailed in the Northeast and the Midwest, while in the antebellum South, the reformers never quite mustered the political and economic support necessary to establish free common schools.

The agenda for reform in the North can be read in state school reports of the 1840s and 1850s, which contain a litany of complaints about local school conditions. Short terms, irregular attendance, bad facilities, shortsighted and penurious district control, poor teachers, insufficient supervision, lack of uniformity, and indifferent parental support were among the chief complaints. Enrollment itself was already high in many areas of the North, but educators periodically expressed concern about children who were not enrolled. Data from Massachusetts and New York suggest that by 1840 the percentage of children annually attending school was equal to about half of all persons under age twenty and that it changed very little during the succeeding twenty years. The figures are crude, however, indicating only that a child was listed on the school rolls at some point in the year; also, such data are not very comparable from state to state. Furthermore, the rise in enrollment rates may have been partly due to better reporting by local officials. Nonetheless, attempts to construct parallel time series on enrollments in other states suggest that the New York and Massachusetts pattern of high, stable enrollments was also true by 1850 for the northernmost of the midwestern states, Michigan and Wisconsin, while in Iowa, Illinois, and Ohio, the 1850s witnessed substantial increases, bringing them up to levels (around 50 percent of all children aged 0–19) comparable to Michigan, Wisconsin, Massachusetts, and New York by 1860. Communities in Pennsylvania and New Jersey appear to have been slower to provide widespread local schooling before state intervention. Rates in these states rose from around 20 percent in 1840 to 40 percent in 1860, still somewhat below the level that had become roughly consistent across the upper North. These data support what is apparent from the reformers' own statements—that enrollment was not the central concern of the common-school movement. An enrollment level of 50 percent, the northern norm by 1850, meant that half of all children under twenty years of age attended school sometime during the year. Since many under five and many over fifteen did not attend, the enrollment rate must have been considerably over 50 percent among the children from age five to age fifteen. Indeed, investigation of enrollments for eight towns in Massachusetts in 1860, for Washtenaw County, Michigan, in 1850, and Chicago in 1860 reveal rates of 85 to 90 percent at the prime common-school ages, seven to thirteen, for all ethnic and occupational groups.[2]

Concern for nonattenders was focused on particular pockets like urban slums and factory tenements, and on particular groups, like the children of freed blacks. In 1830, Charles Andrews, head of New York's African Free School, estimated that there were 1,800 school-age black children, not counting those already in domestic service. Of these 1,800 children, 620 were enrolled at the African Free School and about 100 at private schools, leaving 1,080 to "prowl the streets . . . growing up in habits of idleness and its attendant vices." By midcentury, poor immigrant youth had replaced blacks as the most worrisome of the nonattenders. In the 1860s, urban charity workers took a survey of New York City's horrid Five Points district. Concentrating on 382 families who lived in the tenements of a single block, they discovered that only about ten of the 600 children of the block attended any school. Two-thirds of the adults could neither read nor write. The children, they said, "are too dirty, too ragged, and carry too much vermin about them, to be admitted to the public school."[3]

In factory towns, children often followed their parents to the mills as early as age ten, and legislation making education for factory youths compulsory was generally unenforced before the Civil War. Some of these children, then, were among the small percentage who did not attend school even at the usual common-school ages. Educators warned about these factory children and about the untended younger siblings of families in which both parents worked. The Peltz Committee reported in 1837 on the conditions of child labor in Philadelphia's cotton mills. The working day for children and adults alike ranged from eleven to fourteen hours. One-fifth of the employees were under age twelve, and no provision was made for their education. Of all the employees under eighteen, only one-third could read or write. Manufacturers complained that a shorter work day would harm business, but the committee argued that "in a republic, where so much depends upon the virtue and intelligence of the people, it is far better that we should forego pecuniary advantages, rather than permit large masses of children to become the miserable victims of an oppressive system." But dreary conditions of industrial child labor persisted into the second half of the century.

A mule spinner in Fall River, Massachusetts, testified in the early 1870s that his schedule was typical of English immigrant families who worked in textile mills. He rose at 5:00 a.m., made breakfast for his family, and then went to the mill with his wife and twelve-year-old daughter. They got back home about 7:30 at night. His ten-year-old daughter got herself dressed in the morning, ate leftovers from the table, and went to school. Her father joined her at home for the noon meal. In the afternoon, after school, she went to the mill, got the key from her father, and went home to await the arrival of the rest of the family for supper. On Sunday the children went to Sunday school, while the father did chores and his wife took in washing. When asked why he did not go to church, he said, "I really have not time, because if I went to church, my woman would have all the work to do, and it would take her all the day Sunday, and that would be seven days' work."[4]

Investigations led to legislation requiring a few months of education for young children working in factories in several states, including Connecticut, Rhode Island, Massachusetts, and Pennsylvania. But later inquiries found all such laws to be without teeth. A Massachusetts legislative committee of 1866 heard the following testimony from millworker John Wild:

Q.: Do you know that your children are working contrary to the law?

A.: I didn't know there was any law.

Q.: Did you know that if I should go to Fall River and prosecute their employer, he could be compelled to pay a fine for employing your children?

A.: No, sir, being no scholar.[5]

Such were the protections of early child labor laws. Employers were divided; some rejected employment of very young children and abided by the schooling provisions, while others ignored the laws altogether. Nor was it only ignorance of the laws that made parents violate restrictions on child labor. Factory workers needed the additional income. Finally, school reformers like Horace Mann knew that the proportion of young children in factory labor was small. They were more concerned about youths wandering around city streets than those occupied in the mills, and they were reluctant to advocate compulsory schooling for either group. Instead they exhorted employers to comply voluntarily with labor laws and encouraged local school committees to find ways to increase enrollment among truant youth. The continued availability of jobs for teenagers helped keep school enrollments level rather than rising in industrial areas.

If school reformers were not willing to compel teenage attendance, neither were they on a campaign to recruit toddlers into the public schools. Indeed, they actively worked against the enrollment of very young children. In the 1830s and 1840s, educators throughout the country came to believe that the practice of allowing three- and four-year-olds to attend common schools was wrong. For the sake of their health and the good order of the school, these toddlers belonged at home. As we have seen, very young children had traditionally attended rural district schools with their older siblings, and in urban areas a flurry of enthusiasm for separate infant schools had developed in the 1820s and early 1830s. During the antebellum school-reform period, these practices fell into disfavor. There were several reasons for the gradual exclusion of young children from schooling. Domestic writers argued that young children belonged at home with a real mother, not a surrogate. A rising interest in the causes and possible prevention of insanity led to further speculation about the harmful effects of early schooling. "I am forced to believe the danger is indeed great," wrote physician Amariah Brigham in his influential book, *Remarks on the Influence of Mental Excitement upon Health* (1832). "Very often in attempting to call forth and cultivate the intellectual faculties of children before they are six or seven years of age, serious and lasting injury has been done both to the body and the mind." Finally, professional education journals of the day publicized the naturalistic theories of Pestalozzi and Fellenberg, who argued the need for balanced and unforced development of mind and body. These theories also pointed in the direction of a later entry age for schoolchildren.[6]

Toddlers in ungraded district schools had been a feature of a more casual world, in which the school and the family were not sharply demarcated. Reformers, with much support from teachers, saw the arrangement as not only casual but also ineffective and inappropriate. The arrangement had been largely custodial anyway; it fit neither the ideology nor the structure of the reformed common school. Mothers were supposed to be at home, devoted to the education of their young children. Schools were supposed to classify children for more effective moral and intellectual instruction. Toddlers didn't fit in the new graded schools. School officials expressed this view at the simplest level through their complaints that little children were a nuisance. Jesse Miller, the state superintendent of Pennsylvania's schools, recommended in 1848 that communities raise the school entry age from four to six, saying that the younger pupils "necessarily incommode and retard the progress of the pupils who are more advanced." In some communities by persuasion, in some by regulation, younger children were gradually eliminated from the schools.

Probably only a small minority of children in the North missed going to school altogether. Enrollment says nothing, however, about the quality or quantity of education a child received. Reformers placed their emphasis on matters of quantity and quality. Their general goal was to increase regularity of attendance, that is, to increase average daily attendance among those enrolled, and to increase the length of the school year. They believed that coercive legislation on either issue would be an unacceptable incursion on the family and on local government. But through persuasion and publicity, both average attendance and length of school terms were increased. Both, of course, added to the number of days of schooling the average child received per year in this increasingly schooled society.

Teachers, school-committee members, and state officials complained of the disruptive effects of irregular attendance. "Ne :t to the want of uniform text books of the proper kind," said Pennsylvania's superintendent of common schools, "the teacher meets with no greater obstacle." His counterpart in New York agreed:

"The loss of time, the loss of ambition, and the consequent relaxation of effort . . . which are the fruits of irregular attendance, may be a life-long injury to the pupil," but also "much of the time and labor of the teacher is lost; irregularity of attendances divides and distracts his attention." Different communities tried different tactics to get a higher percentage of enrolled children into school each day. In 1858 the Superintendent of Chicago's schools called irregular attendance "the most dangerous evil that exists in connection with the free school system." In addition to exhorting parents to send children more regularly, Chicago school administrators tried monthly attendance reports to be signed by parents and a rule threatening habitually absent children with expulsion.[7]

Reformers also placed great emphasis on increasing the length of the school year. Rural communities often operated school for eight to ten weeks in summer and a similar period in winter. Common-school reformers wanted longer sessions, both to increase the amount of schooling children received and to enhance the possibility of making teaching a regular profession. Pennsylvania's superintendent complained in 1848 that the average length of the school year was less than five months. "This is an evil of no trifling character," he said, for it was impossible to attract competent teachers unless longer-term employment could be offered. During the antebellum period, there was a gradual trend toward longer school sessions in the North, due to reformers' urgings, an expanding economy, and an increased popular acceptance of more schooling. Children in 1860 attended school longer and more regularly than their parents had in 1830.

The mere fact that more children were going to school more days per year did not satisfy common-school reformers. The quality of the schools did not measure up to their standards. Next on the reformers' agenda came the evils of the district system. They believed that expenditures, teacher training, and the organization of schools could not be improved without changing the tradition of small-scale local control. In fact, district control of schools was not as firmly rooted in history as some of its defenders claimed. Town-wide control of schools in New England had only given way to smaller district control in the eighteenth century as population scattered and neighborhoods pressed to have their own schools closer to home. The same process of decentralization was repeated in some frontier states. In Michigan, official control of common schools rested from 1817 to 1827 with a state body, the university; control by district was enacted in 1827 and endorsed in the state constitution of 1835. Wisconsin entered statehood with a system dividing authority between districts, towns, and the state, but the school code of 1849 transferred most powers to the districts. The district system was obviously popular at the local level; the common-school reformers' challenge to it was the most controversial aspect of their program. Nonetheless, most state officials, writers on education, and school promoters in legislatures supported larger-scale school units and more supervision from above. The effort to centralize control thus proceeded along three parallel lines: consolidating districts into town systems, developing mechanisms for state supervision and regulation, and encouraging the transition from private to public control of schools. The evils of district control became a major theme of state school reports of the 1840s and 1850s. Reformers claimed that control by tiny districts led to the hiring of incompetent teachers because the examining committees were incompetent. The system also led to short school terms, dilapidated school buildings, and lack of equipment because small districts resisted taxing themselves or were indifferent to innovation and sound professional practice. Some also argued that district control perpetuated unequal common-school facilities because districts had unequal wealth and varying degrees of willingness to tax for schools. Consolidation, they said, would both raise and equalize school expenditures.

Vermont's first state superintendent, Horace Eaton, said in 1846 that small districts were the "paradise of ignorant teachers." He urged rural Vermont to follow the example of New York and Massachusetts, where districts were larger. If towns would not consolidate, he urged "at least that limits be set to the prevailing mischievous tendency to multiply school districts." The next year, John Pierce of Michigan lauded the "union school" made possible by town consolidation. Union schools brought together children from several districts, allowing grading of pupils, more advanced instruction, and larger, more homogeneous classes. Ohio's report of 1854 labelled district schools inefficient and ineffective and gave thirteen reasons for the superiority of graded schools. In his 1861 report, the Illinois superintendent called for the consolidation of one-room schoolhouses in rural areas and estimated that switching to town control would reduce the number of districts in Illinois from 10,000 to under 2,000.

Cities, of course, had sufficient numbers of children and taxpayers to satisfy the demands of organizational reform; they pioneered in establishing graded schools and high schools, and in developing professional supervision. Consolidation was primarily a rural issue in this period. But there were different kinds of rural communities. Aside from the population size itself, there were different rural settlement patterns. Where a rural community already had a village population center, it was more likely to adopt school consolidation than a comparably sized township of scattered farms. Wisconsin education reports spoke optimistically about the cities and the rural villages but referred disparagingly to the scattered farming communities. Villages had the necessary concentration of population; they also had a smattering of nonfarm population, and with it usually an element of boosterism. Some people in these villages wanted their communities to grow, to be modern, and to link up with developing networks of commerce and other nonlocal institutions. This brought the dialogue about educational reform into the local scene. In dispersed rural areas, a strong countertrend still operated, especially in frontier states: as population continued to disperse, school districts multiplied and residents clung tenaciously to control of their nearby school.

Common-school reformers of the antebellum period also attempted to influence local education through the creation of state education agencies and the use of state funds. Among the early legislative accomplishments of reformers in all the northern states was the creation of the office of a chief school official, usually called the superintendent of common schools. Sometimes the office was joined with that of the already existing secretary of state. Historians have often focused on these spokesmen for educational reform, and many of the prominent common-school advocates, including Mann, Barnard, and Pierce, served terms as state school officers. The heroic view of Horace Mann was well summarized by George Martin, a later state school superintendent. Mann, he said, was the "Puritan of the Puritans." He was "born to be a champion . . . the stuff that martyrs are made of. . . . He fought the battle of educational reform in Massachusetts through to the end and conquered."[8]

It is difficult to disentangle the unique contributions of these state leaders from general trends in pedagogy and educational systematization that would have prevailed anyway. There is no doubt that they were influential people in their time. They were consulted, quoted, and invited to speak. They shepherded education bills through legislatures and established the rudimentary administrative structures of nineteenth-century school systems. However, some skepticism about the decisive role of heroic state officers is warranted. Calvin Wiley of North Carolina helped persuade his legislature to create a state superintendent's office, to which he was appointed in 1853. He worked as hard as Mann and Barnard, exercised great talent, and mustered the same arguments; yet he came up with different results—less state influence, lower attendance levels, shorter school terms, and lower expenditures. North Carolina was not Massachusetts. The reformers pushed virtually the same program in every state, but the results were shaped by social structure, politics, demography, and resources. The office of state superintendent was not conducive to heroism, though historians have lionized some of its early occupants. Even in education-minded states like Michigan and Massachusetts, the position was weak and vulnerable. Educational improvement had the powerful sanction of native Protestant ideology, and responded to myriad problems of economic growth and population diversity; but centralized state power over such a reform program was not a foregone conclusion, and the attempt to hasten educational improvement through state action politicized the reform movement in its first blush. Legislative battles were waged in many states over the creation of state superintendencies, county superintendencies, and consolidated districts.

Between battles, the state superintendent's job was largely clerical and exhortatory. His task was to gather, summarize, and report annually the statistics on educational practices in the state. He was expected to write essays about good educational practice and to recommend improvements. Most educational legislation in the period was limited to defining the relative roles of district, town, county, and state officers and providing for the maintenance and distribution of small state school funds. Some states experimented with county superintendencies to bolster the state officer's supervisory capacity, but this innovation was everywhere controversial, and local committees retained ultimate authority over expenditure levels, length of school terms, curriculum, texts, and the hiring and firing of teachers. State superintendents were more like preachers than bureaucrats. They traveled about their states, visiting schools, giving speeches, organizing teachers' institutes, gathering data, and spreading the common-school reform gospel. Some of them wanted more coercive authority, and they worked to create a rough hierarchy of professional supervision, but their regulatory power was more form than substance. The Wisconsin state superintendent was charged with hearing appeals in educational disputes, but he complained in 1859 that town superintendents refused to comply with his rulings. In 1857 the Illinois superintendent argued the "utter futility of attempting to operate a Free School System, without proper supervisory agents." School systems were like railroads, he said. They needed "head superintendents, with ample assistants, to attend to their general movements, and watchful agents stationed everywhere."

The history of the county superintendency in the 1840s and 1850s illustrates both the bureaucratic aspirations of the common-school reformers and the mixed results of their attempts to systematize local schooling. Ohio secretaries of state complained throughout the early 1840s that local school officials were so "ignorant" and "sluggish" that they could not "make a report with the form in front of them." They argued for county superintendents to interpret laws, explain procedures for reports, encourage uniformity of textbooks, and examine teachers applying for jobs. But when a state law made the hiring of superintendents a local option in 1848, only one county voted to do so. Legislators in both New York and Vermont established the position of county superintendent during the 1840s and then abolished it in response to the criticism that they were an unnecessary expense. In some states, the reformers met with success. In Pennsylvania, despite some local hostility, the state superintendent reported in 1857 that county officers had improved teachers' qualifications, promoted teacher institutes, fostered uniformity of texts, generated parental interest, and prompted local officials to be more conscientious. Like the state superintendent, the county superintendent's role was more to persuade than to coerce.

The third element in the reformers' program for centralization of control was the campaign against private schooling. The goals of a common-school system—moral training, discipline, patriotism, mutual understanding, formal equality, and cultural assimilation—could not be achieved if substantial numbers of children were in independent schools. For the school reformers of the antebellum period, the phrase "common school" implied an effort to draw all children into public free schools, and they fought the old connotation of "common" schools as ordinary and undesirable. Horace Mann complained that private schooling drew off the support of "some of the most intelligent men," and Orville Taylor said of exclusive schooling, "this is not republican. This is not allowing all, as far as possible, a fair start in the world." Barnard argued that private schooling "classifies society at the root, by assorting children according to the wealth, education, or outward circumstances of their parents, into different schools; and educates children of the same neighborhood differently and unequally." Moreover, argued the reformers, private schools soaked up resources from the public schools. "In those towns where private seminaries have been located and well sustained," said John Pierce, "the free schools will be found, without exception, to be in a miserable condition."[9]

During the antebellum period there was a substantial shift from private to public schooling in the cities. Public school facilities improved and there was a general tendency of urban governments to extend public control of institutions as the population increased. In New York City the percentage of students in private schools dropped from 62 percent in 1829 to 18 percent in 1850. In Salem the percentage in private schools was 58 in 1827, and still 56 in 1837. By 1846, however, Salem's public schools enrolled all but 24 percent of the city's schoolchildren. In the newer cities of the West, the same process occurred. Milwaukee reported 61 percent private enrollment in 1845, but by 1848, when they reported a much larger total enrollment, the private percentage was down to 46. The Illinois superintendent claimed in 1868 "that the public schools are steadily weakening and decimating private schools, and that they will ultimately crowd them almost wholly from the field." The only substantial countertrend against this gradual shift to public schooling in the cities was the development of Roman Catholic schools, but they were not numerous in most areas until after the Civil War.[10]

In the large cities, schools tended to be either entirely free or entirely supported by parental fees. By 1840 the categories corresponded roughly to our modern definitions of "public" and "private." The goal of the reformers, therefore, was to increase the public sector at the expense of the private. Rural areas and smaller towns had few entirely private schools, but their district schools commonly charged some form of tuition. This was done by charging parents "rate bills" for some part of a term, or by extending the regular public term with a "select" or "subscription" school, usually taught by the same teacher and open only to children whose parents would pay the cost. Most school reformers opposed any parental assessments for schooling, and they waged a campaign against the rate bill and the subscription schools from lecture podiums, in annual reports, and in legislatures. It was not simply a disagreement between those who supported more education and those who supported less, though there was that element in it. It was also an argument about whether the state should assume educational responsibilities previously reserved to parents. Eventually the school reformers prevailed. Most northern states abolished rate bills by law in the 1850s and 1860s, although some communities ignored the laws and continued assessing rates. Full tax support for southern public education, even in principle, was a phenomenon of the 1870s and later.

As the public schools of the North became wholly free, the cheaper independent pay schools, previously patronized by ordinary families, declined. A certain percentage of more wealthy families, however, could not be recruited to the cause. Samuel Galloway, in charge of Ohio's schools, complained in 1849 that the "better class of families" would not send their children to public schools. A certain "better" class continued to evade the net of the reformers and support private schooling. Some less wealthy groups also persisted in supporting private schools for cultural and religious reasons, but in general, working-class and middle-class support of cheap pay schools gave way with the advent of improved and free public schools.

The same transition from private to public began in secondary education in the North in the mid-nineteenth century. Reformers' antagonism to independent academies and their enthusiasm for the creation of high schools were part and parcel of the common-school reform program. The public high-school cause paralleled the drive to make elementary education free and publicly supervised. Reformers argued that free public high schools were part of the democratization of education. High schools also fit the bureaucratic impulse in antebellum education reform, bringing the secondary level of schooling into a more coordinated system.

The image of elite military academies or New England boarding schools of the twentieth century tempts us to exaggerate the exclusive character of the academies of the early nineteenth century. Educational reformers contributed to that stereotype. In their campaign against these independent schools, they emphasized the social class bias of academies while ignoring the same selective character of the early public high schools. Even a free secondary school was bound to have a clientele skewed toward the middle class, both because informal class discrimination existed and because many working-class families could not afford to forgo the earnings of teenage labor. For blacks, of course, discrimination was often formal and absolute. Various obstacles to secondary education remained for women, but their opportunities were expanded by academies, and they gradually came to predominate in public high schools.

In their heyday, academies had offered an opportunity for secondary education to children of families with modest means. Ambitious youths, encouraged by common-school teachers, managed to attend academies with support from relatives or by working part of the year. For some native males, like Horace Mann and John Pierce, this path led to college and careers as lawyers or Protestant ministers. Some, including Mann and Pierce, later became critics of academies, but their complaints should be weighed against the rosier picture of some contemporaries. Hiram Orcutt of Connecticut reminisced warmly: "Most of these institutions were unendowed and short-lived, but they were then a necessity. . . . The open door of the old academy, its economical arrangements, and its earnest and devoted teachers invited and encouraged the young men and women of the neighborhood to come up higher." Because a needy student could scrape through, because academies were dispersed in rural areas, and because many received charters and financial assistance from the states, some people argued that the academies were "public" schools. Certainly they fell between the modern categories "public" and "private." Communities sometimes voted subsidies to local academies, or provided a building; the composition of boards of incorporated academies often differed little from those that governed common schools. Indeed, in the 1820s the trustees of several incorporated academies in New York State were also the trustees of the common-school districts in which their academies were located. Erasmus Hall Academy in Brooklyn got local public aid in return for teaching some poor students without fee, and the Pennsylvania legislature gave several academies aid on the same condition in the 1820s. In New York a legislative committee declared in 1838 that academies were related to the common schools "as part of the same system of public and popular education."[11]

Some defenders of academies lived up to the aristocratic image. Edward Hitchcock, president of Amherst College, gave a speech in 1845 in which he lauded academies as perfectly suited to the genius of Protestant, "pure Saxon" Americans. He pointed out that by "Americans" he did not mean the "motley crew—annually disembogued upon our shores." As for the charge of elitism, said Hitchcock, "it is easy to get up a prejudice against men thus thoroughly educated, as if they were aristocratic; but when the people come to look around for those who are to maintain their highest interests, whether in church or state, they are very apt to select those very men." The haughty tone of men like Hitchcock may have lost the academies some popular support. But the establishment of high schools depended more upon the acceptance of full public funding for the education of middle-class children as well as those of poorer parents.[12]

High schools fit the reformers' program of a hierarchical, graded, coordinated system of public schooling. In New York City, educators spoke of the need for a high school "as part of a perfect system," and when it was founded in 1849, they called it "the splendid crown of our Common School system," and "an integrant branch of the whole system for the enlightenment of the people." Connecticut's superintendent, Seth Beers, argued that a high school in a town would enable the teachers of the district schools to teach elementary subjects more thoroughly by relieving them of the smattering of advanced subjects forced upon them by the wide age range of district-school students. H. H. Barney, principal of Cincinnati's high school, loved the symmetry of a school system capped with a high school. The construction metaphor was continual. Independent academies and denominational schools made a "wretched, misshapen, loose-jointed system." Boston's schools, he said, were "so complete and symmetrical in structure that the human being there receives the first rudimental instructions, and is then led along and upward by gradations as simple and beautiful as its own growth, until it steps forth an American citizen complete."[13]

Urbanization, along with the reformers' arguments and the attractiveness of high schools to people in middling occupational groups, combined to create a gradual trend toward the provision of public high schools. Massachusetts, New York, and Ohio led the way, and within those states the innovation more or less followed urban lines. High schools were urban institutions; they required a sufficient concentration of taxable wealth as well as enough students who wanted secondary schooling. After Boston created its English High School in 1821, many Massachusetts cities followed in the 1820s and 1830s, including Worcester, Salem, Springfield, Lowell, and Newburyport. By 1865, 70 percent of the population of Massachusetts lived in towns with public high schools. In New York State the busiest period of high-school establishment was in the 1850s and 1860s. In the five years following the Civil War, the number of high schools in the state increased from twenty-two to fifty-nine, while the number of academies declined from 190 to 132. The state's high schools surpassed academies in number of institutions by 1875 and in number of students by 1880. In other northern states, the development was similar.[14]

Only a small minority of teenagers attended secondary schools of any kind in nineteenth-century America. The establishment of public high schools performed a largely symbolic function in the reform program. They established the opportunity for free local education through the secondary level, even though few used it, and they represented the upper levels of an increasingly graded and coordinated system of public education. These symbolic functions —both democratic and bureaucratic—are clear from the debates about the creation of high schools. Their actual functions are less clear. We are only beginning to understand the social origins and social destinations of high-school graduates. In 1851 Hiram Barney lauded Boston's English High School as "the perfect example of the poor and the rich meeting on common ground and on terms quite democratic," and the principal of that school said "about one-third of my pupils are sons of merchants; the remaining two-thirds are sons of mechanics, professional men and others. Some of our best scholars are sons of coopers, lamplighters, and day laborers." More precise studies of high schools in Chicago, New York, and Salem in the 1850s partially confirm that picture. Sons of clerks, merchants, proprietors, craftsmen, and professionals attended these high schools. A few factory workers' sons appear on the rolls, but the lower working class is severely underrepresented. The trend in graduates' careers was toward white-collar work, both clerical and professional, regardless of whether the boys' fathers worked in manual or nonmanual jobs. The New York graduates of 1858 included a brass turner's son who became a lawyer, a machinist's son who became a lawyer, and a wheelwright's son who became a bookkeeper. Some fathers with such artisan labels may have been substantial craftsmen or even proprietors of their own businesses; however, because of changes from craft to factory production, some members of this upper artisan group may have felt anxious about their positions and their sons' futures. In any case, the high-school graduates' career lines suggest that for a small, middling segment of the population, public secondary schooling fostered intergenerational change from manual to nonmanual occupations, and it may have helped confirm or improve white-collar status for those whose fathers were already in the white-collar ranks. Coeducational and separate girls' high schools soon provided females with possibilities for secondary education in the cities.[15]

The common-school reform program put considerable financial strain on local school districts. In addition to longer school terms, the shift to more public schooling, the abolition of rate bills, and the addition of high schools to the system, antebellum school reformers campaigned for better equipment and better facilities. They ridiculed the crude and simple materials used in rural district schools, and they bemoaned the lack of solid, well-ventilated schoolhouses. New York State school reports charted a gradual increase in schools with decent privies, and Wisconsin reports recorded the increase in brick and stone construction over log or frame houses. Still, complained Wisconsin's Superintendent Barry in 1856, "ninety-nine out of every hundred of them should be torn down or greatly improved." In rural Trempeleau County, teachers complained about the overcrowded "shacks" in which they taught, most without the aid of blackboards, outline maps, or other innovations of the day.

Many rural residents responded to expensive reform demands simply by rejecting them, voting down increased school taxes, and sticking to their ramshackle schoolhouses, old-fashioned slates, short sessions, and tattered family textbooks. Other communities, however, did not wish to appear backward or uninterested in their children. It was hard to ignore a county superintendent like the one in Trempeleau County, who reminded residents that while they were spending $3.33 per pupil, the average town in Massachusetts was spending $22. Meanwhile, in Massachusetts, Horace Mann annually published a list of all the towns, ranked by per-pupil expenditures. In 1851 the school committee of Palmer, Massachusetts, called it a "mortification" that they were lowest of all 316 towns in per-pupil expenditures. "Mortification" was exactly what Mann had in mind.[16]

To some extent, school reform rode the back of economic expansion. In industrial or agricultural communities where productivity was rising, it was not necessary to raise the rate of school taxation on assessed wealth in order to increase the per-pupil expenditures for education. But sometimes school reformers were fighting fiscal retrenchment, declining farm prices, and traditional resistance to school expenditures. Thus they emphasized that some innovations could actually save money. Their favorite example was the introduction of inexpensive female teachers. Samuel Lewis of Ohio said that counties employing females "are able to do twice as much with the same money as is done in the counties where female teachers are almost excluded." The ratio of female to male teachers' wages varied quite a bit from town to town and from state to state, but there was little movement toward equalization during the antebellum period. On the average, female teachers' wages were 44 percent of males' in Michigan in 1845, and the same in 1863. In Wisconsin the ratio was slightly more favorable: 53 percent in 1850, increasing to 62 percent in 1860. In Massachusetts the salary ratio remained around 40 percent throughout the period, while the proportion of females in the teaching force increased from 56 percent in 1834 to 78 percent in 1860.[17]

Opposition to female teachers centered on their alleged inability to teach higher subjects or to control rowdy older male pupils. "Where the mind in its maturing state and fuller development . . . is led onward to the higher departments of literature and science," said the Wisconsin state superintendent, "it is obviously better to employ male teachers." In rural areas the problem of disciplining older boys was limited mostly to the winter term, when there was little farm work to keep teenagers busy. In upstate New York, a county superintendent said in 1850 that "weaker districts" might benefit from hiring women, but that if they did, the more advanced students would need "the more extended advantages of a central town school." The entering wedge for female teachers, therefore, was the education of young children in common schools. The employment of female teachers for younger children was consistent with antebellum notions about domesticity and education. Advocates of female teachers could see the benefit of transferring the savings to other improvements, and they also wished to encourage the more tender, loving pedagogy they associated with female teachers. "Heaven has plainly appointed females as the natural instructors of young children, and endowed them with those qualities of mind and disposition, which pre-eminently fit them for such a task," said the Connecticut Board of Education in 1840. Indiana's first state superintendent exclaimed simply in 1853, "Blessed be he who invented female teachers." The female has "patience and perseverance, quick sensibilities and sympathy with youthful minds," said a Pennsylvania state superintendent in 1857, illustrating the appeal of the domestic stereotype. "Except in the family, she nowhere so truly occupies her appropriate sphere, as in the school room." Barnas Sears, Horace Mann's successor, said in 1851 that the female teacher "paints to the imagination, where the male teacher defines and reasons. She can more easily bridge over the chasm between the natural life of infancy or childhood, and the artificial thing called a school."[18]

The two arguments in favor of female teachers—their cheapness and natural superiority as instructors of young children—appear together so often that it is difficult to determine which was the more important as a motive. Discussions of the issue by rural school committees suggest that women would not have been hired had they not been available more cheaply. Still, if economy and exploitation were the whole story, one might expect the poorest districts, or those that spent the lowest percentage of assessed wealth on education, to convert to women teachers soonest. This was not the case; the picture is more complicated. One factor, obviously, is that the poorest and most penny-pinching districts were often small, rural communities that clung to traditional practices. Ideas about proper female roles died hard; thus a purely economic explanation of the feminization of teaching is inaccurate. A second factor has to do with scale and organization. In the towns and cities, reformers advocated the employment of female teachers as part of the general program for improving and reorganizing the schools. In 1841 the mayor of Salem, Massachusetts, recommended "the system of placing a large number of scholars under the care of male principals with female assistants—the most economical as well as the effective mode of instruction—and of securing the advantages of a division of labor by converting what are now separate schools into co-ordinate departments, under teachers to whom separate duties shall be assigned." In 1853 the Phillips School in Salem had 343 students, with a staff of seven female assistants plus a male principal teacher. The city as a whole employed eight males and sixty females. The modern school principal was a byproduct of the shift to female teachers. The term originally applied to the "principal teacher," who, in the twentieth century, shed his teaching function.

At first glance, it might seem that the feminization of teaching and the professionalization of teaching were in tension, since few people thought of women as having professional status. However, the two trends were compatible and reinforcing. Having created more bureaucratic and highly organized schools, reformers wished to soften the experience for younger children, to bridge the widening gap between family culture and school culture. Educational reformers decided that gender differences coincided with a proper division of labor in education. Having solved the female teacher's problem of discipline by providing a male overseer, they soon learned that supervision had many uses in large schools and that the prospect of such responsibilities might keep men in the profession. On all these grounds, hiring female teachers made sense. In cities and towns, the feminization of teaching was seen as one of several related organizational innovations, tied to grading, efficiency, and supervision. In the country districts, it was seen primarily as an economy move, first for the summer sessions and gradually, after women had proven themselves to skeptical school committees, for winter sessions as well.

In 1800 most teachers had been male, with the exception of the women who conducted neighborhood dame schools or private lessons in female accomplishments. By 1900, most teachers were women—about 70 percent of the precollegiate instructors nationwide. For the North, the period of fastest change in this momentous shift came in the antebellum period. It proceeded fastest in the cities but soon affected almost all districts. It was based on an argument of efficiency but was bolstered by other cultural and pedagogical arguments. It had important effects on the profession—fixing the subordinate role of the classroom teacher, reinforcing the hierarchical organization desired by professional male educators, and underscoring the new, softer approach to educating young children.

The feminization of teaching also had important effects on the lives of the women who taught. The number of women who had some experience in the classroom was quite large, for although the percentage of all women who were teachers at any given time was small, their careers were brief, so it took a very substantial number of young women, each teaching for a few years, to fill the teaching positions of the expanding public schools. Horace Mann estimated that the average length of time in teaching was 2.6 years in Massachusetts in 1845. In southeastern Michigan in 1860, 77 percent of all female teachers were between the ages of seventeen and twenty-four, suggesting the short-term nature of teaching as an occupation for females. In Dane County, Wisconsin (which included Madison, the capital), 27 percent of the female teachers were eighteen or younger in 1860, though there were no male teachers that young. As a superintendent in another county said, female teaching candidates seemed to be just "emerging from a state of childhood." For a brief span, then, at a young age, teaching gave a large number of women a chance to work—for unequal pay and often in subordinate and difficult positions—but nonetheless, to have a daily, nonmanual occupation, outside the home, for wages. For some women it meant a chance to live away from home between parental dependence and marital dependence; however, most female teachers in fact lived with their parents while they taught. In Martha Coons's study of Dane County, Wisconsin, 82 percent of female teachers were single and living with their parents. About 7 percent were married; the remaining 11 percent were single and boarding away from home. In Ann Weingarten's similar study of southeastern Michigan, 67 percent were single women living with their parents, only 1 percent were married, and the remaining 32 percent lived independently. These data suggest that the short duration of female teaching careers was due to the fact that very few women taught after they married.[19]

It is difficult to estimate the impact of a brief term of teaching on the thousands of women who served in antebellum classrooms. Some women testified to its crucial importance in their lives, and some few, of course, made long careers of teaching. In her book *The Evolution of a Teacher,* Ella Gilbert Ives described what it was like to be a student in the 1860s at Mount Holyoke College, "the Mecca for school committees in quest of teachers." She quoted Frances Willard, the temperance crusader, who had declared "not to be at all, or else to be a teacher, was the alternative presented to aspiring young women of intellectual proclivities when I was young." Perhaps this is why some women, starved to use their minds and their talents, were willing to make statements that seem so abject today. At a meeting in upstate New York in the 1840s, Emma Willard, the educator, proposed a resolution to be adopted by the men in the audience, to the effect that they would aid common schooling by asking women in their communities to take on educational activities "properly belonging to their own sphere in the social system." She then asked the ladies to resolve "that if the men, whom we recognize as by the laws of God and man, our directors, and to whose superior wisdom we naturally look for guidance, shall call us into the field of active labor in common schools, we will obey the call with alacrity." Unfortunately, no one recorded whether her tongue was in her cheek on this occasion, but both resolutions passed unanimously.[20]

Despite the discriminatory wages and the moralistic public scrutiny that faced female teachers, some recognized the expanding field as an opportunity. Catharine Beecher said it most directly: "A profession is to be created for women. . . . This is the way in which thousands of intelligent and respectable women, who toil for a pittance scarcely sufficient to sustain life, are to be relieved and elevated." However, Beecher thought it was better tactics to present the idea as a way to solve the problems of public education "rather than to start it as an effort for the elevation of woman. By this method, many embarrassments would be escaped, and many advantages secured." Beecher hinted here that some of the talk about women's natures and destinies was self-conscious posturing. As much as she may have believed sincerely in the domestic ideal, her remark about female teachers suggests that she also knew that the price for a measure of independence and public activity was acquiescence in the prevailing ideology.[21]

While common-school reformers advocated female teachers, they also urged a variety of other changes to bolster the status of teachers of both sexes: longer terms for year-round employment, better wages, improved teacher training through normal schools and teachers' institutes, more communication through professional journals and organizations, and improved hiring practices. These reforms, they believed, would simultaneously raise the quality of common-school education and the status of common-school teachers. Orville Taylor pleaded in 1835: "Teaching should be made a distinct profession. The teacher's employment should be made as honourable and as separate as the physician's, the divine's, the lawyer's. . . . Let teaching be made a profession, and let teachers be united for their mutual improvement." Early state teachers' organizations, always male-dominated, provided a platform for school professionals and visibility for promising men on the rise. Sometimes they had an impact on policy, as when the Illinois Teachers' Association controlled the early normal school, when the Wisconsin teachers endorsed the introduction of county superintendents, or when Ohio's College of Professional Teachers publicized the need for a state superintendent of instruction.[22]

Education journals proliferated during the antebellum period. In some cases they were independent publications, in others they were the organs of state superintendents or teachers' organizations. They promoted the common-school reform program, including increased expenditures, more schooling, improved pedagogy, and the professionalization of teaching. Some state superintendents provided every district school committee with a copy of a state or national journal, to promote innovation and public support. Still, these journals were not read by most classroom teachers. In 1855 one-fourth of Massachusetts' teachers subscribed to the *Massachusetts Teacher*. The editors of the *Maine Journal of Education* complained in the 1850s that their journal was an "orphan" because ordinary teachers were "too indifferent to support it," and in Ohio, an estimated 18,000 of 21,000 teachers in 1863 never looked at the state journal. Using very crude figures, Sheldon Davis, a historian, estimated that about 10 percent of the nation's teachers received an education journal in the early 1850s, rising to perhaps 20 percent by the end of the Civil War. Nonetheless, this was an influential minority of teachers, and the impact of the journals may have been multiplied in discussions and through the sharing of copies among several readers. Henry Barnard's compendious *American Journal of Education* was so expensive that it probably never had more than 500 paid subscribers, but it became a standard reference work in pedagogical libraries and was frequently cited among education professionals.[23]

Another means of disseminating educational reform ideas was

the teachers' institute. Often organized at the county level and endorsed by state superintendents, these meetings consisted of several days' speeches and discussion conducted by some prominent professional educator. David Camp, later the superintendent of Connecticut's common schools, described the teachers' institutes he helped conduct in the 1840s. They lasted four days and featured model lessons and discussions of classroom technique during the day, with guest lecturers in the evening, such as the Reverend Horace Bushnell, author of *Christian Nurture*. When William Mowry landed his first job as principal of a graded school in Massachusetts in 1850, he decided to attend a teachers' institute conducted by Barnas Sears, the new secretary of the state Board of Education. He took notes at the lectures, and he said he "kept the book containing them on my desk for the whole year . . . it had a marked influence on my subsequent teaching." In Illinois the superintendent of public instruction said in 1858 that annual institutes should be to teachers "what the yearly pilgrimage to Mecca was to the ancient Arab—the source whence he renews the spirit and life of his existence." Henry Barnard called teachers' institutes an "education revival agency." They became one of the most popular innovations of the reform program. In 1849, Maine officials reported that 36 percent of their teachers, both male and female, attended institutes. In Wisconsin, superintendent Azel Ladd began campaigning for institutes in 1852, "to mitigate the disadvantages" of teachers being "so diversified in qualifications." The state began supporting teachers' institutes in Wisconsin in 1859. In that year about 1,500 teachers attended institutes in fourteen cities, perhaps 20 percent of the state's teaching force. At the same time in Michigan, about 15 percent of all teachers, male and female, attended institutes.[24]

As teachers' institutes became more popular in the Midwest, reformers in the East pressed for better teacher training through the establishment of normal schools (the term originated in France and meant that teachers should be trained to perform according to high standards or "norms"). Impressed by the professional status of Prussia's normal schools, reformers began to place a high priority on the establishment of similar institutions in America. Horace Mann supported normal schools vigorously. Shortly after he took office as secretary to the Board of Education, Mann attended a meeting at the home of Edmund Dwight, a wealthy industrialist, to discuss the possibility of persuading the legislature to support a normal school. He returned home with a promise from Dwight of a $10,000 private gift for the project, on condition that the legislature match it. In his diary he exulted, "I think I feel pretty sublime! Let the stars look out for my head!" The Whig legislature took advantage of the gift and established the nation's first normal school at Lexington in 1839. Even though the reform forces barely weathered a legislative assault on this "Prussian" institution in 1840, they soon established additional normal schools at Barre and Bridgewater. Classroom instruction at the Lexington normal school, as at most early teacher training institutions, was in academic subjects like geography, grammar, moral philosophy, botany, history, algebra, and political economy. Thirty-five students studied under a single instructor, Cyrus Peirce, regarded by Mann as a master teacher. Teacher training was accomplished in four ways: through the example of the instructor, through his incidental remarks about teaching methods during the regular lessons, through his weekly lectures on the art of teaching, and through practice teaching in the model school, under Peirce's observation. Thus, although the stated curriculum differed little from an academy, teacher training pervaded the day's activities. Henry Barnard called Lexington "the most interesting educational experiment now making on this side of the Atlantic."[25]

In New York, the state regents and legislators decided that existing academies could do the job of teacher training. The superintendent of common schools, John Spencer, rejected normal schools as an "unnecessary expense." Although Spencer's successor supported the establishment of a normal school at Albany, which opened in 1844, New York continued to rely largely upon normal departments within its academies for teacher training during the nineteenth century. Indeed, academies throughout the nation often ran teacher-training departments comparable to the normal schools. For example, a student in the normal department of the academy at Canandaigua, New York, in the 1830s said that the program included "studies and recitations of the common branches; a daily drill upon the best methods of teaching; lectures upon the theory of teaching, and also upon geology, natural and mental philosophy, physical geography and history, upon warming and ventilation, the laws of health, teachers' associations, schoolhouses and blackboards, also upon the teacher's social habits and duties as a member of the community." He added that graduates of the program "were eagerly sought for the best class of winter schools."[26]

New Yorkers continued to debate which alternative the state should support, while the elite of their teaching force received training at the Albany normal school, at the normal departments of academies, and at periodic teachers' institutes. Most teachers, though, had no such training at all. When the teacher training departments of New York's academies graduated 284 students in 1837, there were about 10,000 school districts, most with frequent vacancies in winter and summer teaching slots. In Michigan, the normal school opened in 1853 and was attended by a few hundred students a year. By 1860, when the normal school had been operating for seven years, about 3 percent of the state's female teachers and about 4 percent of the state's male teachers had attended the normal school. Nonetheless, common-school reformers were confident by 1860 that they had their sights on the right institution for professional training. The post–Civil War era saw the proliferation of normal schools throughout the nation, but it was a very gradual development. By 1900, for example, 40 percent of the public-school teachers of Massachusetts had attended normal school.[27]

Journals, teachers' associations, institutes, normal schools— these first instruments of professionalization probably affected the top 10 to 20 percent of the teachers of the antebellum period, the men and women who were more likely to stay in teaching beyond a few years, who were more likely to teach in the larger towns, and who were more likely to have the ambition to rise in the profession. The great majority of teachers, it seems, were either untouched by the new professional communications, or read a bit about education in popular journals, or learned about new practices from school visitors and annual reports sent to the districts. The potential professional networks existed, but the rapid turnover of teachers remained an obstacle to professionalization. In Trempeleau

County, Wisconsin, the turnover rate was as high as 80 percent in the 1860s. The average teacher had less than two years' experience, and many positions were filled by a "brigade of irregulars," who had not taken the certification exam but applied for licenses the weekend before school was to start, in the absence of qualified candidates. The county superintendent labelled these teachers "vampires" and "barnacles." In Clinton County, New York, in 1843, three-fourths of the teachers were twenty-one or younger, and over 70 percent were new to the district in which they were employed. It was a short-lived occupation. Rapid teacher turnover inhibited professionalism, training, and higher pay for teachers. The reformers tried to break a vicious circle: low pay attracted transient, unqualified teachers, who seemed to merit low pay. But the reformers knew that higher pay rates had to be accompanied by longer sessions and an end to alternating men in winter with women in summer. "It is unreasonable to expect, that a person who is qualified to teach, will pursue a profession, if he can only find employment for three or four months in the year," said one Pennsylvania state superintendent.[28]

Henry Barnard linked teacher turnover to the slow progress of another favorite reform, the grading of schools and students. "The evils of a want of proper classification of schools . . . are aggravated by the almost universal practice of employing one teacher in summer, and another in winter, and different teachers each successive summer and winter." The graded school had numerous organizational and pedagogical implications, and it directly challenged the traditional structure of rural schooling. Grading could transform the organization of the school by classifying pupils roughly into levels of achievement. In the antebellum period, the word "grade" applied not to a particular level within a school, but to the practice of having a coordinated set of schools at different levels. The phrase "grade school," meaning elementary school, is also a later usage. Thus, to say in the 1850s that a town's schools were "graded" meant that they were divided into such levels as infant, primary, grammar, and high school. The purpose, of course, was to divide children by level of instruction so that teachers would not have to deal with such a wide range of ages and lessons. In large schools this effort led to internal gradations as well. The schools of Utica, New York, were an example of a budding graded system. In 1854, Utica had fourteen primary schools, each divided into higher and lower levels, six intermediate schools, and one advanced school, divided into male and female sections. Educators congratulated themselves that this sort of system was the beginning of proper classification.[29]

Barnard identified the key assumption behind the graded system: "The great principle to be regarded in the classification, either of the schools of a town or district, or of the scholars in the same school, is equality of attainments, which will generally include those of the same age." Although in most graded systems children had to pass some sort of examination to move from one school to the next, the net effect of grading the schools was to stratify children by age. This had a profound impact upon the social experience of schooling for children. In the ungraded, one-room district school, students had been in close contact with older and younger children, sometimes in a cooperative relationship. In the new graded schools of the antebellum period, students increasingly related only to other children their own age, and often in a deliberately competitive situation. Educators lauded competition as a "natural and commendable motive," certainly better than the fear of physical punishment. George Emerson, writing in the *Common School Journal,* urged teachers to try to "prevent the competition becoming personal," but he concluded that the graded system was desirable because in "a system of several connected schools, examination for each higher one may be rendered a strong motive to study."[30]

Reformers believed that graded schools were not only a great pedagogical invention, consistent with principles of efficiency and division of labor, but that they spurred industry and were therefore morally sound. Furthermore, they believed that they were an essential expression of democracy in education. In his *Report on the American System of Graded Free Schools* (1851), Hiram Barney argued that free schools graded into levels would give all children the opportunity to advance according to their merits. All would be on an equal footing. Happily, said Barney, the graded system was even finding some acceptance in rural districts and in the South. Nonetheless, many rural areas still refused to consolidate and grade their schools, adding to the reformers' growing impatience with rural schooling and their admiration for the more complex urban systems.[31]

Reformers coupled the drive for classification with a desire to see more uniformity in classroom programs. They did not want lock-step conformity, to be sure. They were for innovation, change, and the adaptation of schools to local circumstances; but they also thought that there were desirable standards of quality and that consistency was a virtue. Having made the assumptions that more schooling was better, that modern teaching aids like blackboards and outline maps were essential, and that some methods were demonstrably better than others, it was easy for them to see their desire for uniformity as a desire for higher quality. The most common issue of uniformity arose from the fact that parents provided textbooks for their own children. Students often had different texts in a given subject, even at the same level. This made it doubly difficult for the overworked teacher to group children for instruction, or to plan lessons. Diversity of textbooks undermined efficiency and professional expertise.

In Vermont the legislature attempted to impose a law for textbook uniformity, but a local official warned in 1846 that it would take "time and skill to bring about this change without giving occasion to opposers of the state regulations to arm themselves against the law," and in 1851 the state superintendent wearily advised that Vermont should guarantee to people "the peaceful possession of their schoolbooks." In New York a law specified that town committees, on the advice of teachers and the town superintendent, were to "determine what textbooks shall be used in each study, and require every child thereafter coming to the school to be provided with the designated books." Despite the law, implementation of the practice was very slow. A Wisconsin law of 1849 gave the state superintendent the power to "recommend" texts, but in a rural state, with transient teachers, it was nearly impossible to require uniform textbooks until school districts began to purchase the books themselves, a practice not authorized until 1874. Pennsylvania passed a law in 1854 calling for uniformity of texts, but it was widely ignored. If educators could not even get children at the same level in the same school to use the same spelling book, dreams of further uniformity in public school curriculum had to be postponed. A few states prescribed subjects for study, but such laws also turned out to be exercises in persuasion, not regulation. In the larger cities, however, one could see visions of the bureaucratic future. For example, the board in New York City decided in the 1840s to employ a supervisor to identify the best practices in the city, directing that they then be approved by the board and taught to other teachers. In the post–Civil War era, city superintendents would forge stronger procedures for uniformity, invoking visions of clock-like school systems, only to be criticized by a new generation of critics around the turn of the century who argued for more flexible systems sensitive to individual student differences. In the antebellum period, reformers did not argue for more diversity.[32]

Normal schools, education journals, professional supervision, uniform textbooks, higher teacher wages, and other antebellum reforms were designed to bring a measure of consistency and quality to a collection of local institutions that the reformers considered uneven and largely inadequate. Theirs was a program of assimilation, centralization, and standardization, a program of government encouragement and organization designed to make public education in different communities increasingly similar as well as more substantial, and to make schooling more responsive to the political, economic, and cultural tasks that Anglo-American Protestant educational leaders believed were necessary to preserve and improve their society. On the purposes of common schooling, there was much popular agreement, and when they argued for their innovations, school reformers invoked the necessity of universal schooling in a republic of diverse peoples. There was less agreement on the specific proposals of the reformers. They encountered inertia and resistance on matters of centralized control, nonsectarian religion, full tax support for common schools, and the establishment of new institutions like high schools and normal schools. Nonetheless, they had achieved many of their objectives by 1860 in the North, and they congratulated themselves on a successful campaign.

7

Ins and Outs: Acquiescence, Ambivalence, and Resistance to Common-School Reform

COMMON-SCHOOL reformers were fond of battle metaphors. Surveying the field in 1860, they believed that they had carried the day. Except in the South, state legislatures and local school committees had accepted much of the reform program. Most towns provided free common schooling, and most states employed a superintendent of common schools. But we should not imagine that there was general agreement about public education by the end of the period. Opponents of state school systems began as a majority in many states, and in 1860 they remained a strong minority, even in the Northeast. The battles had not been imaginary; the warfare metaphor reflected real conflict. Although few critics assaulted the educational reform program as a whole, there were continuing skirmishes fought by different groups on different issues.

It is easy to underestimate the resistance to state school systems. State superintendents usually publicized only the arguments in favor of more highly organized common schooling, and most newspapers and journals supported the reforms. Many speeches against school reform were lost to history once their echoes died in town meetings or legislative halls. The reformers' characterizations of their opponents prevailed. Horace Mann called his foes "political madmen," while Henry Barnard labelled his enemies "ignorant demagogues" and "a set of blockheads." George Martin, writing in the 1890s, said that opposition to antebellum school reform stemmed from "hide-bound conservatism, niggardly parsimony, sectarian bigotry, and political animosity." Until the middle of this century most historians equated common-school reform with progress, and they perpetuated the stereotype of the reformers' opponents as hack politicians, penny-pinching bumpkins, unassimilated foreigners, and undemocratic elitists. The historians were not entirely wrong. Some hard-pressed rural towns opposed increased school expenditures, some immigrants resented public-school attitudes, and some wealthy people were indifferent to tax-supported, free schooling. But these groups were not unanimous, and others also dissented.[1]

One important set of questions has to do with class, specifically with whether middle-class people imposed public education on working-class people in order to maintain social control in a changing industrial society, whether working people resisted the reforms, or, alternatively, whether public schools resulted from the conflicting interests of workers and the elite. Public common schooling was indeed devoted to moral education and discipline. Textbooks glorified American politics and social relations, and they often perpetuated demeaning ideas about immigrants and racist ideas about nonwhites. But it is quite another matter to demonstrate widespread class resistance to public schooling. For the most part, generalizations about the attitudes of ordinary workers must be gleaned from the observations of middle-class writers or inferred from fragmentary evidence about working-class behavior, such as voting lists or school enrollment records.[2]

Let us consider some of the evidence about the attitudes of manual workers toward common-school education, using the term *working class* synonymously with *manual workers* and *middle class* to include all white-collar workers except the very wealthy, mindful of the problem of the ambiguous and changing class status of some artisan proprietors on the one hand and some salaried white-collar workers on the other. A possible third or upper-class group, rich people, did not constitute a very distinct class in antebellum America. Despite statements by some wealthy individuals in support of public schooling, many were also indifferent or merely acquiescent in the creation of public schooling. Both workingmen's spokesmen and middle-class reformers, however, expressed hostility toward elite education. In the late 1820s and early 1830s American labor spokesmen railed against private education for the rich. They demanded common public schools, freed of the stigma of charity education, and an end to public subsidies of colleges and academies. Focusing on these statements, earlier historians assigned a key role to labor in wresting tax-supported education from reluctant and conservative legislatures. They believed that workingmen's groups, far from being suspicious of public education, were centrally important in its triumphs. Although it is difficult to judge how crucial labor's support for public education was, there is no doubt that between 1825 and 1835, workingmen's associations helped popularize tax-supported common schools.[3]

In 1828 the editors of the *Mechanics' Free Press*, complaining about the pauper stigma of charity schools, said, "Give us our rights, and we shall not need your charity." In 1829 they urged every man to "come forward and use his utmost exertions to procure a system of education, where the children of the rich and the poor shall receive a national education, calculated to make republicans and banish aristocrats." The same year a convention of workingmen in New York City predicted that the existing system of education, which separated the children of the poor and the rich, would "eventually lead us into all the distinctions which exist under the despotic governments, and destroy our political liberties." The Albany Mechanics' Society, protesting a public subsidy to the local academy in 1830, asked readers to imagine how greatly the virtue and well-being of the public might have increased if the "immense sums now perverted to the aristocratical nurseries of the wealthy few, had been judiciously and economically applied to the really useful instruction of all." Workingmen in New Castle, Delaware, pledged to support only those political candidates who favored "a rational system of education to be paid for out of public funds," and in 1834 members of the National Trades Union declared that the education system of the United States was "destructive of the Equality which is predicated in the Declaration of Independence."[4]

The workingmen's contribution to the nation's material progress was a central theme in statements by workingmen's groups. Despite some middle-class writers' stereotypes of working-class people as hard-drinking and profligate, many manual workers prided themselves on hard work, frugality, morality, and enterprise. The hero in workingmen's literature was the self-educated "mechanic" (a craftsman in the mechanical arts). While the later heroes of Horatio Alger's novels attained positions of respectability through hard work, honesty, and luck, the antebellum mechanic made it through self-improvement and inventive genius. Successful, real-life mechanics were called to the podiums of workingmen's lyceums, and they wrote their memoirs for apprentices' magazines. Their lives represented a working-class translation of the dictum, "Knowledge is power." The emphasis on self-education derived from the necessity for workingmen to leave school at a young age and from their desire for practical learning in mechanical subjects. "What is the education of a common school?" asked the *Mechanics'* *Magazine* in 1834. "Is there a syllable of science taught in one, beyond the rudiments of mathematics? No." The Mechanics' Institute of New York was formed "with the view of carrying the mechanic to something beyond the mere knowing how to read, write and cipher." Professionals, ministers, and manufacturers encouraged the establishment of organizations that would foster the self-improvement of skilled workers, and they frequently cited examples of success through diligence and reading. A judge in Salem, Massachusetts, told a lyceum audience that Isaac Newton had succeeded more by hard work than by genius and that John Locke relied more upon self-teaching than upon his Oxford teachers. "Innumerable are the instances of successful self-instruction," he said, even "among those of apparently moderate powers."[5]

Timothy Claxton, who was born in England in 1790 and finished his career in Boston, is a perfect example of the self-taught artisan hero. His father was a gardener, and both parents were illiterate. His own schooling ended after three years but sufficed to get him started reading, and he learned arithmetic as far as ratios. He worked at several jobs as a little boy, then did a full apprenticeship to a metal worker. Because the other apprentices were illiterate, the master chose Claxton to help keep accounts of work completed. The boy started studying again, borrowing books on surveying from a journeyman carpenter in the neighborhood. In his spare time he tinkered, proving his perseverance by building a clock. He taught himself mechanical drawing. As a journeyman in a London machine shop, he started reading and going to lectures on chemistry and natural philosophy. Among his evening projects, he invented a mousetrap in which the mouse first reset the trap and then drowned. In 1823, Claxton emigrated to America, and he spent the voyage learning to use a slide rule. Beginning as a journeyman machinist, he eventually gained prominence as a manufacturer of school and scientific apparatus. A tireless self-improver, Claxton helped found the Boston Mechanics' Institution, the Boston Mechanics' Lyceum, and the *Young Mechanic* magazine, all active in the 1830s. A factory manager summed up the ideal when he introduced Claxton at a lyceum lecture: "He is a man we admire, a self-made man, a mechanic—an industrious, persevering, indefatigable student . . . one of the most scientific and intelligent mechanics in the city of Boston."[6]

Workingmen's organizations of the 1830s also supported a more egalitarian public school system. The workingmen's criticism of exclusive educational institutions and their demands for tax-supported common schools were consistent with their general political goals: to eliminate monopoly and special privilege, to remove disabilities in the lives of workingmen, and to provide all youths with an equal chance for advancement. These organizations flourished for a brief period, particularly from 1828 to 1834. During that period, the workingmen's groups stridently publicized their demands for tax-supported common schools. Through political alliances the early workingmen's groups achieved some legislative victories, but by the late 1830s they were torn by factions and had lost workers' votes to the two main political parties. They were succeeded by trade union organizations that eschewed direct political involvement and concentrated more on working conditions. To some degree the early workingmen's groups were victims of their own successes. In the case of education most states moved toward public support of common schools. Even in the states where resistance to free schooling lingered, organized labor lost interest in the issue. As the hard times of the early 1840s turned workers toward issues of wages and hours, and as the industrial work force became more proletarian, the old workingmen's crusade against privileged education was inherited by such middle-class school reformers as Horace Mann, Henry Barnard, and John Pierce. By 1850, the trades unions were almost silent on educational issues. In that year, New York State voters chose by referendum to repeal the unpopular 1849 free-school law; organized labor played no role in the attempt to save the common schools from a reinstatement of tuition bills. By midcentury spokesmen for organized labor viewed public education neither as a panacea nor as a threat.

Like their English contemporaries, American artisan leaders of the 1830s criticized aristocratic education and supported free schools. Unlike the English, however, few drew a line between appropriate middle-class and working-class education. Workingmen's parties acted on the assumption that if abuses in the economy and workplace were rectified and if free common schools were established and were attended by children from all classes, the American economic order could be a just and rewarding one for workingmen. In England the privileges of the aristocracy and the abject conditions of labor had combined with long-standing class traditions to create a context of greater class consciousness, in which working-class radicals eventually saw middle-class educational reform as invidious. In America, there was virtually no overt working-class resistance to middle-class reformers' proposals for state-sponsored schooling. Working-class and middle-class educators shared the goals of morality, respectability, and self-improvement. Even if the concepts meant somewhat different things in the different class structures, many parents of both classes saw free common schools as desirable instruments of moral education. These shared commitments, sometimes reinforced by religious and ethnic identities that crossed class lines, produced an alliance in the 1820s and 1830s between American workingmen's groups and middle-class reformers in favor of tax-supported common schooling. Because the workingmen's political parties were dominated by upper-status craftsmen and included merchants and professionals, there is even less reason to expect in their statements alienation from middle-class educational institutions and values.[7]

Not all spokesmen for workers acquiesced, though. Some challenged capitalism itself, with its individualistic values and unequal distribution of wealth. Among the most widely publicized radical challenges were those of Robert Owen and his followers. Although the ideas of these socialist dissenters did not gain the allegiance of very many people, they are worth remembering because they represented alternatives to the policies and ideological perspectives that dominated school reform in antebellum America. Robert Owen was a successful factory owner who had created at New Lanark, Scotland, a paternalistic, cooperative, workers' community. Owen was convinced, however, that a cotton manufacturing town was not a promising environment for complete social reconstruction, so he decided to create an agrarian, socialist community on the American frontier. Owen purchased land in Indiana and began recruiting settlers for the community, which he named New Harmony. It was to be based on the ideas he had set forth in his *New View of Society* (1813) and on the critique of competitive capitalism that he and his followers developed in the years before his departure for America in 1824. In America the prestigious Owen spoke before the House of Representatives and the President. His educational ideas were publicized by reform-minded educators like Boston's William Woodbridge, editor of the *American Annals of Education*, and John Griscom, chemist and patron of common-school reform in New York City.

Among Owen's important English followers was William Maclure, another wealthy philanthropist. Maclure worried that the beliefs and habits of the adults who would populate New Harmony would be "stubborn, crooked, and too often bent in the opposite direction from their own most evident interest." Nonetheless he went to New Harmony to head up the educational and scientific activities of the community. He believed in the central propositions of Owenite socialism: that social relations could be based on rationality and interdependence, but only in a reformed community in which all shared property and all shared work. Only a loving, rational, and egalitarian education could rid individuals of the false conventions and destructive motives brought about by private property and acquisitiveness. Convinced that Pestalozzian pedagogy was the perfect means to such an education, Maclure had earlier patronized the schools of outstanding Pestalozzian teachers in France and in Philadelphia. Three of these teachers— Marie Fretageot, William Phiquepal, and Joseph Neef—joined in the New Harmony adventure.[8]

Because Pestalozzian education seemed more effective to them, the Owenites thought it was automatically a threat to the old economic order. In a sarcastic comparison, Maclure said that "to multiply and exaggerate the difficulties" of educating a child was "perfectly consistent with the principles of all commerce and trade, to buy cheap and sell dear." What else could explain such useless and ineffective educational practices? Traditional schools, he said, were devoted to the "killing of time" and to the "imprisoning of children for four or five hours in the day—after which they are let loose on society for eight hours, full of revenge and retaliation against their jailors." Schools at New Harmony would be "bottomed on free will, by the total exclusion of every species of correction." Children would be "constantly occupied with something useful." The schools would omit everything "speculative and ornamental." Girls, like boys, would get a practical education. Because everyone would share manual labor, menial work would be less onerous. Indeed, a proper Pestalozzian education could render "all the useful and necessary operations of both males and females, a pastime and amusement, converting life itself into a play."[9]

It was not to be. New Harmony failed. Disputes, misunderstandings, and schisms began almost immediately. Owen himself, too often absent, was contentious and inconsistent when he was on the scene. Maclure's worst fears about the resiliency of a competitive value system were realized; idealism was ground into the Indiana soil as dissenting groups organized, voiced their complaints, and seceded. Maclure pursued his educational and scholarly ventures at New Harmony after the breakup of the experiment, but they had lost their moorings to an actual reformed community. Owen, wiser and poorer, returned to England, where he pursued his socialist theories through the labor movement. Some of the New Harmony leaders transferred their efforts to New York. This group included Robert Dale Owen, the founder's son, Robert Jennings, a member of the community's governing board, Frances

Wright, the ardent socialist and occasional resident of New Harmony, and William Phiquepal, the Pestalozzian teacher who later married Frances Wright. Wright had co-edited the *Free Enquirer* with Robert Dale Owen at New Harmony, and with Jennings as an assistant, she had lectured and published essays attacking Christianity, asserting women's rights, and advocating family limitation and universal equal education. She was, to say the least, controversial.[10]

These tireless socialist reformers moved their newspaper to New York City and forged an alliance with the leaders of the new Workingmen's Party. Although the *Free Enquirer* group agreed with many workingmen's demands, their central focus was on equal education as the key to a reformed society. "All the reform must be wrought where the corruption has generated—in education," said the *Free Enquirer* in 1829. They disavowed the more radical solutions of Thomas Skidmore, who favored redistribution of land and the abolition of inheritance. The Owen-Wright supporters tried to distance themselves from this position, but their own educational proposals were radical, and they had difficulty escaping the label. They proposed a national system of boarding schools for all children aged two to sixteen, designed to eliminate the unequal influence of family wealth and culture.[11]

For a brief period in 1830, Robert Dale Owen enjoyed great influence in the Workingmen's Party. The Owenites' boarding-school plan seemed at least tentatively acceptable as an education plank. But in the spring of 1830, the majority abandoned it. They were put off by the charge of atheism that plagued Owen and Wright, and they were uncomfortable with the boarding schools' proposed elimination of family influence. The Workingmen's Party adopted a subcommittee report advocating a more moderate endorsement of free public day schools. After a series of acrimonious and sometimes tumultuous meetings, Frances Wright realized that she was doing more harm than good to the education cause in New York. She married Phiquepal and moved to Paris. Robert Dale Owen returned to England briefly; he later settled in New Harmony. Most of the Workingmen's Party members apparently returned to the folds of the Democratic Party.

Radical social reform did not survive in this early labor organization, dominated as it was by middling-status artisans and absorbed as they were in tough practical issues like mechanics' lien laws and ten-hour days. Frances Wright's attacks on clerical influence in American institutions invited the charge of infidelity against all of the Owenites' plans. Influential evangelical clergymen saw in Frances Wright's popular lectures an anticlerical threat, and they too pressed the counterattack. In a Boston sermon, Lyman Beecher further displayed the connection of assertive Protestant religion to other ideological commitments. Political atheism, said Beecher, aimed at "nothing less than the abolition of marriage and the family state, separate property, civil government, and all sense of accountability." Political atheists, he charged, were engaged in "an effort to turn the world upside down, and empty it of every institution, thought, feeling, and action, which has emanated from Christianity." According to Lyman Beecher, Frances Wright believed that "atheistical education must and will come, either by public suffrage or by revolution."[12]

An attack on Protestant influence in government and schooling was an attack on a coherent ideological perspective in which republicanism and universal education were nurtured by Protestant Christianity and all three were linked in a view of progress and morality. The claim that the Owenite socialists were attempting to "turn the world upside down" had some truth to it. Their social beliefs were indeed linked, just like those of the mainstream Protestants they opposed. Although Frances Wright was more radical and outspoken than her colleagues, they shared several basic beliefs: religion was superstitious, traditional education irrational, capitalism unnatural, the subordination of women artificial, and all of it inequitable. Through the proper sort of education, said Wright, "a revolution would indeed be effected; the present order of things completely subverted."

The brief crusade of the Free Enquirers was as sustained and comprehensive an assault on mainstream Protestant ideology and institutions as anything that appeared in the antebellum period. It failed as the basis for a utopian community at New Harmony through poor planning, dissent about organization, personality clashes, and, as William Maclure had feared, persistent traditional habits of mind. It also failed in its urban political phase. It was too comprehensive a critique of existing institutions. Workingmen were not in general committed to religious skepticism, to women's rights, or to attacks on marriage and the family. Owen, Wright, and their sympathizers had tried to engraft a thoroughgoing critique of capitalist society onto a stripling labor organization whose members were largely motivated by specific work-related grievances. The effort proved futile.

Antebellum workingmen's groups enthusiastically endorsed tax-supported public education in the 1830s and displayed moderate support or indifference thereafter. But the early labor organizations were dominated by middling-status workers, and therefore their statements do not tell us much about the attitudes of the large group of less skilled manual workers in the cities, nor anything about the large number of farm laborers in the countryside. If we look instead at public-school enrollment rates by occupational groups, the pattern of enrollment by children of manual workers is very similar to those of white-collar groups, except for the teenage years, when the parent's occupational group appears to have affected a child's school-leaving age. But the school enrollment patterns speak only indirectly and uncertainly about attitudes. What other sort of evidence exists about working-class acquiescence or opposition to public schooling? Michael Katz has argued that there is very revealing evidence in a case where the individuals' votes on an important local school issue were recorded—the vote to abolish the high school in Beverly, Massachusetts, in 1860. In that controversy, shoemakers and fishermen voted to abolish the high school by about three to one, while artisans and businessmen split, and professionals generally voted to continue the new institution. A vote against public secondary schooling is, of course, not necessarily an indicator of working-class attitudes toward common elementary schooling, but it does indicate dissent against one particular reform at this point in Beverly's history. In a separate analysis of the same information, however, Maris Vinovskis has demonstrated that while the negative vote correlates with occupational and wealth status, the best predictor of how one voted on the Beverly high school issue was the voter's neighborhood. It appears that the Beverly vote depended to a great extent upon the fact that voters in outlying districts opposed the maintenance of this town-wide institution.[13]

The Beverly high school had been promoted for some years by a small group of ministers and other prominent citizens who threatened to invoke a poorly enforced Massachusetts law requiring towns the size of Beverly to support a high school. In 1857 they made good on their threat, and the suit that followed largely accounted for the reluctant establishment of the high school in that year. The 1860 vote, which defied the law and reversed that decision, indicates an element of resentment against imposed reform, deepened by the hard times of a shoemaker's strike. But there was a more long-standing tension involved. Beverly still had a district system. At midcentury, each of its ten districts controlled the expenditure of its share of the town's school funds. The districts hired teachers and determined the length of the school year. District committees guarded their autonomy and periodically complained of inequities in the distribution of funds. In contrast, the town-wide school committee, which included some of the Protestant ministers, urged not only more expenditures for common-school education, which the districts were prepared to support, but innovations like the abolition of the district committees, the hiring of a professional superintendent, and the establishment of a public high school. Although during the 1850s the town meeting acquiesced in the hiring of a superintendent, the majority resisted incursions on the districts' control of funds, and when they were bullied into establishing a high school, they located it in an unlikely and inconvenient spot at the edge of town. When it was abolished in 1860, only seventeen students were attending.

Beverly soon changed policies again, reopening its public high school in 1861. However, the skirmishes of the period—not just over the high school, but over other reforms associated with centralization—suggest that the main issue was localism, one of the most enduring and pervasive sources of conflict in American educational history. Reformers in Beverly and across the nation called for more state regulation, the consolidation of small districts into town units, the replacement of private schooling with one inclusive public system, and the development of a more professional corps of teachers and administrators. A wide variety of groups opposed one or more of these goals during the antebellum period. Sometimes the tension coincided with class differences, sometimes with religious, racial, or ethnic conflict, and sometimes it ran along urban-rural lines. In some cases, class, race, or ethnic tensions appear to be the crux of the situation.

On the one hand, issues of control, centralization, and bureaucratization had an independent importance. On the other hand—and equally important—those who favored the centralized solutions were more often insiders, who had more power, while the groups who dissented were characteristically the outsiders. Despite their shared sense that state-regulated schooling was not in their interests, dissenters were drawn from very different groups, and in each of these groups—whether Illinois farmers, Beverly shoemakers, New York blacks, or Minnesota Norwegians—there were some who supported reformers' plans for inclusive public schooling. Opponents in these groups did not think of themselves as a common force; their solutions were inherently local and largely negative. They shared a desire to limit the increasing consolidation and the increasing cost of public education; they argued variously on the basis of tradition, parents' prerogatives, minority rights, religious freedom, and theories of limited government. The diversity of the opponents and their independent orientation spelled their defeat in the long run. But this was not self-evident to the cosmopolitan school reformers. The outcome was far from certain at the beginning of the antebellum period. The opponents, though scattered, were vocal, and in the short run they succeeded in delaying or modifying some aspects of the reform program.

One hotly debated issue was the provision of tuition-free schooling for all children. Despite the Puritans' devotion to education, common schooling supported entirely by general taxation had not been characteristic of the colonial period, even in Massachusetts and Connecticut, and many people in the early nineteenth century did not want their property taxed for the education of children whose parents could afford to pay part of the costs. "The habits of the people were formed by the custom which prevailed from the settlement of the province," wrote Pennsylvania's state superintendent in 1842. "Provision for general education was a private, not a public duty." Opponents of general taxation for free schooling were not necessarily opposed to education under parental control or to charity schooling for the poor. But their opposition to general taxation for a free school system meant a rejection of the educational reform program. The general property tax, said Henry Barnard in his 1842 Connecticut report, was "the cardinal idea of the free school system."

In the opponents' view, state and town governments had no business regulating common schooling. Parents and neighborhoods, they argued, should decide how much schooling to have and how to divide the cost. Schooling should not be free for those able to pay for it, nor should the state compel communities to provide schooling. These traditional views meant trouble for free-school bills in various state legislatures. In Pennsylvania, lawmakers created a tax-supported system of common schooling between 1834 and 1837, but it was voluntary, and many communities chose not to tax for common schools, particularly where dissent was bolstered by German immigrants and religious groups who wanted to preserve their independent schools. By 1847 the "nonaccepting" districts, however, had decreased to 158 out of 1,225. The provision of completely free schooling was also optional for Connecticut towns until 1868. Despite Henry Barnard's campaign against the rate bill and the unusually large amount of aid provided by the state's school fund, many communities refused to use local property taxes to end tuition payments to public schools. About half of the state's 1,600 school districts provided tuition-free schooling by 1860.[14]

Most opponents did not reject all property taxes for common schools, but preferred a combination of general community support mixed with charges to the families whose children benefited. Rate bills accounted for about 10 percent of public-school resources in Rhode Island in 1852, about the same in Connecticut in 1856, about 15 percent in Michigan in 1850, but 40 percent in the average New York town in the same year. Where tuition payments were high, they probably deterred the attendance of children from poor families. Rate bills also tended to discourage regular attendance because towns usually charged parents according to the number of days their children attended. In some places, the acceptance of fully tax-supported schools was a seesaw process. In Kenosha, Wisconsin, voters created a free school system, abolished it, and recreated it in the 1840s. In New York State the issue was in doubt for over twenty years. A provision requiring full free schooling failed in the constitutional convention of 1846, but the legislature passed a law to the same effect in 1849. Much traditional opposition remained, however, and the details of the tax law were highly controversial. One tiny upstate district angrily resolved "not to raise no money for teacher's wages." An opponent wrote the *Rochester Daily Democrat* that "the new school law takes A's property without his consent and applies it to the benefit of B, which is unconstitutional, arbitrary, and unjust." A petition from Onondaga County said that the law created "strifes, jealousies, divisions and animosities in every district" by authorizing people "to put their hands into their neighbors' pockets." Some opponents believed rate bills for education were fair and should be retained, others preferred county or state level taxes instead of local taxes, and others were upset by the state's property valuation system. The referendum for repeal in 1850 succeeded because of these multiple frustrations.[15]

Opposition in New York had an effect on the deliberations of the Michigan constitutional convention in 1850, which debated the free-school tax issue at great length. Democrats John Pierce and Isaac Crary, who had helped create the state system, argued against a constitutional requirement for district taxes, claiming that New York's free-school experiment had been "disastrous." Delegate Joseph Williams, though, argued that the matter should not be left to the timid legislature or the reluctant districts because "the most backward, the most ignorant, the most indifferent, are the very portion of the population we wish to enlighten. The state wishes to stretch its paternal arms around them. It wishes to educate all, willing and unwilling." There was much resistance to this "paternal arm" of the state. When some delegates argued that the tax should be statewide rather than district-by-district, members from the western counties argued that a state tax would drain money from their part of the state to educate children in the populous eastern counties. Some members said they were for free schools by law but not through a constitutional requirement. However, Mr. D. C. Walker charged that these members were really opponents of free schooling, like the man with "a bottle under his cloak" at a temperance meeting. In the end, the convention adopted a weak clause stating that any town not providing three months of free primary schooling could lose its state funds. It left the details of taxing to the legislature. Walker predicted that "violent opposition will be got up when it shall be attempted in legislature to establish free schools throughout the state. Men of capital, and men without families, will resist."[16]

Arguments persist in the twentieth century about the inequities of property taxes, about the proper relative state and local share of school expenses, about "double taxation" for those who patronize private schools, and about the heavy school-tax burden on childless and retired property owners. It is not surprising that the original implementation of full tax support encountered resistance, but educational reformers worked hard to devise acceptable schemes of local taxation and to persuade people that public schooling benefited everyone, not just those who received the education. Their arguments prevailed by the 1870s, when the last of the northern states abolished public-school rate bills. Even in the late nineteenth century, however, some communities followed tradition, not the law.

Although tax support was a necessary condition for a free school system, it was only the beginning, and it was only one aspect of the tension between reformers and independent-minded dissenters. The reformers had a long agenda. Two key items affected local control of public schools: the substitution of town control for district control and the creation of state departments to oversee common schools for the legislature. Both innovations prompted vigorous and outspoken opposition. Town government may seem close to the people from a twentieth-century perspective, but nineteenth-century towns were often very large and encompassed people who had little contact. In Boxford, Massachusetts, residents said that some people spent their lives without visiting the other side of town; in Wisconsin, district-school advocates complained that towns measured forty square miles and were often not communities at all. As late as 1865 the Wisconsin state superintendent reported that almost half of his county superintendents were opposed to the township system. Robert Lees of Buffalo County called it "but another step toward the concentration of power, and all concentrations of power have ever proved destructive to republican forms of government." The superintendent of Columbia County echoed the fear. The township system would place control "one step farther from the people."

In most states the abolition of district control did not happen in one dramatic stroke. The districts had control on some matters while the town controlled others. Legislation gradually reduced the autonomy of the districts, but not without opposition. The Massachusetts legislature passed a law requiring town-wide committees to visit and report on district schools, but in 1841 the townspeople of West Springfield voted that their committee would make no such inspections. When Newbury, Massachusetts, abolished district control in 1851, one of its districts claimed control of its schools and appointed a committee to hire teachers. In many other towns, school committees reported no such opposition and welcomed the transition to central control. The town committees were in the middle of the drama between the defenders of local control and the advocates of statewide school reform. The town committees often included ministers and other prominent citizens, and they typically acted like local agents of the reform program, pressing for more expenditures, longer sessions, better teachers, and town-wide supervision. On the other hand, they were elected and had to be responsive to popular opinion in towns where resistance to reform was clear and vocal.

The debate continued well beyond the antebellum period. In many states, legislation on school district powers was like a tug of war. Massachusetts passed legislation urging the voluntary abolition of districts in 1853, required their abolition in 1859, repealed that law in the same year, required the abolition of districts again in 1869, allowed their reestablishment in 1870, and finally abolished them again in 1883. Many other states made town-level control mandatory by the 1890s, but related debates about centralization continued into the twentieth century. Centralized control, avidly pursued by professional educators and spokesmen for "progress," was the most controversial of the antebellum reforms. As its opponents emphasized, it removed educational control "one step farther from the people."

In addition to town consolidation, reformers supported the creation of state school boards and professional state school officers to gather statistics, urge improvements, recommend legislation, and implement state school laws. Reformers equated the appointment of state school officers with progress, efficiency, and improved quality. Opponents labelled the innovation undemocratic and unnecessary. In Massachusetts, localists mounted an effort to abolish the Board of Education in 1840, two years after its establishment. The legislature's Education Committee, on a 4–3 vote, approved a report that characterized the board as "the commencement of a system of centralization and of monopoly of power in a few hands, contrary, in every respect, to the true spirit of our democratical institutions." The majority report praised the district system and denied the need for a state board or state normal schools. It recommended the abolition of the board and the dismissal of its Secretary, Horace Mann. In the vote that followed, the board survived on a vote of 245–182. The roll-call vote reveals some of the characteristics associated with opposition to state involvement in education. The rural source of the opposition is indicated by the fact that farmers in the legislature voted more heavily against the board than other legislators, as did members in general from rural towns. Legislators who lived farthest from Boston, the capital, tended to vote against the state educational involvement. Legislators from the most highly developed commercial and manufacturing centers generally rallied to the support of the board. But the best single predictor of the vote on the board was the legislator's political party. About four-fifths of the Whig members voted to save the board, and about two-thirds of the Democrats voted to abolish it.[17]

The political parties played a key role in the debates about educational policy between conservative localists and cosmopolitan reformers in the 1840s. Both Democrats and Whigs favored free common schools, and they shared much of the general ideological perspective associated with school reform. Spokesmen for both parties stressed the sacredness and fragility of the republic, the great destiny of America, the sanctity of property, a commitment to universal male franchise, and fair economic opportunity within a free wage-labor market. But to the extent that the cultural core of that ideology was native and Protestant, it was more comfortably and unequivocally the ideology of the Whigs. Democrats adopted a more pluralist and egalitarian expression of the same commitment to republicanism and capitalism, and they generally opposed centralized regulation of education.

Leaders and supporters of both parties came from a wide socioeconomic range, yet the parties differed in ways that made the Whig ranks attractive to the more conservative, native elite and made the Democratic Party attractive to much of the immigrant working class, particularly Roman Catholics. The Whigs favored government intervention on a wide range of issues. They believed that state governments should finance canals and railroads, regulate banks, build asylums and penitentiaries, and regulate public morality on such matters as temperance and Sabbath-keeping. The Democrats, in keeping with their more diverse constituency and their Jeffersonian philosophy of government, supported these activities less enthusiastically and less often. They urged limited government intervention on most issues and opposed the drift toward centralization in areas where they felt government action was necessary. Their political philosophy has been aptly summarized as "negative liberalism," emphasizing individual liberty and limited government, while the Whigs' "positive liberalism" stressed public morality and state action on many fronts. The Whigs were government activists and were mainly responsible for the translation of Protestant native ideology into state government policy. And in education, they were the ones who turned to the cosmopolitan solutions of centralization and professionalization. They were the modernizers, who believed that social planning and state regulation were essential to progress in both the moral and the economic sphere.[18]

But what were Democrats to do about public education, believing as Robert Rantoul of Massachusetts said, that "the whole object of government is negative"? Government, said this prominent Democrat, should "remove, and keep out of the citizen's way, all obstacles to his natural freedom of action." A few hardheaded Democrats applied this doctrine to public education. John Bigelow, a radical Democrat and writer for the *New York Evening Post*, said that government aid to canals, railroads, and common schools was "downright dangerous." He argued that the entire existing New York State school fund should be applied to the state debt and that the state should cease all involvement in education. Most

Democrats, however, looked upon locally controlled common schools as a necessary and proper government activity. The reason, according to Rantoul, was that people "have a right to have the career kept fairly open to talent, and to be brought equally and together up to the starting point at the public expense; after that we must shift for ourselves." Differences in party philosophy emerged not on the issue of public education per se, but in debates about how public education should be organized.[19]

In Connecticut the focus of the debate was the same, and the party split was even more absolute than in Massachusetts. The Hartford *Times*, a Democratic paper, attacked the Whig centralizing reforms as "despotic" and "Prussian." During 1840 and 1841 it called Henry Barnard's salary exorbitant, his efforts useless, and his powers dangerous. When Democrats captured the legislature and the governorship in 1842, they abolished the board and the position of secretary and repealed the previous year's legislation encouraging district consolidation. In New York State, too, the centralizing orientation of the Whigs and the localist orientation of the Democrats affected educational politics. Opponents of centralized educational supervision had succeeded in 1821 in combining the job of common-school superintendent with that of Secretary of State. Under Martin Van Buren's "Regency" Democrats, who controlled the state government from the late 1820s until 1839, only staunch localists held the combined position. John Dix, Secretary of State from 1833 to 1839, criticized Prussian-style centralization, and in 1837 he criticized the legislature for increasing state aid to common schools. William Seward, a Whig, became governor in 1840 and immediately set out to introduce the cosmopolitan school-reform program to New York, recommending a separate state superintendent and the introduction of county superintendents. In Vermont, educational reform was similarly spearheaded by Whig Governor William Slade and superintendent Horace Eaton, a protégé of Horace Mann. In Ohio, their Whig counterparts were Governor Joseph Vance and superintendent Samuel Lewis, a lawyer born in Massachusetts and devoted to temperance, common schooling, and the abolition of slavery. Whig reformers across the North played the key role in establishing state school systems.[20]

Democrats criticized professionalization as well as centralization. In Massachusetts the localists opposed state normal schools, arguing that existing academies and high schools furnished competent teachers for the common schools. It was "not desirable," they declared, "that the business of keeping these schools should be~ome a distinct and separate profession." In Connecticut the Hartford *Times* argued in 1850 that there was "just as much reason for asking the State to instruct young men in making shoes and hats, as to require it to fit them for teaching." To the localists, teaching a common school was something any competently educated person could do; pedagogy was not to be elevated to the level of a science in order to make education a profession, especially if it involved costly government intervention.[21]

It seems, then, that Democrats favored local control of common schooling and emphasized the theme of opportunity, while the Whigs favored organized state systems of education and stressed public morality and social stability. But local and state control could be mixed, and the themes of opportunity and stability were not mutually exclusive. These were matters of emphasis. Horace Mann was a Whig, but there is much in his writings about opportunity, freedom, and respect for diversity, just as there is much about public morality and social stability in the arguments of Michigan's Democratic state school superintendent, John Pierce. In the Illinois constitutional convention of 1847, the strongest advocate of mandating a state school superintendent was the Democrat Thompson Campbell. There were Democrats in other states who, like Campbell, supported the increasing involvement of state government in local schooling. They believed that a strong public school system was compatible with their Democratic philosophy. They joined with reform-minded Whigs in support of temperance, antislavery, and public schooling. This bipartisan support helped to create state school systems in the North in the face of localist opposition.

The cosmopolitan solution aimed in theory at getting all white children—rich and poor, rural and urban, immigrant and native—into one uniform system and imparting to them similar values and similar opportunities. While the egalitarian aspect of that proposition appealed to many Democratic spokesmen, the assimilationist aspect of it had a special appeal to the Whigs, who generally believed that outsiders should conform to the dominant culture and that schools should take on the task of assimilation. Nonetheless, Whig politicians were not predictable on issues of cultural pluralism. After a year as New York's governor, William Seward aimed a message at New York City's immigrant Roman Catholics and declared that they should have "schools in which they may be instructed by teachers speaking the same language as themselves and professing the same faith." Seward's Secretary of State and ex officio superintendent of public instruction, John Spencer, produced a remarkable report condemning the "educational establishment" in New York City and recommending a decentralized, pluralist, "voluntary" system that would accommodate the immigrants' religion and culture. Party affiliation was thus not always a reliable indicator of how antebellum politicians faced educational issues, but these pluralistic Whigs were exceptions to the general orientation of their party.

School reformers attributed localist opposition to petty politics or to popular ignorance. To try to get their message across, state superintendents crisscrossed their states like circuit-riding preachers. Samuel Lewis, Ohio's first superintendent, rode as much as thirty miles a day, speaking in small towns in the evenings. Once, in the more hostile southern part of the state, he arrived unannounced at a meeting that had been called to protest the new state school system. Not aware of Lewis's presence, a committee presented resolutions "which opposed the School Law, demanded its repeal, and the repeal of all school taxes, censured the Superintendent in the severest terms, and imperatively demanded his withdrawal from office." All speakers supported the resolutions, and when Lewis introduced himself and asked to speak on behalf of the laws and the superintendency, only a bare majority approved. But then, according to his son, he delivered a brilliant speech, after which the original resolutions were tabled, new resolutions of praise were passed, "and the crowd gathered around Mr. Lewis with tears of sympathy and pledges of support." Although the story may be exaggerated, it accurately portrays the reformers' perception that the common-school struggle was one of enlightenment against ignorance. They failed to see that there were principles on both sides of the debates over common-school organization. The effort to professionalize, homogenize, and organize common schooling threatened highly prized local control.[22]

Localism was reinforced by resistance to the reformers' pan-Protestant approach to morality. The policy of a generalized Protestantism for schools found opponents not only among Roman Catholics but among Lutherans, Congregationalists, and other groups, especially where communities were religiously homogeneous and people often wanted sectarian religion kept in their schools. Frederick Packard, a critic of Horace Mann, believed that local majority rule should prevail instead of Mann's policy on moral education, which, he charged, "makes natural religion and ethics the basis of the system." "What doctrines of revealed religion will remain, to be connected with a system of public instruction, after subtracting those about which there are conflicting creeds among men?" he queried. As for excluding books with sectarian religious content, Packard declared, "neither the legislature nor the Board of Education can control a district in this matter." The reformers' view prevailed among most professional educators, but the views of men like Packard continued to have much support at the local level, and many communities quietly continued to include the prayers, catechisms, or storybooks that reflected prevailing religious views.[23]

The local-control tradition left much of the responsibility for schooling to parents. Parents decided when and for how long their children would attend, and they paid partial tuition costs. Parents had great influence over the hiring, retention, and behavior of teachers. Groups of parents sometimes boycotted unpopular teachers, forcing committees to dismiss them. Although teacher-parent conflict was not new to the antebellum period, school reform created a new element of tension between the state and the parent. School reformers argued the precedence of state responsibility over traditional parental responsibility for education. Hiram Barney, Ohio's school commissioner in 1854, wrote that "for educational purposes, the State may with propriety be regarded as one great School District, and the population as constituting but one family, charged with the parental duty of educating all its youth." The Wisconsin Teachers' Association declared in 1865 that "children are the property of the state," an argument often heard in favor of more state activity in common schooling.[24]

Some parents resisted these arguments. The county superintendent of Allen County, Ohio, reported in 1854 that people opposed the school law "because they think its principles subversive of their constitutional and parental rights, in that it takes away the right of the parent to decide as to the manner and the quality of his child's education." Local school reports in antebellum Massachusetts reveal widespread parental resistance to the authority of teachers and school committees. In turn, their resistance prompted frequent complaints by town school officials against uncooperative parents. "There is a class of parents in all communities, who have little or no control over their children," declared the Lynnfield, Massachusetts, school committee in 1853, and it is just these parents who "join, to prevent a teacher from opening a school, or during the term impair its usefulness by continual opposition."[25]

School officials urged parents not to believe their child's version of classroom incidents because children were biased and given to lying. In various reports, children were characterized as "prejudiced witnesses" with "groundless complaints" and "improbable stories" about what goes on in school. If parents wanted the straight story, they were to come to school and get it from the teacher. School committees emphasized that the teacher's authority was crucial and therefore must under no circumstances be challenged. They complained that some parents criticized teachers in front of their children at home and even encouraged them to misbehave in school. Corporal punishment, although considered a last resort, was generally defended by local school committees in the face of parental challenges. School officials complained that petty factions of parents supported favorite teachers for appointments, and that when they failed, they subverted the rival teacher's success by encouraging the disobedience or absence of their children. Over and over, school committees urged parents to come supportively to school exhibitions when invited but never to come angrily supporting their children's complaints. "Most of the difficulties that occur in schools," said the Chicopee, Massachusetts, school committee in 1851, "may be traced to one single source, and that is the undue interference of parents with their government." In a prize essay written for the Essex County Teachers' Association, the principal of a Salem grammar school wrote that students whose parents "violently and unreasonably interfered" with a teacher's rightful authority, "have, almost without one exception, 'turned out badly' in life."[26]

Some parents reacted contentiously to this anti-parental campaign. They took their children's side in cases of school discipline, disrupting school sessions to argue with teachers, in some cases assaulting the teacher and in others having the teacher arrested and brought before a magistrate. In 1842, a Lynnfield youth insulted a teacher who had criticized him for persistently misspelling the word "Broadway," which apparently had made the other children laugh. The next day, the altercation continued, and the teacher eventually beat the boy with a stick after enduring various insults and profanities. The parents had the teacher brought to trial for assault and battery. Disgruntled parents encouraged their children's absence, sometimes in sufficiently large numbers to force the dismissal of a teacher. Mr. Cutler's harsh discipline in Boxford's winter school in District 7 in 1844 resulted in "the ill will of the scholars, and also of the parents. The scholars withdrew themselves from school, so that only thirteen were present at the close." In the summer of 1851 the parents of Boxford's District 3 evidenced such "prejudice" against the teacher that only nine children remained at the end of the session.

Parents and teachers in the antebellum Northeast were not in a state of declared war, but neither was their relation blissful. The indifference of many parents to school exhibitions, the persistent belligerence of some others resisting school discipline, and the anti-parental propaganda of antebellum educators belie the notion of consensus and collaboration. The adjustment between the family and the antebellum school occasioned sporadic conflict between self-consciously "modern" school spokesmen and stubbornly traditional parents. In general, parents in nineteenth-century America wanted schools to take custody of their children, and they wanted schools to train their children in basic skills and attitudes. The eventual price that they paid was the loss of authority and control over their children's education. The trade-off was made. The state successfully exerted its right to discipline all children in values that served the necessities of the school but also served social leaders' notions of appropriate adult behavior and parents' notions of appropriate childhood behavior. Parents' acquiescence in the loss of control and involvement in schooling was often reluctant, but ultimately it was insured by the schools' promise to confer opportunity and status. It was sweetened by some shared goals, chiefly literacy and character building. School discipline offered something to everyone in a time of rapid change: obedient children for anxious parents, malleable students for efficient schools, productive workers for the emerging capitalist economy, and acquiescent citizens for the frail republic. The need for discipline was a bridge over a widening gap between family and school; it was a bridge that some families crossed reluctantly, however, for there was a sign at the other end reading "children proceed, no parents beyond this point."[27]

Some of the parents who resisted the assertion of teachers' authority and the erosion of district control were white, Anglo-American, middling-status Protestants. But outsiders had even more potent reasons for resisting state-controlled common schooling. For European immigrants the culture of the public school was often alien and the benefits uncertain. Still, the common school offered English literacy, math training, and an introduction to American society at little or no direct expense. Many immigrants therefore sent their children enthusiastically or obediently; others hesitated or resisted. The American immigrants' confrontation with the dominant culture involved a mixture of accommodation and resistance, of assimilation and cultural maintenance, of cooperation and conflict. The blend of these opposing tendencies differed not only from one immigrant group to another but from one geographical setting to another. Within immigrant groups, clergy and lay people often disagreed about public schooling. Even among the clergy, there were Americanizers and traditionalists. It is thus impossible to assess as a general matter how popular the American common school was among immigrants. Instead, different degrees of acceptance and participation can be illustrated by looking at different groups in different settings.

In the urban Northeast, public-school educators put much emphasis on the assimilation of immigrant children. When large numbers of foreigners began arriving in the industrializing cities, people looked to education as the best way to transmit Anglo-American Protestant values and to prevent the collapse of republican institutions. Holyoke, Massachusetts, provides a dramatic example. Basically rural until the 1840s, Holyoke had a traditional district school system, and its few mills employed native farmers' daughters. The arrival of the railroad, the presence of strong water power, the construction of elaborate canals, and the availability of plentiful Irish labor changed the town's character almost overnight. By 1850 half the factory operatives were Irish. The farmers' daughters, said an employer in neighboring Chicopee, no longer found the workplace "congenial to their tastes and feelings." One-fourth of Holyoke's school-age children were not enrolled in school, and employers were lackadaisical in enforcing the education provision of the child labor law. The School Committee complained that "free institutions cannot be sustained by ignorant or vicious men" and declared that only education could "perpetuate our republican form of government." But the public schools had to compete with payrolls and priests for the time of the Irish children. Bobbin boys, who worked from 5 a.m. until 6:30 p.m., could supplement the meager wages of their parents. Furthermore, the priest of the newly established Roman Catholic church criticized the public schools' use of the Protestant Bible and reportedly discouraged his parishioners from attending. In the 1860s the School Committee adopted two key reforms. They abolished the district system and created a paid superintendent. At the same time, though, Catholics established schools for both boys and girls. By 1873, when the city had 2,300 children aged five to fifteen, 975 were enrolled in public schools and 700 in the parochial schools. Most of the rest were working in the mills or were perhaps, as the superintendent of schools said, "students in the public or private haunts of vice and crime."[28]

Other cities approximated the Holyoke experience. Rapid immigration, the equation of immigrant status with ill-paid manual labor, the deteriorating environment of factory and tenement, widespread child labor, the anxious rhetoric of a school committee, and the resistance of the Catholic church were common features of cities in the industrial Northeast. In Lawrence, Massachusetts, another new factory town, the Irish were paid low wages, consigned either to tenements or a shanty town, and then criticized for their unhealthy "habitations, habits and peculiar modes of living." Anxious natives proposed public schools to combat "idleness, truancy, falsehood, deceit, thieving, obscenity, profanity, and every other wicked and disgraceful practice." But some Irish Catholics had a different idea. In 1848 the Lawrence *Courier* reported that "the Irish have, during the past season, maintained a large school, and we are informed that it is the determination of that portion of our population to continue the instruction of their children and youth in schools of their own, so far as they may be able to support them." The *Courier* article stated that the teachers, Mr. O'Connell and Mr. Bresnihan, were very popular. The town's School Committee, however, did not share this sanguine view of the Irish Catholic school. In their 1850 report, they raised the problem of immigrant children who were "incipient rogues and vagabonds," and in 1855 the city's school superintendent bemoaned the growth of Roman Catholic schools among the Irish. Nonetheless the Roman Catholic schools of Lawrence continued to grow, providing immigrants with an alternative.[29]

In New York City the foreign-born comprised over 50 percent of the population by the 1850s. An alarmed state assembly committee warned: "We must decompose and cleanse the impurities which rush into our midst," and *Putnam's Monthly Magazine* provided the answer: "There is but one rectifying agent—one infallible filter—the SCHOOL." The Irish Catholic bishop, John Hughes, protested against public-school textbooks that slurred immigrants and Catholics; one book said that Irish immigration would make America the "common sewer of Ireland." Some German and Italian parents petitioned to have dual-language schools for their children, but public-school officials rejected this policy after a brief trial. Those "who come to this country to be Americans and not foreigners," they said, should be "attending the common schools and mingling with our children." Many immigrants acquiesced in the demand that they become more American by becoming less European, but not without some private anguish and much public debate. Irish children in the public schools are called "Paddies," said New York's Thomas McGee. "Here," he said, "is precisely where the second generation breaks off from the first" and "our children become our opponents." A nun in Hartford complained that poor Irish children in the public schools "see their parents looked upon as an inferior race," and an immigrant paper in Chicago complained that public schools taught children "to feel ashamed of the creed of their forefathers, which is often assailed."[30]

Immigrant resistance to common schooling was not restricted to Catholics or to cities. In southeast and central Pennsylvania, German Lutherans, Reformed Protestants, and Mennonites in small towns and rural districts resisted the introduction of free schools in the 1830s and 1840s. In contrast to the immigrant Catholics of industrial New England, who had started new parochial schools as alternatives to existing public schools, German pietists and other immigrant Protestants of Pennsylvania had supported their own schools long before the creation of public schools, and they had withstood efforts in the eighteenth century to assimilate their children through English-language charity schools. In the antebellum period, these German religious groups staunchly resisted the creation of a unitary, free school system, preferring parochial schools that combined religion, basic skills, and German language. In 1830, 217 of Pennsylvania's 294 Lutheran churches operated day schools. Despite the antebellum public-school crusade, there were still about 100 Lutheran schools in 1850.[31]

In the Midwest, there were similar efforts by immigrant groups to maintain language and religion through independent schools, but tension with public-school advocates was generally more muted. In the middle decades of the century, at least, the region was characterized by more cooperation and compromise on immigrant cultural issues. Wisconsin, with 36 percent of its population foreign-born by 1840, is a good example. Unlike the urban Atlantic-seaboard states, Wisconsin could not count on a supply of immigrant laborers and settlers without some enthusiastic recruiting and some cultural concessions. Also, the European migrants who made it as far west as Wisconsin were often those with more financial resources or saleable skills, so they did not get concentrated as heavily in the ranks of unskilled labor. The Midwest thus provided a different context for immigrant adjustment and resistance than the Northeast.

In Wisconsin a vague phrase in the state's 1848 education law allowed districts to provide public-school instruction in languages other than English, and public-school officials in some areas took a relatively accommodating position about foreign-language instruction or religious observances in accord with local preferences. They did not want to foster the development of nonpublic alternatives to the fledgling public schools. In the countryside there were many different patterns. In some communities, children of several different nationalities mixed in the district schools, which were taught in English. In District 5 near Kenosha, for example, there were Germans, Welsh, Irish, and "Yankee" pupils in a typical one-room school. In one Pierce County district, most of the pupils were Norwegian, but the school also enrolled some Irish, French, Germans, and "Americans." In other communities, a single immigrant group dominated, and the district schools reflected its language and religion. A variety of bilingual schemes existed in such immigrant communities. Some schools had English instruction for part of the day and German during the remainder; some had German for a specified portion of the year. Some predominantly German towns had instruction entirely in German, despite a revised education law in 1854 requiring that basic subjects be taught in English. Elsewhere, immigrants supplemented English-speaking public schools with other institutions for the maintenance of culture. Nils Haugen learned to read Norwegian at home before he went to school. Church services were in Norwegian, and Norwegian children spoke their native language during school recesses. Norwegian children also attended church schools in the summer, where laymen taught them Norwegian history and Lutheran doctrine. Norwegian ministers criticized the public schools and feared their influence. In 1857 a conference of Norwegian Lutheran clergy, meeting at Coon Prairie, Wisconsin, said that rapid assimiliation had become "idolized by the Norwegians." They envisioned a system of parochial day schools to stem the erosion of language and religion. Nonetheless, a majority of Norwegian lay people seemed to favor participation in the free common schools.[32]

In yet another type of community, Yankees and immigrants in comparable numbers competed to control the hiring, curriculum, and language in the district schools, sometimes compromising, sometimes appealing their disputes to the state superintendent. In Herman, Wisconsin, Yankees successfully challenged the teaching certificate of a non-English-speaking Lutheran minister whom the residents had hired to teach the district school. They wanted "an English school and not a forked tongued one." In another town, near Milwaukee, a petition complained in 1852 that the teacher had been installed by "a clan of foreigners." Sometimes local officials would settle the conflict by redrawing district boundaries to set up "foreign districts," or by providing public funds for foreign-language schools after the common-school session ended. Until the 1860s, both the state teachers' association and the state superintendent encouraged bilingual arrangements where possible. Some immigrant groups, of course, established wholly independent parochial schools, and when the spirit of accommodation in the public schools turned to a more uncompromising Americanism in the postwar decades, the independent alternatives became more popular with immigrant dissenters.[33]

In Wisconsin and around the country, Roman Catholic immigrants established and supported the largest number of independent schools, and ultimately they were the only group to organize and sustain a sizable number of schools outside the public system. Ethnic pride played a role, as we have seen in the case of the Irish, and language maintenance reinforced the support of parish schools among non-English Catholics. Indeed, ethnic segregation and rivalries among Catholic immigrants often spurred the proliferation of Catholic parish schools. But Roman Catholic schooling was also generated by the historic enmity between Protestants and Catholics and by the Catholics' philosophical objections to state-regulated common schooling.

During the early nineteenth century, the distinction between private and public schooling was still fuzzy. Many independent schools, including some church-affiliated schools, received government funds. The Catholic charity schools of New York City got aid until 1825, along with schools run by Methodists, Episcopalians, and other groups. Public funds were also granted to support Catholic schools in Lowell, Massachusetts, in the 1830s and 1840s, in Milwaukee, Wisconsin, in the 1840s, and in Hartford and Middletown, Connecticut, in the 1860s. In New Jersey the apportionment of public funds to denominational schools was not abolished until 1866. The idea of separation of church and state with regard to education did not spring full-blown from the United States Constitution. It was a public policy developed gradually and unevenly at the local level during the nineteenth century. The relevance of the federal constitution to the matter was asserted only in the twentieth century. The first impulse of state or city officials interested in subsidizing schooling for the poor was to give aid to existing institutions. In some cases this included religiously sponsored schools. In the antebellum period the idea of a unified public school system gained ground. Still, people could only accept the common-school plan if they agreed that moral education could be separated from doctrinal religion. As we have seen, some Protestants as well as Catholics resisted this view. Eventually, most Protestant leaders acquiesced in the common-school concept, while many Catholics, especially the clergy, looked upon the public common schools as either godless or Protestant. If the schools were Protestant, they were a threat to Catholic children's faith and culture, a slur on their parents, and an injustice to Catholic taxpayers. If the common schools were nonreligious, they could not carry on proper moral training, and it would be a sin to send a Catholic child to them.

The more the common-school concept gained, the more the Catholic leaders urged the establishment of parish schools, and their convictions were reinforced by periodic eruptions of anti-Catholic feeling and violence. Shrill nativist warnings increased apace with immigration. Native laborers were often hostile to immigrants because they accepted low wages. Newspaper commentators worried that Catholic Europe would dump its paupers and criminals on American shores. The 1830s saw an increase in violent incidents and anti-Catholic literature. The Catholic population was growing rapidly. In the hostile environment of Protestant America, the education of Catholic children became a pressing public question. Parish schools served some families, and others willingly sent their children to the public schools, but others faced a choice they found unsatisfactory: Protestant-oriented public schools or none.[34]

Governor William Seward's sympathetic remarks on this subject in 1840 encouraged New York City Catholics to petition for a restoration of public funds to religious schools, which had been discontinued in 1825. In a series of petitions and public debates, the Catholics made their case against New York's public schools, which were still governed by a self-perpetuating philanthropic board called the Public School Society. John Hughes, the fiery new bishop of New York, attacked the schools' use of the Protestant Bible, their practice of Bible-reading without accompanying doctrinal instruction, and the frequent slurs upon Catholics in their textbooks. The public schools, charged Hughes, taught children that Catholics were "necessarily, morally, intellectually, infallibly, a stupid race." After much debate, the state legislature passed a bill in 1842 ending the reign of the Public School Society and establishing public control of New York City's schools, with some decisions to be made at the ward level and some by the central, elected board. In a few wards, Catholic children were subsequently allowed to substitute the Douay version, but Bible reading "without note or comment" remained the official policy of New York's public schools. Many Catholic leaders saw the legislation as a signal that they would have to embark on the development of parish schools without public assistance. The First Plenary Council of the Church, meeting in Baltimore in 1852, urged Catholics to "encourage the establishment and support of Catholic schools; make every sacrifice which may be necessary for this object."[35]

Bishop Hughes of New York was the most outspoken, but not the only separatist. Like-minded Catholics challenged public schooling root and branch, criticizing its commitment to the superiority of native Protestant culture and its new claim that moral education could be conducted apart from religious doctrines. Although these alienated Catholic spokesmen assaulted the common school's cosmopolitan solution on religious grounds, they also made some of the same arguments as democratic localists. Hughes warned in 1840 that the common-school idea had spread "from the dark regions of Prussia." Orestes Brownson, who was both a Catholic and a critic of centralization, charged in the *Boston Quarterly Review* in 1839 that the "Whig Board of Education" was trying "to imitate despotic Prussia."[36]

Catholic opponents of public schooling shared another complaint with localists: the infringement of parental responsibility in education. "To you, Christian parents, God has committed these His children," said the First Plenary Council. "You are to watch over the purity of their faith and morals with jealous vigilance. . . . Listen not to those who would persuade you that religion can be separated from secular instruction." The precedence of parental responsibility in education was a common Catholic argument against taxation for public schools. A related argument, shared by other religious groups, was that the state should not enjoy a monopoly in education. Just as the Baptists had argued in 1824 that competition in schooling was healthy and spurred efficiency, Bishop Hughes and Seward's Secretary of State John Spencer both criticized the Public School Society as an inefficient and improper "monopoly."[37]

In reply, public school defenders asserted government's responsibility in education and the efficiencies of a large-scale, unified system. The right of the state to intervene to guarantee minimal education for citizenship, said Theodore Sedgwick, "no longer admits of argument." In 1853 the Hartford *Courant* lamented that Catholics in Cincinnati, Detroit, and Baltimore seemed determined "to break down the Common School System of this country," a system which should be allowed to proceed with "the rapid amalgamation of our different races." Horace Bushnell criticized Catholics for accepting "the common rights of the law, the common powers of voting, the common terms of property, a common privilege in the new lands and the mines of gold, but when they come to the matter of common schools, they will not be common with us there." He warned against recent attempts by Catholics in Michigan, Ohio, and Pennsylvania to get a share of public school funds.[38]

But not all Catholics were separatists. Catholic reactions toward public schools ranged from resistance and separatism, to ambivalence and compromise, to outright acceptance and endorsement. In New York, Hughes's subordinate, Father Varela, pressed for changes in public-school textbooks to make the schools more tolerable for Catholics. The Philadelphia clergy did not at first establish separate schools, attempting instead to gain concessions from the public-school board, which in 1843 ruled that Catholic children could read the Douay Bible and be excused from other religious instruction or exercises. Unfortunately this compromise led to further misunderstanding and tension. The American Protestant Association charged that Catholics were attempting to exclude the Bible altogether from the public schools. Arguments turned to demonstrations and demonstrations to violence. Before the Philadelphia Bible riots of 1844 were over, thirteen were dead and St. Augustine's Church was in ashes. This tragedy turned Philadelphia's Bishop Kenrick toward the development of independent Catholic free schools. In Cincinnati, Catholics objected to Protestant Bible readings as early as 1839; but not until 1855 did the public board relent and allow parental choice of scripture, in a belated attempt to stem the rapid growth of parochial schools in that city. Nonetheless, pressure by Catholics did have some effect on public schools. Horace Bushnell reluctantly suggested that while the public schools of New England had changed from being Puritan to being Protestant, they now had to try to be more generally Christian in order to avoid the desertion of Roman Catholic immigrants. School officials in some cities began heeding this advice.[39]

Compromises on religious practices in the public schools were often begrudging, imperfect, and transient, but they illustrate a general point about the development of public schools. In some communities, there was a process of give-and-take that softened the native Protestant emphasis of common schooling during the critical mid-nineteenth-century decades of immigration. Negotiations and concessions helped attract some newcomers to the public schools even though the schools continued to base instruction for morality and citizenship on Anglo-American, pan-Protestant culture. The process that Bushnell articulated, from Puritanism to Protestantism to Christianity, was characteristic of the cosmopolitan program for common schooling. School officials from Horace Mann to the present have tried to make public schools as inclusive as possible by making them as uncontroversial as possible and by devising a curriculum as universally acceptable as possible. As part of this process, nineteenth-century schoolmen sometimes made concessions, allowing scriptural choice, restricting prayer, or expurgating offensive religious and ethnic slurs from textbooks.

Sketchy evidence suggests that many Catholic parents sent their children to public schools. In New York City, the Irish newspaper supported public-school attendance, and in Kenosha, Wisconsin, the German priests acquiesced in the development of a common system. In Boston in the 1840s, 7,000 children, about one-third of all public-school pupils, were Catholic; and in Chicago in the 1860s, over 80 percent of Catholic elementary schoolchildren were in the public system. Nonetheless, disputes and incidents continued. In Oswego, New York, a Catholic student was whipped and expelled from a public school in the 1850s for refusing to read the King James Bible, and a similar refusal in Boston prompted a teacher to beat eleven-year-old Thomas Wall for thirty minutes. Legal action against the teachers failed in both cases, and in another case from the 1850s, the Maine Supreme Court upheld the right of public-school officials to compel all children to read the Protestant Bible. Despite this bias, parochial-school development was slow in many areas. By the 1860s, Massachusetts had only fourteen Catholic parish schools, Connecticut had about twenty, and Wisconsin about the same. Chicago had fourteen schools in 1865, while New York State had about thirty. In Pennsylvania, only fourteen parish schools were founded between 1830 and 1850. Cincinnati had seventeen Roman Catholic schools by 1860; St. Louis and Baltimore were also centers of parish-school enthusiasm before the Civil War, and in territories where there were large numbers of Catholics, as in Louisiana and the Southwest, priests attempted to establish parish schools. Still, in the judgment of James Burns, a historian of Roman Catholic education, "parochial education on a large scale did not begin till after 1870." Roman Catholic religious leaders had set out on a separatist educational course by 1860, but resources were slim and Catholic lay people had varying opinions about public schools. Thus the establishment of independent Catholic schools was slow in most areas.[40]

A similar pattern of ambivalence and resistance occurred in the case of American blacks. While historic religious conflict made it difficult for Protestants to apply the cosmopolitan educational reforms in a tolerant way to Roman Catholics, racism made it even rarer for antebellum public-school advocates to argue for the integration of black children into common schools. The same ideology that promoted the idea of a common-school system prevented it from being cosmopolitan in the best sense of the word because that ideology, in all its variants, featured a belief in the racial superiority of whites. Because they were excluded from most northern common-school systems, blacks were faced with a strategic dilemma, whether to make the best of separate-and-unequal black schools or to press for integration into white schools. Some blacks supported the common school as an ideal; some argued for the value of separate black institutions in a racist society. In either case, their relationship to the emerging public common-school systems of the North was pervaded by conflict and disappointment.

In the early national period, schooling for blacks was supported either by private black efforts or by white philanthropy. In this respect it was like schooling for poor whites before the advent of the public common school. From the 1790s to the 1820s, whites helped to found charity schools for blacks in many cities. In a few small towns these were integrated; generally they were separate. Meanwhile, blacks, like whites, supported inexpensive pay schools taught by teachers of their own race. In other ways, of course, black education was not at all like white education. Segregation and racism permeated northern society, and this was a central problem for black parents and educators. Except in New England and New York, whites barred blacks from voting, denying the relevance for blacks of one of the major goals of common schooling, participation in political institutions. Opportunities for most jobs and for most higher education were also closed. Speaking in 1839 at the funeral of a black Revolutionary War veteran in Newark, New Jersey, a minister noted that William Stives's children had been refused admission to local schools. He bemoaned the fact that although Stives "had purchased the country with his sacrifices, toil and blood," his family had been "proscribed out of all their civil rights and privileges." Even where laws sugggested that blacks had rights, they were often denied. As John Jay Smith commented to Tocqueville in 1831, "the law with us is nothing if it is not supported by public opinion—the people are imbued with the greatest prejudice against Negroes, and the magistrates don't feel strong enough to enforce the laws favorable to them." When an 1845 Massachusetts law stated that all children had a right to attend neighborhood public schools, the Boston School Committee vigorously denied its applicability to racial segregation.[41]

Education had little effect on job discrimination for blacks. Although African free schools of northern cities were the focus of some high-sounding egalitarian statements by enlightened white philanthropists, they were also the cause of considerable frustration for black parents and students. In 1842 a black newspaper in Albany demanded to know how many abolitionist merchants and lawyers had chosen their clerks from graduates of the African free schools started by abolitionists. The question was purely rhetorical. The main rationale for charity schooling was moral education. Black parents, however, complained about the lack of job opportunities for educated blacks, and they complained about the mechanical nature of the Lancasterian system used almost universally in African free schools. Where they could, blacks started their own schools. As with most private schooling, no systematic evidence has survived, so the extent of these educational efforts is impossible to gauge, but sketchy evidence indicates that independent day schools run by blacks existed in New York City, Brooklyn, Columbus, Philadelphia, Pittsburgh, Cincinnati, Troy, Rochester, New Brunswick, Princeton, and most other northern cities with a sizable black population.[42]

In Boston, black initiative mixed with public financial assistance in the development of segregated black education. In the 1790s, blacks requested public aid for separate schools, saying that the black children who went to town schools met with prejudice. The city refused, but blacks started a school on their own with some help from white philanthropists. In 1812 the town reversed its decision and agreed to an annual subsidy. By 1830 the School Committee had established black primary schools in the growing ghettos. Some blacks viewed separate schools as merely better than none. It was a choice involving the "least between two evils," said a black teacher in New York. Because of their depressed economic condition, blacks could not go it alone; they needed free public schooling. Recognizing this need, officials of northern public-school systems gradually absorbed the black charity schools. Although these systems were generated by the common-school ideal, very few whites thought that common schools ought to integrate the races. The absorption of African free schools by public systems had nothing to do with common schooling. It was simply part of a trend toward public administration of schools and the waning of independent philanthropic effort to provide charity schools. It was a change of mode, not a change of philosophy, and many of the same prominent white citizens were on both the charity-school and the public-school boards. In Detroit, independent black schools became public in 1842; in Poughkeepsie the public school board adopted the African free school in 1843, and in Schenectady the same process occurred in 1854 upon the creation of a unified public-school system. Thus systems that boasted their commitment to efficiency and the promotion of common culture absorbed segregated schools that were neither efficient nor common.[43]

Black parents did not merely acquiesce in the meager segregated schooling provisions of northern public-school systems. New York City provides a good example of black initiatives and black resistance in the development of public schooling. By 1820 there were 10,000 black people in the city, and the succeeding decade witnessed the development of important black community institutions. In 1823 the African Methodist Episcopal Zion Church split from the Methodists and established an independent black church, and in 1827, New York blacks established *Freedom's Journal*, the first black newspaper in the country. Leaders associated with these institutions also took a strong interest in the schools of the Manumission Society, mounting a successful attendance drive in 1827 and providing winter clothing for poor schoolchildren.

Charles Andrews, a white Englishman, had been the head teacher of the Society's schools since 1809. Like other charity-school teachers, he emphasized moral education, but he also opposed slavery and stressed black achievement. He enjoyed the support of most New York black leaders until 1830, when he became convinced that the future of free blacks lay in African colonization. Because many colonization advocates discouraged the development of black educational institutions as a diversion that would dissuade blacks from emigrating, the movement was anathema to most black leaders. Andrews's colonization views led to declining enrollments at the Manumission Society schools. In 1832 the Society announced his resignation due to the "prejudice now existing against him among the coloured population." They replaced him, at the urging of black leaders, with a black man, James Adams. The schools continued to expand and hire teachers who had "the confidence of the coloured people." Soon, however, black community leaders had a new organization to reckon with. In 1834 the Manumission Society transferred its schools, with an enrollment of 1,500 children, to the Public School Society. By this time, the Society had developed a near-monopoly on free schools. Without consulting black leaders, the trustees reduced the status of all but one of the black schools to the primary level. Enrollments dropped, and some black families turned to private schooling again. In the quarter-century between 1835 and the Civil War, the enthusiasm of New York City black leaders for the black public schools waxed and waned. Some radical blacks espoused a separate, nationalist course; of these some eventually emigrated to Africa. The moderates, who predominated in New York City and in the nation generally, advocated public-school attendance, moral education, intellectual improvement, parental involvement, and the appointment of black teachers in public schools for blacks. School boards were often receptive to the suggestions and petitions of such groups, partly because they wanted to avoid black boycotts of public schools and partly because they much preferred such compromises to radical demands for integration.[44]

Some black leaders began to press for truly common schools. They had to wage two debates, one against white segregationists and one against blacks who preferred separate public schools. The integrationists' arguments centered on two main points: that segregated schools were by definition unjust and that segregated black schools consistently received poorer resources. The first point was stated in a hundred ways by frustrated black integrationists and a handful of white allies throughout the nineteenth century. The very existence of segregated public schools offended justice, they argued. It impeded the acquisition of political rights and prevented the contact between the races that might ultimately reduce prejudice. The second point, about unequal resources, was a commonplace. "Conscious of the unequal advantages enjoyed by our children," said two angry Philadelphia mothers, "we feel indignant against those who are continually vituperating us for the ignorance and degradation of our people." Philadelphia officials continued the Lancasterian method in black schools after they had abandoned it for whites, provided infant schools for whites but not for blacks, denied blacks admission to the public high school, and in general starved the black school facilities. An angry and militant integrationist, Robert Purvis, wrote the Philadelphia tax collectors in 1853 that his "rights as a man and a parent have been grossly outraged" by such a system.[45]

Blacks who favored separate schools countered integrationists' arguments with two compelling arguments of their own. Black children in white schools were subject to insults and racial stereotypes, and to white teachers' low expectations. Moreover, even if white school officials would integrate children, they certainly would not integrate teachers. Thus there would be little employment for blacks in teaching, one of the few professions open to educated blacks. Black parents placed great stress on the importance of having black teachers for their children, and they often fought hard to replace insensitive white teachers with black teachers in the segregated schools. The prospect of losing these teachers was one of the most agonizing drawbacks to integration. Whites seized upon black sentiment for separate schools. Boston officials reminded black integrationists that the segregated public schools had been established "at the urgent and repeated requests of the colored people themselves." In Providence the president of Brown University observed that segregation "works well" and that Negroes preferred it. Whatever the preferences of blacks, they faced overwhelming white opinion against integrated schools. The confrontation between black integrationists and white public-school officials is most dramatically illustrated by the case of Boston, a city with a large, vocal black minority, a city with a reputation both as the cradle of liberty and the seat of deep racial animosity.[46]

After years of mixed results from their efforts to improve the segregated black schools of Boston, a growing number of parents decided to press for integration. A group meeting in the Belknap

Street Church resolved in 1849 "to contend for equal school rights, until the schemes of prejudice and expediency are alike driven to the wall." They had been frustrated by unsatisfactory concessions regarding teachers at the black schools, and they were encouraged by the relatively peaceful integration of schools in the nearby Massachusetts cities of Lowell, Nantucket, New Bedford, and Worcester. In Salem, after a decade of agitation of the school-integration question between blacks and whites, the city's attorney had written a stirring opinion in favor of integration, which the School Committee accepted in 1844 by a vote of seventeen to two. The opinion was reprinted as a pamphlet in Boston and in the *Common School Journal*; the attorney, Richard Fletcher, went on to become a state supreme court justice. "Perfect equality is the vital principle" of a common-school system, said Fletcher. All must have an opportunity to gain power and wealth, or to be trained for public office. Without this equality of opportunity, there would be class oppression and class war. Black people could not be an exception, argued Fletcher, especially because Massachusetts recognized them as voting, tax-paying citizens. Fletcher rejected the separate-but-equal argument. He doubted that the black schools had resources equal to the white schools, but even if they did, he declared, "it would in no way affect the decision of the question. The colored children are lawfully entitled to the benefits of the free schools, and are not bound to accept an equivalent." Finally, argued Fletcher, "the people can be lawfully taxed, only for the support of the public schools." A segregated school, he concluded, "is not a public school."

Boston integrationists were encouraged by the Salem decision, but the Boston School Committee did not find Fletcher's logic persuasive. Their segregation policy was unswerving. The Primary School Committee stated their reasons for rejecting integration in 1846. Blacks' "peculiar physical, mental and moral structure require an educational treatment different" from whites. Although black children can memorize and imitate, "when progress comes to depend chiefly on the faculties of invention, comparison and reasoning, they quickly fall behind." Thus, integrated schools don't work. Expressing the view of most Boston whites, they declared that "amalgamation is degradation."

The segregation issue split Boston's black community. The integrationists were led by Benjamin Roberts, a printer who had long been active in black educational causes. The separatists were led by Thomas Paul Smith. Smith had attended Boston's black grammar school under the hated white teacher Abner Forbes. Refused admission to the public high school, Smith had attended nearby Andover Academy and became a successful clothing dealer in the city. When Roberts became disgusted with the School Committee and led an effort to boycott the grammar school, Smith labelled the tactic "suicidal." Roberts soon concluded that no amount of petitioning or boycotting would move the Boston School Committee toward integration, so he sued them to recover damages for the unlawful exclusion of his daughter, who had to pass several white elementary schools on her two-and-one-half–mile walk to a segregated school. Smith opposed Roberts's goal as well as his tactics. A black child, he argued, was far better off "taught by those who felt his elevation their own, cheered on by the unanimous shout of encouragement by all his fellows." In his harshest statement, Smith declared that the integration movement "injures, it lies." One of Smith's allies said that black children in a white school would "be under the constant criticism of the whole school." This would cause poor achievement, which would in turn be "falsely attributed to a natural inferiority."

Fears of racism in integrated schools did not deter Benjamin Roberts and his supporters. They engaged two lawyers, Robert Morris, a black member of the Massachusetts bar, and Charles Sumner, a white. Sumner, later a radical Republican in the United States Senate, was a rising young Boston lawyer. He had been defeated as a candidate for the Boston School Committee only a few years earlier. The Roberts case was heard in the Massachusetts Supreme Court in 1850. Sumner argued along the same lines as Salem's attorney, Richard Fletcher. After describing the history of freedom in America, and the schools' role in preserving it, Sumner compared the Boston School Committee to Southern slaveholders. They had no legal right to "brand a whole race with the stigma of inferiority," Sumner argued. Racial segregation was based on unreasonable prejudice and was therefore illegal. Like Fletcher, Sumner rejected the separate-but-equal argument. Because segregated schools stigmatized black children, they were not equivalent. Chief Justice Lemuel Shaw disagreed. He admitted that segregation constituted a caste system, but he held that the schools did not create and could not alter racial prejudice. Nor was classification by race arbitrary; it had the sanction of tradition and culture. He upheld the Boston School Committee. Defeated in court, Roberts and his followers soon won in the legislature. Integration had been implemented in many Massachusetts communities voluntarily, and in 1855 the legislature made it mandatory. Boston school officials complied reluctantly but without further open resistance.[47]

In the long run, Boston whites found new ways to restore school segregation through residential segregation and other tacit public policies. In the short run, black public-school enrollment picked up, and a sprinkling of black students graduated from Boston's high schools. The rest of the North did not follow Massachusetts's lead in integration. In an editorial illustrative of blatant northern racism, the *New York Herald* reacted to the Massachusetts law: "Now the niggers are really just as good as white folks. The North is to be Africanized. Amalgamation has commenced. New England heads the column. God save the Commonwealth of Massachusetts." The Pennsylvania legislature declared itself against such "amalgamation" with an 1854 law permitting segregation. The state's superintendent of public instruction explained that blacks were "destitute of either moral or intellectual culture." That they provided a large share of paupers and criminals was no surprise, he said, since blacks were "naturally indolent, and perhaps improvident," and "their resort to vicious practices is, perhaps, no more than could be expected." Ohio likewise sanctioned separate schools, in a law that was sustained by the state supreme court in 1849. Most states were simply silent, allowing segregation to stand. At the time of the Civil War, blacks were afforded separate and unequal public schooling throughout most of the North. Blacks remained outside of the cosmopolitan rationale of antebellum school reform. In the face of this racist reality, black leaders remained ambivalent toward public schooling.[48]

Northern blacks were not the only group outside the assimilationist policy of early public-school reform. Most poor southerners, whether white or black, lacked common schooling, for in the ante-bellum South, school reform had only modest success, even for whites. American Indians faced a policy of extinction and removal, not of assimilation. Hispanic Americans, largely beyond the scope of this book in space and time, waged the same sort of uneven contest with white governments that black Americans waged in the East and the Midwest. Women, the largest out-group, were dispersed across racial, ethnic, religious, and class lines. Even more than other out-groups, therefore, they tended not to speak and act as a group on issues of common schooling. Some women objected to the whole ideology and structure of female education in antebellum America, but many more accepted the prevailing ideal of domesticity and its educational implications. Those who accepted native Protestant ideology and cosmopolitan school re-form fought for more access to schooling for girls, more practical education for women's roles, and the development of teaching as a woman's profession. Many women believed that these policies would improve women's lives. This does not mean that middle-class antebellum spokeswomen merely acquiesced; their efforts helped to shape the outcome and to win concessions about women's intel-lectual and professional capabilities.

There were, then, a variety of dissenters, and they had some impact. Catholics forced some concessions on Bible-reading prac-tices, black boycotts prompted the hiring of black teachers, and rebellious rural parents expelled unpopular district teachers. In the countryside less assertive forms of opposition were often suc-cessful. State school officials, empowered to regulate local school-ing in a variety of ways, often had little actual impact at the local level. Admonitions, laws, and occasional missionary sweeps could be ignored if the local population concurred. In small-town Amer-ica, school reforms succeeded only where influential local residents became the agents of change. No matter how much circuit-riding the superintendents did, they could not accomplish their mission alone, and some rural communities simply ignored all but the most mandatory common-school reforms. Similarly, there was tacit op-position among urban workers. Manual laborers' families were not served as well by the new public-school systems as were middle-class children, and the costs of sending their children were greater.

But open conflict on educational issues rarely took the form of white-collar versus blue-collar interests. Blue-collar people expressed their support, indifference, or alienation about common schooling in family counsels more often than in organized groups. They expressed their challenges to educational policy through individual choices and family strategies.

The combination of tacit and expressed opposition was enough to give cosmopolitan school reformers the impression they were fighting a war, but it was a guerrilla war. The opponents were scattered; their goals and their cultures differed. Localists wanted small-scale majority rule, separatists wanted independent group control. Integrationists protested not the principle of common schooling but its failure. Some opponents were as alienated from each other as from the educational reforms. Local ward control advocates in the cities had little else in common with rural people clinging to district schools; urban blacks and Irish Catholics were in conflict because of historic racial animosity and the competitive position in which the capitalist economy placed them.

There was very substantial opposition in antebellum America to the creation of state school systems. Although some opponents gained concessions and some others successfully ignored the reform program, they did not prevent the establishment of a state school apparatus, the beginnings of professional training, the shift from private to public administration, the consolidation of districts, and a substantial increase in the amount of time and resources spent on public schooling. Opponents of this program of common-school reform shared some philosophical objections to a state monopoly in education, but their circumstances and goals varied, and they were predominantly outsiders with less power and influence than those who supported the reforms. The reforms prevailed, gradually and imperfectly, sometimes with compromises. The reforms prevailed because they served the predominant ideology and because a majority of people in the North appear to have been convinced that a cosmopolitan common-school system would serve not only the collective goals of republicanism, Protestantism, and capitalism, but individual goals of enlightenment, morality, and personal advancement as well.

8

Regional Differences in Common-School Development

IN the Midwest, the creation of state common-school systems proceeded along lines very similar to those in the Northeast. In the 1840s, legislatures in the Midwest created state superintendencies and provided state support for common schools. Bureaucratic and professional development followed in the 1850s, including more effective reporting requirements, teachers' institutes, state support for school libraries, experiments with county-level supervision, and other hallmarks of eastern common-school reform. In the antebellum South, in contrast, most states did not adopt common-school legislation despite continual efforts by public-school advocates. Schooling in the South differed markedly from that in the North in both amount and organization. In most southern states, the public purse provided elementary education only for poor whites. Others fended for themselves wholly on a fee basis.

According to the traditional interpretation of these regional differences, public common schooling began in New England as a result of English democracy, Anglo-Saxon initiative, and Puritan commitment to learning. After a period of slumbering indifference to schooling in the eighteenth century, New Englanders woke up to their responsibilities and nurtured common schooling to its full flowering by 1860. They also tried to spread the idea, through correspondence with educators, speaking tours, and the training of young educators for the South and the West. In the South, continues the traditional story, this missionary effort faltered. Neither economic conditions nor accompanying attitudes encouraged common-school legislation. Slavery, sparse population, periodic economic crises, and aristocratic attitudes frustrated the plans of New England–style reformers. The Midwest, by contrast, benefited from the large migration of New Englanders and New Yorkers, who brought their notions of republican institutions with them. Thus, in the northern tier of the Midwest, settled predominantly by northeasterners, the states adopted common-school systems early despite the difficulties of frontier life. In the southern part of the region—Ohio, Illinois, and Indiana—the population included migrants from the South, and the development of common-school systems was slower and more controversial.[1]

There is much truth to the traditional explanation of why the Midwest was similar to the Northeast and why the South was distinctive in common-school development. New England and New York migrants were conspicuous in midwestern school reform. There was in general a North-South gradient in the support of state common-school laws as well as in school enrollment. But by conceiving of common-school systems as the transportable property of New England migrants, this explanation obscures indigenous regional causes of educational development and tends to paint an overly homogeneous picture of each region. It ignores the seesaw battles on educational issues in all areas of the country. The New England migrant theory overlooks substantial opposition to common schooling among New Englanders and among upper midwesterners, while it suggests a monolithically hostile South. To gain a more sophisticated understanding, we must analyze why the advocates of state-supported common schooling tended to succeed in the North and tended to fail in the South.

Historians often begin the story of common schooling in the Midwest by noting the educational provisions of the Northwest Ordinances of 1785 and 1787. Designed to shape the settlement of the area, the ordinances decreed that one of the thirty-six sections of land in each township was to be set aside for purposes of common schooling. Technically, this legislation remained in force into the statehood period of the old Northwest, but it had very little effect on the actual support of schools. The school lands were supposed to be rented and the proceeds devoted to common schooling. The dedication of land rentals to educational purposes was a time-honored English practice, common in colonial America. Connecticut's Manasseh Cutler explained its incorporation into the Northwest ordinances as a way to promote the "religion, morality, and knowledge necessary to good government." But Cutler's best intentions bore little fruit during the decades of settlement. Unimproved land often went without renters in a region of abundant cheap land. The meager proceeds from the lands went into state school funds that remained unused because the capital did not generate enough interest to begin a common-school program. The lands and the funds were often mismanaged, sometimes fraudulently. By the mid–1820s Congress recognized that the system of renting school lands was a failure and authorized the sale of school lands to establish permanent school funds. These funds remained subject to fraud, diversion, and neglect. In 1843, Ohio's state auditor told the legislature, "The lands have been squandered and the fund has been plundered until it is now merely nominal." A general history of these state educational lands, written in the 1880s, reads like a catalog of disaster. The author discussed "New Evils" and "Hasty Sales" in Ohio, an "Attempt to Divert the Fund" in Indiana, and "Illegal Use of the Fund" in Illinois. In some scattered instances money from land sales actually fostered local school development. In general, however, funds from school lands were insufficient and ineffective.[2]

The failure of education land policy demonstrated the futility of an old English funding device in a frontier with plentiful cheap land. It is also a comment on the low priority given to statewide educational organization among settlers intent on more immediate tasks, such as clearing land, building roads, and organizing territorial governments, in a region where all land affairs were characterized by speculation and special interest. Schooling remained a local, voluntary, and largely entrepreneurial undertaking.

The image of New England migrants planting free common schools in the towns of the American Midwest deserves our skepticism. Not only were the early settlers' efforts at public-school organization and funding unimpressive, but the northeastern states imagined to be the models had not themselves adopted free, universal, or state-mandated schooling at that time. The New England public-school model was something of a myth, the ordinances of 1785 and 1787 were ineffective, and the use of state taxes for common schooling was still in the future. The true models were the customary rural and urban modes of education of the early national Northeast. In rural town meetings, frontier families made short-term arrangements with schoolmasters and paid them through a combination of general town taxes and tuition charges to parents of schoolchildren. In urban settlements, charity and pay schooling combined to provide a modicum of elementary education for most families who wanted it and whose children could afford the time. These two modes existed in the Midwest as in the East, but on the frontier, sparse population and preoccupation with other tasks made schooling less accessible to children and less important in the priorities of adults.

It is difficult to generalize about local education conditions in the Midwest, but school practices in this largely rural area seem to have been very similar to those in the rural Northeast. Memoirs of frontier Wisconsin provide examples. Common schooling began in Manitowoc in 1837 with twelve pupils in part of a warehouse. In Paris, Wisconsin, the first district school met in a living room. In Sawyer County, schools were generally in session for three months, taught by men who farmed in the summer. Sometimes Wisconsin teachers were paid in goods, such as vegetables or meat; one town offered to pay the talented Pestalozzian teacher Charles Lau a salary of $25 "whenever there is money in the treasury." When state laws requiring local school funding appeared in the 1840s and 1850s, small communities often dodged or met them minimally. Merle Curti discerned a pattern of "indifference and parsimony" toward public common schooling in Trempeleau County, Wisconsin. Most districts eventually built schoolhouses, however, and in some ways, the schoolhouse played a more important role than schooling itself. In the woods outside of Platteville, Truman Douglas recalled, a social life developed around the log schoolhouse, including evening spelling bees, debating societies, and neighborhood prayer meetings. Douglas, who was a young boy in the 1840s, said that he and his neighbors rarely went into Platteville, the bustling and somewhat less "Puritanical" town center.[3]

Many midwesterners, like their countrymen in the East, resisted the systematization of education at the state level; but local schooling seems to have been on the rise by the 1830s in the more settled parts of the Midwest. As in the Northeast, enrollment increases due to local schooling arrangements preceded the effective creation of state school systems. The state school-reform movement, which eventually led to free education in all communities, subsequently encouraged increased participation, longer school years, and higher expenditures. However, antebellum school reform does not account for the initial development of local common schooling in the Midwest any more than in the East.[4]

The reform movement went through two main stages in the midwestern states, similar in broad outline to eastern reform. Early school bills were often permissive, allowing towns to tax local property for schooling. Some early bills were mandatory but remained unenforced. In either case, they usually aimed at only partially offsetting the cost of tuition, and they provided for little state-level bureaucratic oversight. Nonetheless, even these rudimentary bills failed at first. As in the East, people resisted state involvement in local education, and they resisted new taxes. Eventually voters succumbed to appeals about the necessity of education on the frontier. After securing such initial legislation, common-school reformers attempted to get bills passed requiring free schooling and erecting a structure of state supervision, including a state superintendency and a state school fund. The permissive first stage was ineffective; the more coercive second stage was controversial. A few examples will illustrate the seesaw process between common-school activists and conservative localists. Ohio, admitted to the Union in 1803, passed a voluntary school bill in 1821, authorizing local districts to tax property for common schooling. School reformers succeeded in replacing that in 1825 with a bill requiring towns to provide schools, to tax property for part of the cost, and to set up a mechanism for teacher certification. This bill was unpopular and unenforceable. In 1830, then, Ohio still had no operating state school fund, tuition fees for attendance were universal, and local schools held short sessions in informal settings or ramshackle schoolhouses. As much as these features of a local school tradition distressed reformers, they were very similar to conditions in the East.

In the mid–1830s, Ohio witnessed a flurry of reform enthusiasm. In the wake of Calvin Stowe's influential and admiring report on Prussian schools, the legislature passed by one vote a Whig school bill that provided for a state superintendent. After two years the office was abolished, in 1840, the same year that Henry Barnard's position was eliminated in Connecticut and Horace Mann narrowly averted a similar attempt in Massachusetts. Ohio's retired incumbent, Samuel Lewis, exhausted by the missionary job and discouraged by the ignominious abolition of the state authority, had nonetheless been able to help increase attendance and improve facilities. In 1847 the legislature tried voluntary centralization, authorizing county superintendents, but few counties adopted the innovation. In 1850, Ohio saw yet another attempt to create a state superintendency, through a bill that was not even implemented. Finally, in 1853, Ohio's legislature enacted its basic antebellum state school-reform law, requiring free schooling through local taxes, division of authority between town and district committees, county examinations for teachers, segregated schools for blacks, and a state commissioner of education. The cosmopolitan structure had arrived in law—fifty years after statehood, and thirty years after Ohio's first permissive common-school bill. The manner and the timing were almost identical to the East.[5]

In Illinois an 1825 bill allowed localities to tax for common-school provision. Being permissive, it succeeded only modestly, and its unpopular taxation provision was quickly repealed in 1827. Common-school reformers, in Illinois as elsewhere, complained throughout the 1840s that Illinois schools were primitive and behind other states. An 1845 law declared that the Secretary of State would serve as superintendent of common schools, but provision of schooling was still local, voluntary, and partially fee-based. In 1854, Illinois passed a bill, which, like Ohio's of 1853, provided for a state superintendent, town control over districts on some matters, and taxation to provide wholly free schools. In Michigan the territorial legislature passed a school bill in 1827 which, like colonial Massachusetts statutes, required towns to provide schools but not necessarily free schools. Any town could opt out of the law by a two-thirds vote. The state constitution established tax-supported free schools, but rate bills were reauthorized in 1839. Like many other northern states, Michigan ended the antebellum period with a state superintendent presiding over a local district system that still featured rate bills and racial segregation. Nonetheless, school participation had risen, school sessions were increasing in length, and expenditures were up.[6]

The midwestern experience in creating state school systems was similar to the eastern experience, but the question of eastern influence remains. Was the similarity due to conscious imitation of New England and New York institutions by migrants from the Northeast, or was the similarity caused by underlying social and political factors common to both regions? The logical starting point is with direct evidence of northeastern influence on the development of midwestern common-school systems.

There is no doubt that New Englanders and New Yorkers were prominent in school reform and teaching in the Midwest. The triumvirate of Ohio's early educational reformers—Caleb Atwater, Nathan Guilford, and Ephraim Cutler—were New England–born, as was the first state superintendent, Samuel Lewis. Michigan's chief heroes, John Pierce and Isaac Crary, were both New Englanders. Pierce had been sent West as a minister by the American Home Missionary Society in 1831, and when he was selected as state superintendent, he made a tour back east in 1836 to study educational developments in the more settled states. William Larrabee, first state superintendent of Indiana, was born and educated in Maine and taught in Connecticut and New York before moving west in 1841. Michael Frank, born in Connecticut, followed a similar migration pattern through New York State, where he became a Whig editor and reformer in Cortland County. He finished his career as the father of common schooling in Kenosha, Wisconsin, and a leading legislative proponent of free schooling in that midwestern state. All but one of Wisconsin's state school chiefs were born in New York or New England through 1880, as were all of Michigan's superintendents.[7]

Correspondence between Midwestern educators and educators in the East was frequent, and explicit references to northeastern models abound, though the admiration was sometimes mixed with criticism. In 1825, Nathan Guilford of Ohio recommended the good examples of Massachusetts, Rhode Island, New Hampshire, and Maine but listed as bad examples New York and Connecticut.

In the later antebellum years some of the leading eastern reformers travelled west and spoke in the reform cause. Barnard urged the establishment of normal schools on a trip to Illinois in 1855, and in 1857, Horace Mann consulted with Iowa's governor on a revision of that state's common-school system.[8]

New England migrants were not the only free-school enthusiasts in the Midwest. In a compendium of outstanding Ohio educators of the antebellum period, James Burns chronicled many who were Ohio-born. Although some of these educators may have had parents born in the Northeast, this heritage would have predated by far the development of common free-school systems in the Northeast. Typical were Lorin Andrews, born in Ashland County in 1819, who taught in an academy, became a lawyer, then superintendent of schools in Massilon, and in the 1850s went on as an agent of the Ohio Teachers' Association to publicize and develop support for the 1849 school law; William Hinkle, born in Springfield in 1828, who taught district schools, became a high-school principal, superintendent of Salem, Ohio, schools, and President of the Ohio Teachers' Association; Elizabeth Russell Lord, born in Kirtland, Ohio, in 1819, who became a high-school principal and then the superintendent of a school for the blind; and Emerson White, born in Mantua, Ohio, in 1829, who began by teaching district schools, became the head of grammar and high schools, then superintendent in Portsmouth, Ohio, and during the 1860s editor of the *Ohio Education Monthly,* crusading for normal schools, teacher certification, and the further codification of school laws.[9]

Midwesterners were not passive recipients of northeastern practice. They studied education from many sources. The Michigan system was based explicitly on the Prussian model, publicized by Victor Cousin's reports. The Ohio legislature sent Calvin Stowe to Prussia, and his report of 1836 became immensely influential throughout the nation. Ohio's Hiram Barney cited Switzerland as the model for normal schools in 1855. Common-school reform was a national movement despite the prominence of the Northeast, and it took its models from the European continent as well as the East Coast. And when easterners like Catharine Beecher proposed to train teachers for the West, the idea attracted frequent dissent.

A judge wrote in the Belleville, Illinois, *Advocate,* "We want teachers raised up from among our own people, teachers acquainted with our habits, customs, and modes of life." Michigan's superintendent, Ira Mayhew, warned in 1847 that Beecher's Board of National Popular Education was a bad idea. The West, Mayhew believed, might look to New York and New England for ideas but not for its trained teachers.[10]

Whatever their New England connections, many midwesterners shared the same culture that bolstered common schooling in the East. They had the same commitment to an informed citizenry and to self-government. The themes of freedom, order, industry, and free enterprise are well expressed in Pierce's 1837 report: "In an educated and virtuous community there is safety; the rights of individuals are guarded, and property is respected and secure. Every man sits quietly and peaceably under his own vine and fig tree, regaling himself with the fruits of his own industry and labor." Along with the theme of individualism, though, Pierce emphasized education for justice: "Justice, truth, and equity are the glory of a nation, but these attributes of virtue are not to be found among an ignorant and vicious people." Boosterism and competition also affected educational development of the West, as in the towns of the East. In his second annual report, Samuel Lewis told Ohioans that they were "as much indebted to our common schools and their reputation, for a rapid increase of population and wealth as to any other cause," and an Illinois report claimed that education had brought wealth to the rocky, barren soil of New England.

As the midwestern states developed, and population centers sprang up, the old urban custom of mixing charity schooling with independent private schooling came under attack. Assailing "pauper" schools and "private" schools, Ninian Edwards advised Illinois to "make the schoolroom just as free as the air we breathe. Let the poorest child feel that he has just as much right to be there as the child of the millionaire, and that the only distinction known is that of merit." The Midwest was not free from the problems of large cities—poverty, squalid environment, ethnic and racial tensions, and the strains on early industrial workers. Not surprisingly, some cities eliminated rate bills before rural communities and attempted to make public schools a common system. In his 1847 report, Michigan's superintendent Mayhew marvelled at Chicago's free schools and urged Detroit to follow its example. There is an urban tone to the discussion; citizens in a threatening urban setting become "subjects" to be controlled. In Chicago, said Mayhew, not only do the schools reform children, "but through the influence of children attending them, their degraded parents, in not a few instances, have been reformed and become law abiding subjects."[11]

The development of Chicago, Milwaukee, Detroit, Cincinnati, and Cleveland was not fundamentally different from cities in the East, nor did their similar educational development depend upon Yankee migrants. The region was developing into the nation's major area of commercial agriculture, with urban centers for regional manufacturing and for the processing of food and raw materials. Culturally and economically, it was part of the capitalist nexus. Capitalism created a world of increasing productivity and specialization, in which people sought ways to improve transportation, communication, enterprise, and growth. Education fit into this nexus. It made sense. The logic of progress seemed to demand it.

At the same time, however, there was opposition to common-school reform in the Midwest as well as in the East. Earlier historians placed considerable emphasis on southern migrants' opposition to public free schooling in the Midwest. This was not a chimera. Indeed, southerners were more resistant to state involvement in education. They were also, on the whole, less accepting of the notion that all should be taxed to provide for the schooling of others' children. But this was not a uniform view. In some cases, such as Grant County in the southwestern mining region of Wisconsin, southern migrants were dominant, local taxation was established early, and rate bills were uncommon. In other areas, such as Macoupin County in central Illinois, settlers from the South fostered local school provision. Also, although local expenditures and support for state legislation tended to follow a north-to-south bias, in Illinois, for example, the northern part of the state was also more wealthy and commercial. Southern opposition to school reform in the Midwest was real, but it was not unanimous, and it cannot be entirely disentangled from other indigenous conditions.[12]

There was also opposition to common public schooling among some midwestern religious and language groups, such as Norwegian Lutherans and German Catholics. Catholics provided the most vocal and persistent criticisms of the state school systems. In Ohio the 1851 constitution forbade public aid to religious schools, and then the 1853 school law made taxation for common schools mandatory. Archbishop John Purcell of Cincinnati protested, to no avail, that the public schools were sectarian institutions in which the Protestant Bible was used and that Catholic parents should be exempted from school taxes. Bible wars and Protestant-Catholic tensions continued throughout the nineteenth century. Other forces inhibited state school reform. The population was young, which meant that many voters were not financially secure and that there was a high ratio of children to adults, making public education relatively expensive. Periodic economic crises and hard times frustrated reformers' plans, particularly in the late 1830s and early 1840s.

In sum, the story in the Midwest is much like that of the East, not so much because of direct influence (though there was much of that) but because the regions were similar in fundamental ways. The cosmopolitan formulation of republican, Protestant, capitalist ideas found a congenial environment in the Midwest. The belief that equity, progress, and cohesion depended upon state-regulated common schooling eventually prevailed. Opposition was not just southern, nor did it stem merely from selfishness, ignorance, or clannishness. As in the East, some people had principled objections, variant ideologies, and different cultural needs. As in the East, there was much more consensus on the provision of rudimentary local schooling than on state organization. Thus a rise in school enrollments preceded the widespread acceptance of state involvement.

In the South there was less enthusiasm for local common schooling and more successful resistance to the creation of state systems. Before the creation of state-sponsored common-school systems in the South, children were educated by local schooling arrangements similar to those in the North, though the mix of schooling institutions was different, and a lower proportion of children went to school. Wealthy planter and professional families provided their children with private tutors, but this did not affect the vast majority of southern children. For the large middling group of white southerners, schooling was available from academies, denominational schools, and subscription schools. The South's most characteristic and visible secondary schools were academies. By 1850 the number of academies in the South as a whole (2,700) surpassed the number of academies in the Middle Atlantic region (2,100) or New England (1,000). Academies flourished not only in cities but in small and medium-sized towns. The stereotype of antebellum southern society, picturing nothing but large plantations and coastal seaports, neglects the vast areas of small-scale farming dotted with small towns. Typical, perhaps, was Talladega, Alabama, which in 1853 boasted a population of 1,200 and the following secondary schools: the East Alabama Masonic Female Institute, the Talladega Male High School, the Southward Select School, and the Presbyterial Collegiate Female Institute. Religious groups were active in sponsoring education. Episcopalians, Lutherans, Methodists, Presbyterians, Quakers, Moravians, and others operated day schools as well as Sunday schools. Church and local government were not always rigidly separate. In the early national period, Episcopalian ministers or lay readers sometimes taught local day schools. In Georgia, denominational sponsorship led to the founding of at least twenty academies and several colleges, with the Methodists in the lead. Denominational efforts in Virginia focused mainly on colleges and theological training, but Episcopalians, Presbyterians, and Baptists founded a few academies. Virtually all academies, religiously affiliated or not, stressed moral education, Bible study, and often some sort of catechism.[13]

More transient and cheaper than the academies were the "old-field schools," so named because they were taught in log cabins built in old, fallow fields. Small communities subscribed to engage teachers. The tuition rates and length of term were specified in "articles" signed by the teacher and the neighbors. Unlike academies, old-field schools taught elementary subjects, and sometimes a smattering of other subjects as needed. There are many memoirs describing such rural neighborhood schools in the South. A Georgian recalled: "There was no school in the Goosepond neighborhood on Broad River from its first settlement, in 1784, until 1796. The first teacher was a deserter from the British navy whose only qualification was that he could write. He whipped according to the navy practice." Governor George Gilmer of Georgia, who grew up in prosperous Wilkes County in the early nineteenth century, recalled a series of old-field teachers—a handsome, kindly man from North Carolina, a loud, violent Irishman, an impoverished Virginia gentleman who drank too much, and a well-qualified, sober Georgian—all of whom came and went in annual succession.[14]

In states that had a fund for teaching poor children, old-field teachers could apply for reimbursement for the tuition of their pauper students. County officials in Virginia were required to file reports on the use of the state's charity education money. Some of these provide brief descriptions of old-field schools. In Lunenberg County, District 5 Commissioner Richard Jeffries reported in 1848 that "eight poor children attend Mr. Hardy's school, which was visited in July. They were employed in spelling, reading, writing, cyphering, and one had commenced the study of English grammar. Several are intellectual in appearance, and all I think were learning tolerably fast. Mr. Hardy had 38 scholars, and though experienced and well qualified, must I think have had his hands rather full." Sometimes a state's meager aid to pauper education helped to establish a subscription school. In Virginia the Greenbriar County commissioners reported in 1825 that "schools have, by the aid of a few indigent children to make a sufficient number, been established in almost every section of the county . . . thus affording the industrious but poor farmer and the middle class of people opportunities of having their children educated." By the 1840s, middle-class spokesmen in Virginia opposed charity education and argued for a state-supported common-school system; but earlier, pauper school aid had indirectly benefited some middle-class families by creating a smattering of pay schools in the countryside, where poor and middling-status children attended school together.[15]

In southern cities, benevolent societies sometimes created separate charity schools for the poor, though the practice seems to have been less frequent than in the North. Alexandria, Virginia, operated male and female charity schools on the Lancasterian plan in the early nineteenth century, combining philanthropic donations and city grants, while Norfolk ran free evening schools for the children of the poor from the 1830s to the 1850s. Petersburg, Virginia, officials reported in 1823 that "all" of their poor children had gone to the Lancasterian school. Governor David Stone of North Carolina caught the Lancasterian enthusiasm and founded a monitorial free school in 1814, but the movement did not spread in his state. At about the same time, Charleston, South Carolina, opened five free schools for poor white children at public expense. In Georgia the pauper school fund supported special free schools for the poor, but the money was also used to fund poor children's tuition at old-field schools.[16]

These various institutions provided some poor white children with rudimentary education. For most of the South's poor children, however—the children of slaves—access to the three R's was slim and getting slimmer. The suppression of slave education grew worse as southern slaveholders came to fear subversion from within and without. Nor did southern whites' attitudes about slavery and education affect only the education of slaves. Slavery influenced educational attitudes and institutions for the whole South.

At the time of the American Revolution, some slaves received education in the Christian religion and the reading and writing of English. Although no statistics are available, there is scattered evidence of literate slaves. Reward notices for runaway slaves in the eighteenth century sometimes refer to fugitives who spoke "remarkably good English," "a little French," or "tolerable German." Others were said to be able to read and write; the benefit of such talents is indicated by a typical runaway notice describing a slave who "can write a pretty hand and has probably forged a pass." Other evidence of education comes from the talents of intellectually accomplished slaves, who demonstrate that some masters allowed and even encouraged the education of promising slaves in the late eighteenth and early nineteenth century. The black ministry was the most common beneficiary of such talent, but James Durham of New Orleans became a physician and Benjamin Banneker of Maryland became an astronomer.[17]

Literate slaves seem to have learned their initial skills either from their masters in the household or in regular neighborhood schools along with their masters' children. More organized efforts aimed specifically at schooling the slaves were begun in the eighteenth century by two groups, the Quakers and the Society for the Propagation of the Gospel in Foreign Parts (S.P.G.), the missionary arm of the Anglican Church of England. S.P.G. missionaries, sent out to bring God to the American Indians and to keep Englishmen from forgetting God on the frontier, often also led classes for Negro slaves. Their emphasis was on conversion, and the training took the form of catechism and Scripture memorization. Nevertheless, many slaves learned to read the Bible in the catechism classes. Also, by emphasizing the desirability of converting slaves to Christianity, the S.P.G. underlined the existence of the blacks as people rather than property. However, the S.P.G. classes also inculcated acceptance of slavery, obedience to the masters, and reliance on a better life in the next world. They gave to slavery the sanction of religion, helping slave owners to defend the institution.[18]

The Quakers, in contrast to the Anglican missionaries, were more uncomfortable with slavery and by the end of the colonial period had given up their slaves in almost all areas. Their educational efforts were closely associated with their belief in manumission, and in the North they were in the forefront of the movement to establish manumission societies and free schools for blacks. In North Carolina, a Quaker, Levi Coffin, opened a Sunday school for slaves in 1821 and persuaded a few "lenient" slaveholders to send slave children to learn to read the Bible. But other slaveholders in the neighborhood said the existence of the school "made their slaves discontented and uneasy, and created a desire for the privileges that others had." The school was discontinued; Coffin, true to his Quaker views, later became active in the underground railroad.[19]

Slaveholders perceived a connection between slave literacy and strivings toward freedom. The connection was not fanciful. When Frederick Douglass's outraged master exclaimed that the boy's newly acquired literacy would "unfit him to be a slave," Douglass called it a "new and special revelation." "From that moment," he recalled, "I understood the pathway from slavery to freedom." In response to the slave revolts of the late 1820s and the increase in abolitionist publications in the North, southern states passed laws prohibiting anyone from teaching slaves to read. Louisiana in 1830, Georgia and Virginia in 1831, Alabama in 1832, South Carolina in 1834, and North Carolina in 1835 prescribed stiff fines for whites and whippings for blacks who attempted to teach slaves to read. Although these laws were enforced unevenly, they were enforced widely. Some masters still supported slave literacy after the reaction set in, but they often faced criticism from their neighbors. Interviews with former slaves, conducted by the Federal Writers Project in the 1930s, include many references to the enforcement of the slave codes against reading. Elijah Green of South Carolina, born in 1843, recalled, "for God's sake don't let a slave be cotch with pencil and paper. That was a major crime. You might as well had killed your master or missus." George Rogers, born about the same time in North Carolina said, "I cannot read and write. Dey did not allow no niggers to handle no papers in dem days."[20]

A few white southerners criticized the ban on reading. J. B. O'Neill, referring to South Carolina's law, wrote in 1852 that "this act grew out of a feverish state of excitement. . . . That has, however, subsided, and I trust we are now prepared to act the part of wise, humane, and fearless masters, and that this law, and all of kindred character, will be repealed." O'Neill claimed that "the best slaves in the state are those who can and do read the Scriptures." The Baptist General Association of Virginia and a few other religious groups criticized the prohibition of literacy, but few slaveholders agreed, and the codes remained in force. After 1830 most masters allowed only oral instruction for slaves, usually in Sunday schools and worship services conducted by carefully screened white clergy. Southern religious spokesmen acquiesced in this practice. The editor of the *Christian Index* told plantation missionaries in 1845 that they should be "prudent . . . carefully abstaining from all intermeddling with the affairs and regulations of the plantations upon which they preach." A slave from Mississippi recalled, "Twan't no teachers or anything like dat, but us sure was taught to be Christians. Everything on that place was blue stockin' Presbyterian. When Sunday comes us dressed all clean and nice and went to church."[21]

Despite the slaveholders' delusion that such enforced participation in a decorous, pro-slavery Christianity could enlist the loyalities of black field hands, a vigorous alternative culture existed in the slave quarters. The slaves' culture emphasized the immorality of slavery, the importance of black solidarity, and the value of various talents, including healing, preaching, conjuring, and reading. The white pro-slavery sermons and tracts emphasized the common interests of master and slave; but mutuality of interest with whites was no more a part of slaves' lives than common schooling. Instead, as historian Thomas Webber has concluded, "the members of the quarter community, especially at night and during their leisure time, were able to create their own institutions within which whites had little, if any, influence."[22]

This then, was the situation in most of the South throughout most of the antebellum period: there was almost no schooling for slaves, a modicum of state aid for the schooling of paupers, and the rest of education fell to independent institutions, principally the old-field school and the academy. Reformers like Jefferson, concerned about the future of republican government, had advocated common free schools in the South since the time of the Revolution. As in the North, the early plans failed. Subsequent reform efforts went through the same stages as those in some northeastern and midwestern states: free schooling for paupers only, often through land-based state aid, then permissive laws authorizing local taxation for free schools along with bills attempting to establish a state superintendency, teacher training, and other features of state systems. Sketches of reform efforts in three southern states will illustrate these patterns. Then we can ask the question: why did the pauper-schooling concept hang on so tenaciously in the South and why did tax-based common-school proposals usually sputter?

In 1806, after several unsuccessful attempts to get the Virginia legislature to pass a free-school bill, Thomas Jefferson wearily wrote:

> There is a snail-paced gait for the advance of new ideas on the general mind, under which we must acquiesce. A forty year's experience of popular assemblies has taught me, that you must give them time for every step you take. If too hard pushed, they baulk and the machine retrogrades.

At that point in Virginia's history, Jefferson remarked, "people generally have more feeling for canals and roads than education." It took another forty years before the Virginia legislature enacted a weak free-school bill. In the meantime, there was a great deal of debate on the issue. In 1811 a Literary Fund was established for aid to pauper education. In 1817 a bill for free primary schooling for all children failed in the Virginia Senate. The bill, brought forward by Charles Mercer, provided a state board of education and matching state aid to localities. Jefferson and his ally, Joseph Cabbell, therefore opposed it as overly centralist. The Mercer bill passed the House by a vote of 66–49, but it lost in the Senate on a 7–7 tie. Instead the legislature passed a bill clarifying the system of pauper education under the Literary Fund. The failure of the Mercer bill illustrates how close some of the southern votes on free schooling were. It also reinforces the point, equally applicable to the North, that just because a person believed fervently in republican government and was concerned about wide diffusion of knowledge, that did not dictate how he would vote on matters of state intervention in education. Despite Jefferson's reputation as the frustrated advocate of public schools in Virginia, he opposed the Mercer bill; elsewhere the same individualistic, cautious attitude about state government reinforced opposition to state-regulated free school systems, in the North as well as in the South. Republicanism lent support to schooling, but not necessarily to school systems.[23]

The next attempt to muster republican ideals on the side of a state school system came in 1826, the year of Jefferson's death. Calling republican government "the proudest triumph of reason and philosophy," Governor John Tyler appealed to Jefferson's memory and called for a system like New York's. He asked the legislature's committee on schools to recommend a system "embracing all, and alike available to all." The committee's report echoed Tyler's concern to support the education of "the industrious and numerous Yeomanry" of the state and warned that without a strong school system, Virginia's "relative influence and importance in the Union must rapidly decline." Both their bill and Tyler himself were soon defeated, and in 1829 the legislature instead passed a complicated, voluntary, common-school system adopted only in four counties. In the late 1830s and early 1840s, free-school advocates mounted a sustained campaign for a state system of free schools for all children. Criticism of pauper schooling became more frequent and more shrill. Appeals to New England or New York systems became common, and in 1839 Benjamin Smith made a report to the House of Delegates that praised the Prussian school system and argued the propriety of general taxation for schooling on the grounds that universal education would protect property, lessen the need for courts and prisons, and contribute to national wealth. Smith, like others, complained that the State of Virginia supported a university for the wealthy and charity schooling for the poor, "while the middle classes, who mainly support the whole burden of government, are left to provide for themselves." Governor David Campbell, who had commissioned the report, was from the southwestern part of Virginia, where free schooling was popular. In the wake of Smith's report, Campbell called for a statewide system, and in 1841, reformers staged three education conventions around the state, which produced proposals for northern-style school systems. The legislature's committee on schools took a compromise position, recommending a state superintendent and county-level taxes, but not wholly free tuition. James Brown, the state auditor who was in charge of the Literary Fund, defended the pauper education system and advised the legislature to leave well enough alone.[24]

Despite reformers' cries in the 1840s that Virginia was "the banner state of ignorance" and that its pauper school system "pines of moral atrophy," the legislature failed to make any fundamental change. Rural opposition to new taxes, urban indifference to educational innovation, and elite domination of the legislature spelled frustration for common-school advocates. In acts passed from 1846 to 1849 the legislature again created a voluntary system of taxation for common schools in counties where two-thirds of the voters approved. Ten counties and four cities adopted such plans, but even in some of those areas, the plan was not implemented or was held up by legal challenges. In 1850, the U.S. Census figures suggest, about twenty percent of Virginia's school-age children attended such common schools. In 1853 the school commissioners of Harrison County were still wishing that Virginia would "shake herself from her slumbering state, and do something on the subject worthy of her name," but educational organization and practice in Virginia did not change substantially again until after the Civil War. The reasons for this inaction will be examined after outlining common-school developments in two other states.[25]

Georgia started out auspiciously for school systematizers but soon settled into a pattern like Virginia's. Its constitution of 1777 specified that there should be state-supported schools in every county. The legislature began to translate this clause into law in 1783 by authorizing the governor to grant school lands to counties that applied. In 1785 they passed a bill to create the University of Georgia, which would not only conduct higher education but oversee the state's educational system. This plan was not implemented, and there is no evidence that any land grants were made for primary education. There were no further attempts to change pre-Revolutionary educational practices until 1817, when the legislature created a school fund to aid pauper schooling and academies. This support program seemed to spur the growth of academies more than free schools. The number of operating academies grew from forty in 1820 to ninety in 1830. The number of free schools was about fifty in the mid–1830s. In 1837 a common-school act passed, but it did not provide for local taxation. In any case, the law was repealed in 1840 in the midst of the serious depression following the Panic of 1837. In 1843 the legislature allowed counties to levy local taxes for pauper education to supplement the state grants, but two years later Governor George Crawford noted that only fifty-three of Georgia's ninety-three counties had even applied for the state aid. In 1858, Georgia's lawmakers passed a permissive common-school law increasing state aid, allowing counties to establish common schools if they desired, and allowing them to tax localities for either common or pauper schools. The decision in each county was left to a grand jury, acting as school commissioners. About eighteen of Georgia's 132 counties established common schools in the following few years. In 1859 an influential report by David Lewis declared that common-school legislation in Georgia had failed. Lewis called for a statewide system with a superintendent and a normal school, but reformers' plans were again disrupted, this time by the Civil War.[26]

Educational reform in North Carolina followed similar lines

and encountered similar constraints, but common-school advocates were more successful in the late antebellum period. The early years were similar to Georgia and Virginia. Early governors and legislatures cited the need for widespread education in a republic, but took no action other than to support a university. In 1817 a state senator named Archibald Murphey, keenly in support of internal improvements and public schooling, presented a report that lauded the ideas of Pestalozzi and Lancaster and proposed a state system of common schools free to the poor and partially subsidized for others. The Murphey Committee's bill and other similar bills failed to pass the legislature in 1817, 1818, and 1824. In January, 1826, however, the North Carolina legislature established a Literary Fund, allocated various state land revenues and license fees to it, and directed that it be invested in bank stocks until sufficient capital accumulated to distribute funds for "the support of Common and convenient Schools." No distribution of these funds was made until 1839, when the legislature passed its first common-school law. The bill called for a vote in every county. If a majority favored the arrangement, school districts were to be created, a county superintendent chosen, and a local tax authorized. Each district in a complying county had to raise $20 and provide a schoolhouse in order to qualify for $40 in state aid.

Unlike Virginians, whose response to voluntary common-school legislation was lukewarm, a majority of North Carolinians in every county had voted "yes" by 1846. Nonetheless, common-school advocates considered it a weak law, and most educational policy debates in the 1840s centered on the method of apportioning state funds to the counties. In 1852, J. B. Cherry succeeded in shepherding through the North Carolina legislature a bill creating a state superintendent of schools, the *sine qua non* of northern systems and, in the eyes of reformers, the solution to North Carolina's weak school system. To this post the legislature elected Calvin Wiley, a lawyer, novelist, and House member from Guilford. Wiley accomplished quite a bit, and he could legitimately claim in his reports of the late 1850s that North Carolina compared favorably to most southern states and to some northern states on matters of attendance and expenditures for common schools.

Still, bills for increased state funding (1854) and training of teachers (1855, 1858) failed during Wiley's regime, and the system may not have been as "public" in reality as it was on paper. In 1856 a school commissioner in Lincolnton wrote to Wiley that "it has been customary here to get up a School in the Academies (we have two, male and female) for five months, on subscription (these schools were controlled by trustees), and there was generally one or two petty schools in town (besides, taught by female teachers on subscription). The District School Committee would distribute the Free School fund among all these schools, and the teachers would divide it as they pleased." In the early days of public schooling, localities often modified the state's intentions to fit local institutions. Independent tuition schools performed desirable "public" functions, and some state aid found its way to these schools, which we would call "private." Nonetheless, North Carolinians had done what few other southerners had done: appointed and sustained a vigorous state superintendent and voted in favor of tax-supported common schools.[27]

Alabama, Louisiana, and Kentucky also had fledgling systems with state superintendents when the Civil War interrupted. Moreover, in states that did not have effective statewide school systems, some particular areas, such as southwestern Virginia, were developing common-school facilities. Many cities had free schools available to the poor, and some, like Charleston, South Carolina, and Nashville, Tennessee, were attempting to make their free schools into genuine common schools. The antebellum South was a diverse area. Educational ideas and practice varied from state to state, from rural to urban places, and from big plantation country to small farming areas. Yet one generalization stands: southerners displayed more reluctance than northerners to tax property for school costs and to erect state-level supervisory mechanisms for common-school systems. An explanation of this generalization must touch upon the region's demography, its economy, the ideology and practice of slavery, the politics of seacoast-upcountry rivalry within southern states, and the effect of North-South sectionalism upon the politics of education in the region as a whole.[28]

The South was sparsely populated and experienced little urbanization during the antebellum period. Low population density in rural areas was an inhibiting factor in school attendance, local school support, and state school reform efforts. Stephen Elliott and James Thornwell advised the South Carolina legislature in 1839 that the Prussian model was useless because of their state's sparse population. In his plan for Virginia education, written in 1841, Henry Ruffner tried to downplay the difficulty, but in doing so he dramatized it. "Youngsters between eight and fifteen years of age often make light of crossing rivers and mountains about home," he said. Parents who complain of great distances to schools should either improve the road system or "provide cheap water craft." As officials in Nansemond County, Virginia, commented in 1852, however, many children did not attend school regularly because they lived too far away. Nonetheless, people in the frontier Midwest attained higher levels of school attendance and school organization than people in the South, despite similarly sparse population. Had this been the only factor inhibiting educational development, southerners too would have overcome the problem; but it was one problem among many.[29]

The economy of much of the South was based on cotton and on slavery. This had several effects on economic and political developments. Because the cotton states were so heavily dependent upon a single price determined by conditions outside the region, it was difficult for southerners to respond to cyclical downturns. Hard times like the period from 1838 to 1843 were more devastating in the South and had lasting effects on state funds, including those earmarked for schools. In Georgia the correlation between rising prosperity and common-school reform is striking, the strongest thrusts coming around 1822, 1836, and 1856, when good cotton prices prevailed. In the first case, a conservative majority defeated a common-school system; in the second case, the subsequent depression contributed to its repeal; and in the third case, the Civil War interrupted. Of course, hard times affected school reform elsewhere. Retrenchment in 1840 led to the elimination of the state superintendency in Connecticut and Ohio and gave Horace Mann a good scare in Massachusetts. Economic troubles are not the whole answer to the South's slow acceptance of educational reform, but they did blunt the reformers' momentum at some key points.

The dominance of slave labor and the cotton cash crop meant that wealthy planters, who dominated southern politics, had little economic interest in the education of white labor. White education as an investment in human capital had little relevance to large plantation owners. But states outside the cotton belt, like Virginia, shared the South's general aversion to state-regulated common schooling, so the human-capital argument is not a sufficient explanation either. Common-school proposals were affected by ideological and political tensions that transcended the cotton economy and characterized the whole region, tensions between slaveholders and nonslaveholders, between wealthy aristocrats and middle-class democrats, and between coastal plains and piedmont regions of the southern states.[30]

Antebellum southern legislatures, journals, and pulpits were dominated by pro-slavery ideology. The defense of slavery rested sometimes on aristocratic arguments, sometimes on racist arguments, and sometimes on the perverted democratic argument that black slavery allowed more equality among whites. Southern ideology at its most aristocratic was critical of northern industrial capitalism and did not draw the same conclusions northerners did about the educational implications of Protestantism. Although the wholesale theoretical critique of capitalism by Virginia's George Fitzhugh was not typical, many defenders of slavery attacked the morality of the North's competitive, individualistic economy and its free-market, wage-labor system. They argued that slavery was a superior labor system because it emphasized reciprocal responsibilities and communal welfare. Under free-labor capitalism, wrote Henry Hughes, the interests of capitalists and laborers are antagonistic. "Want is not eliminated. . . . The young, the old, and other inefficients" are not supported. "Pauperism is not eliminated." But under slavery, wrote Edmund Ruffin, "there is no possibility of the occurrence of the sufferings of the laboring classes" that characterize the "class-slavery of labor to capital."[31]

Slavery dominated southern conservative social thought. The tragedy of it was unwittingly expressed by the trustees of a female academy in Fredericksburg who said that the South without slavery would be like Shakespeare's *Hamlet* without a Hamlet. Because of slavery, Protestantism could never be wedded to republicanism and to education as vitally in the South as in the North, and its duties in the service of slavery were strained. There were, of course, many Protestant lay people and ministers who saw the relationship between religion, education, and social philosophy much as the northern reformers did, but in the South they had to contend with a large, influential, conservative elite and with the morass of slavery.[32]

Pro-slavery arguments had effects on educational attitudes beyond the question of slave literacy. The fear of incendiary publications and revolutionary ideas among slaves made some planters nervous about the free circulation of dissenting ideas anywhere in southern society. Frederick Law Olmstead, a northern traveler in the South, remarked that the "habitual caution imposed on clergymen and public teachers must and obviously does have an important secondary effect, similar to that usually attributed by Protestants to papacy, upon the minds of all the people, discountenancing and retarding the free and fearless exercise of the mind upon subjects of a religious or ethical character." In responding to reformers who urged slave literacy, some southerners defended the prohibition of slave education with an argument that did not depend upon race and that could extend to free whites. These writers began to sound like the nervous English Tories of a generation earlier who had argued that laboring people were better off uneducated because they escaped the weighty responsibilities and perplexities of wealth. In the 1830s, southerners commonly applied this argument to slaves. Learning brings "more anxiety than enjoyment," said a widely read pamphlet. Cultivating a slave's mind would "unfit him for his station in life." But would not the same concerns apply to free white labor? A few southern writers made this striking extension. William Harper, a pro-slavery lawyer from South Carolina, argued:

> The Creator did not intend that every individual human being should be highly cultivated. . . . It is better that a part should be fully and highly cultivated and the rest utterly ignorant. To constitute a society, a variety of offices must be discharged, from those requiring but the lowest degree of intellectual power to those requiring the very highest, and it should seem that endow-

ments ought to be apportioned according to the exigencies of the situation.

This, of course, assumed that children would inherit the status and role of their parents, a fundamental aristocratic assumption. Despite the increasing democratization of southern politics, this conservative economic idea had a long currency in the South. When Philadelphia workingmen demanded equal education in the 1820s, an anonymous writer in the *Southern Review* queried, "Is this the way to produce producers? To make every child in the state a literary character would not be a good qualification for those who must live by manual labor." *De Bow's Review* argued in 1856 that although the state should provide some education for all whites, "beyond that it must educate the wealthy in order to maintain their position as members of the white, privileged class of our society."[33]

Aristocratic, pro-slavery, anticapitalist ideology was not monolithic in the antebellum South any more than the reformist cosmopolitan version of native Protestant ideology was universal in the North. The aristocratic defense of slavery was in fact born in an uncomfortable setting and warred against republican ideals held in the South as well as in the North. Although anticapitalist social theories might have sounded all right when intoned to planters on the veranda of a plantation big house, much of the South was not populated by large landholders. Although the big planters held disproportionate political power, they had to reckon with dissenters in their midst, a countryside filled with whites who farmed their own land, and an increasingly assertive urban middle class. Ultimately slavery was rationalized on racial grounds. Unlike George Fitzhugh and some other aristocratic theorists, many writers defended the restrictions on slave education not on the grounds that all people should know and keep their place but that slaves and free blacks should. They appealed to the alleged common interests of slaveholders and nonslaveholders. This line became more effective as Northern criticism grew. A correspondent in the *Southern Recorder* in 1860 said that he would fight to preserve slavery because slavery "gives independence and dignity to the poor man of the South. It is that which makes him feel his equality with the slave owner, for however poor the [white] man in the South may be, he can stand erect when he looks down and knows . . . the negro is below, and will remain so." By 1860 even Fitzhugh was citing racial theories to defend slavery.[34]

Large plantation slave owners were ultimately able to close ranks with most white Southerners in defense of slavery, but on many other matters they were not able to command their loyalty or their votes. Politics differed from state to state, but in most of the old South, political tensions took a regional form. The geography of the coastal states was such that large slaveholders concentrated near the coast and smaller farmers with fewer slaves occupied the piedmont and mountain regions inland. The political dominance of the wealthy slave owners was bolstered in several ways: in most states representation in the lower house of the legislature was based on "federal" population, that is, each slave counted as three-fifths of a person. In some states there were substantial property qualifications to vote for senators, and in some states the governor or federal legislators were elected by the state legislature, not by popular vote. Throughout the old South these constitutional features were attacked by the disgruntled upcountry middle class. Intrastate regional politics was not confined to the old Atlantic-coast states. In Tennessee, for example, sectionalism played a key role in politics, although the economic sections were geographically reversed. A more prosperous west was pitted against a mountainous east. "We are a divided people, distinguished in our rules of policy by sectional feelings and principles," complained an east Tennessee common-school advocate in 1821. In Alabama the major parties aligned more or less with a belt of slavery and cotton in the south on one side and the more mountainous northern areas on the other. Other states were similarly divided.[35]

Virginia, Georgia, and North Carolina illustrate the effect of class and regional politics on common-school development. Virginia is the most dramatic case of the coincidence of class, section, and educational philosophy. Western Virginians continually and loudly called for equitable representation and free common schools. The Constitution of 1830 failed to eliminate federal-basis apportionment, thus guaranteeing eastern dominance for the succeeding three decades. Western citizens protested that a constitution "composed of such ingredients is unfit for the government of a free people," and the *Wheeling Gazette* dared to suggest that western Virginians should negotiate "with the eastern nabobs for a division of the state—peaceably if we can, forcibly if we must." Westerners continually pressed the interests of the middle class in education. Attempts to establish free schools in the early years, with strong western support, had led only to university and pauper-school aid. In 1838 a western governor, David Campbell, was elected, and he placed a high priority on the issue of common schools. The state should support education for "small landholders and others of inconsiderable incomes." Easterners in the legislature buried all such bills and provoked a torrent of complaints and educational reform demands from the West. Critics labelled the pauper aid system "abortive," complained that its effects in the West were "not appreciable," and demanded a system "something like the schools of the New England states." The Reverend Alexander Campbell, keynote speaker at an 1841 education convention in western Virginia, declared that unlike the aristocrats of the East, westerners "would be glad to send our children to the same good common school, and we would have no patrician scrupulosity of conscience in permitting them to read the same primer or Greek testament with those of mere plebian honours." He urged western Virginians to forge ahead without delay to establish common schools on their own. But when the law of 1846 provided that chance on a voluntary basis, western reformers encountered difficulty in their own backyard. The law was drawn so that a one-third minority could block adoption. In many counties the opposition to new taxes was sufficient to defeat the option. Elsewhere in western Virginia, legal challenges delayed implementation of county-funded common schools. During the 1850s, easterners scuttled further western proposals for common-school legislation. The east-west split in Virginia dramatizes the southern conflict between a vigorous, powerful slaveholding elite and a rising middle class of western small farmers and professionals, and it demonstrates the great appeal of northern-style common-school plans to the western middle class. When West Virginia actually went its own way in 1860, the crucial issues were slavery and secession, but the *Wheeling Intelligencer* also noted among the westerners' grievances that eastern Virginia had denied them common schools.[36]

Sectionalism was less decisive in Georgia. An analysis of an 1831 Senate bill to establish a common-school fund reveals the expected associations: senators from counties with low slave holdings and small farms generally voted for the bill, and the staple-crop, cotton-belt senators generally voted against it. The bill was defeated in the assembly, which, like that of other states, had an apportionment bias toward the slave counties. But these alignments faded during Georgia's subsequent antebellum educational history. Georgia politicians did not face a planter aristocracy as securely entrenched or as conservative as the one in Virginia. Both parties, therefore, muted regional issues in an effort to gain votes across regional lines. Neither party opposed the Common School Act of 1837, but neither worked hard to save it from repeal in 1840. One historian of Georgia politics has concluded that "neither party regarded free public education for white children as a necessity." Economic fluctuations, sparse population, resistance to new taxes, and preoccupation with other issues combined to frustrate the reformers' schemes. Georgians' local arrangements for educating children did not change very much between 1820 and 1860.[37]

Southern states differed in their legislative provisions for pauper schooling or voluntary common-school options, but none of the original states had a broadly accepted system headed by a state superintendent in 1860 except North Carolina. It is thus an exception to the general southern resistance to common-school systems. Still, in many ways, North Carolina's history is similar to that of other southern states. Sectional antagonism extended back to the embittered western regulator movement of the 1760s. In the nineteenth century it took on the same political and economic guises as elsewhere in the South. Western agitation for fairer representation began in the 1790s and heated up in the 1820s and 1830s. Demanding a constitutional convention in 1834, a writer in the *Western Carolinian* said, "Justice is all we want. If we are refused it, I hope my countrymen will show that they still possess the same abhorrence of oppression that distinguished their fathers." Yet in the Constitution of 1835 the federal basis for apportionment of the lower house was retained, as in other states. With this history of sectional antagonism, and the constitutional basis for eastern planter dominance, why did North Carolina's educational history turn out differently from that of her neighbors?[38]

North Carolinians had long displayed more moderate attitudes about slavery, class, and education. Manumission societies enjoyed a longer and more substantial history there prior to the 1820s, and North Carolinians showed distaste for nullification and secession philosophies. The piedmont and middle plain covered a larger geographical proportion of the state, and a smaller percentage of the white population owned slaves than in Virginia or South Carolina. Some evangelical Baptists and Methodists added to the mildly anti-slavery and egalitarian sentiment in the state. The Quakers' manumission work was strong in North Carolina before 1830, and they were strong supporters of public education.

For a variety of reasons, then, North Carolina legislators were more favorably disposed toward the creation of a state common-school system. The Whig party was strong in the west and strongly pro-Union on national issues. Given North Carolinians' general aversion to fire-eating pro-slavery, it was possible for the Whigs to attract enough eastern support to dominate North Carolina politics from 1835 until 1850. Like Georgians, they passed a common-school law in the late 1830s; unlike Georgians, they did not repeal it in the hard times of the depression. In contrast to Virginia's law, the North Carolina option did not require a two-thirds vote in the counties. A majority in favor sufficed to begin common schools. The question was put bluntly; those who favored the law wrote "school" on their ballot, those opposed had to write "no school."

Whiggery broke apart in North Carolina in the 1850s, but westerner J. B. Cherry managed to get his bill for a state superintendent through a Democratic legislature in 1852. The legislature elected Calvin Wiley, a Whig school reformer, to the post. Wiley organized the first state teachers' organization, established a state education journal, and crisscrossed the state, evangelizing the common-school idea. He complained later that people had been "tenacious of old habits, conservative to the point of stubbornness," but these impediments had been overcome by northern school enthusiasts too. North Carolina lacked the abject sectionalism of Virginia, the monolithic, defensive racism of South Carolina, and the roller-coaster cotton economy of Georgia. North Carolina's milder versions of southern conditions provided Wiley with an auspicious field for action.[39]

It is possible that more Southern states would have implemented state school systems in the 1850s had it not been for a second sort of sectionalism, that between the North and the South as regions. As the slavery crisis deepened in the 1850s, northern institutions and ideas came increasingly under attack in the South. As in the Midwest, there had been much New England and New York influence among common-school reformers in the South. Reformers had corresponded with their northern counterparts, and they had held northern systems up as models for the South. As tension with the North increased, especially after 1850, southerners faced a dilemma: they wanted to develop their sectional pride and independence by developing educational institutions, but all the familiar models were associated with their antagonists in the North. In *DeBow's Review* in 1859 a Dr. Cartwright argued that the meager establishment of rural schools under Louisiana's common-school law demonstrated conclusively that "the New England system of public education is not adapted to Louisiana and the South." Planters could take care of education in their communities better than "theoretical, burdensome, troublesome, expensive" government intervention. Speaking in the U.S. Senate against Justin Morrill's proposal for land-grant colleges, Senator James Mason of Virginia expressed the fear that such federal involvement might presage an effort to impose on the South "that peculiar system of free schools in New England States" which would, he said, "destroy that peculiar character which I am happy to believe belongs to the great mass of the Southern people."[40]

Not only the northern models of school organization but other educational influences came under frequent criticism in this decade. Writers bemoaned the South's dependence upon northern teachers, northern textbooks, and northern colleges. New England teachers in New Orleans were called "mischievous spies and agents." In Memphis, teachers imported from Connecticut (the "Nutmeg

State") were labelled "a gang of low flung nutmeg agents." Frustrated southern loyalists called for more training of home-grown teachers. The *Kanawha Valley Star* argued in 1859 "that the influence exerted in the trans-Allegheny by Yankee teachers is entirely too great and that it behooves every true Virginian to correct this evil. No education is better than bad education." There was similar agitation against northern textbooks. A convention at Knoxville complained of the "vicious theories and principles" purveyed in northern books and resolved "that the South should publish her own books." Georgians complained that "we have no Georgia school books. We depend upon Boston publications." J. D. B. DeBow, a University of Louisiana professor and editor of the popular *DeBow's Review*, launched a big campaign against "humiliating dependence" and "vassalage" to northern publishers. He asked a commercial convention in 1852, "Is there any reciprocity, sirs? Who of the North reads a Southern book?"[41]

Large numbers of young southern gentlemen attended northern colleges, and some southern women were sent to northern academies. This practice increasingly came under attack. Criticizing the abolitionist views of Yale's Professor Benjamin Silliman, the Reverend C. K. Marshall of Mississippi declared in 1855, "I do not believe a young man can be safely educated in the North at the present time." A University of North Carolina alumnus charged that Harvard and Yale "have been turned from their legitimate channels and been perverted into strongholds of fanaticism." Again and again southerners were urged to educate their sons and daughters in the South.[42]

Although these anti-northern sentiments reinforced the opposition to northern-style common-school systems, the particular complaints about northern teachers, textbooks, and colleges had surprisingly little effect. The northern contacts had coexisted with southern slave society for decades, and many people, apparently, did not share the orators' fears. Some southern textbooks were produced, such as Calvin Wiley's *North Carolina Reader* and William Gilmore Simms's *History of South Carolina*, but the South could not develop a competitive publishing industry overnight, and northern schoolbooks remained popular. No less a southern patriot than Jefferson Davis, on the very eve of the Civil War, blithely claimed that "above all other people we are one, and above all books which have united us in the bond of common language, I place the good old Spelling-Book of Noah Webster." The sectional anger of the 1850s did not obliterate long-standing northern influences in southern education. Similarly, southern urban school systems such as Charleston continued to import teachers as late as 1857. Nor did the enrollment of southerners at northern universities decline noticeably, even in the late 1850s. In North Carolina, John Gilmer said that fathers who refused to send children to northern colleges were "silly men," and the president of Davidson College told an audience of young southern women that he did not share the prejudice against northern teachers and doubted "that they have ever accomplished anything to our detriment."[43]

Nonetheless, there was an obvious tendency for pro-slavery ideology to move more vigorously to the center of southern discourse in the 1850s. Although some moderates said they could separate desirable northern educational influences from the threat of abolitionism and industrial capitalism, the connections made by fire-eating orators were not entirely imaginary. Northern-style free-school advocacy and abolitionist sentiments were indeed mingled in the social thought of several southern educational reformers. In Virginia many Hampton-Sydney graduates of the early nineteenth century favored gradual abolition, among them John Holt Rice, who taught slaves to read, prominently supported the Mercer common-school bill of 1817, and wrote in 1827, "I am fully convinced that slavery is the greatest evil in the South, except whiskey. . . . The problem to be solved is, to produce that state of public will, which will cause the people to move spontaneously to the eradication of the evil." After 1830 the expression of such views became more risky. Henry Ruffner, a leading Virginia common-school advocate, wrote to Mann in 1848, "You will observe how carefully I guard in my Address against being identified with Northern Abolitionists. This was absolutely necessary to any good effect," in order "that the opponents of our cause have nothing to lay hold on." Little could Ruffner know that Mann faced a similar tactical choice in Boston when integrationists pleaded for his prestigious support in the 1840s. One of them later recalled, "Mr. Mann was with us in sentiment," but he "declined to say anything or take part on the question, for it was an unpopular matter, and might . . . impair his influences on other questions connected with his official duties" as secretary of the state Board of Education. Racial justice was a liability in cosmopolitan school reform. Both Horace Mann, a timid integrationist, and Henry Ruffner, an abolitionist slave owner, dropped it lest it threaten their common-school reform program for whites.[44]

If the Fitzhughes and the DeBows could detect a connection between common schooling and abolition in the prominent reformers, they could also see that the strongest popular support for common free schools came from middling-status southerners, small farmers and professionals in the upcountry, many of whom opposed the extension of slavery, who were hostile to the slaveholding aristocracy, and who favored more democratic political institutions. In the 1850s these forces did not prevail in the South, but in the long run the big planters' fears were realized. After a cataclysmic war, and the failure of Reconstruction, a new generation of southern cosmopolitan school reformers, including Ruffner's son William, went to work. Blacks in the South, as in the North, were left out of the cosmopolitan solution, and it took a long time for reformers to persuade white voters to levy local property taxes for free schools, but this too came to the "new South" of the early twentieth century.

Regional differences in the fate of antebellum common-school reform arose from differences in the economics, demography, ethnic mix, and subcultures of the three areas. At first glance it seems that the Midwest was quite different from the Northeast and shared some characteristics with the South. Both the Midwest and the South were heavily agricultural and sparsely populated. They had few city dwellers compared to the Northeast. In both regions, funds from school lands were mismanaged and failed as the basis of school systems, and in both regions there was considerable local resistance to full property-tax support for common schooling. Yet by 1860 all the midwestern states had established state-regulated, tax-based school systems while few southern states had. In the Midwest, northeastern influences and models prevailed; in the South, they were resisted and rejected.

The similarities between the two agricultural regions were superficial; the differences were fundamental. The Midwest was more diverse than the South and was undergoing a more dramatic economic change. From frontier subsistence farming in the early nineteenth century, the region moved to commercial grain farming for large and distant markets. Extractive industries, food processing, and light manufacturing spurred the development of young cities like Chicago, Detroit, and Milwaukee, which were more industrial and more ethnically varied than southern cities. The region was linked to the Northeast not only by migration patterns and cultural heritage but by trade routes and marketing. The Midwest was solidly engaged in the developing capitalist system of the United States. Furthermore, unlike the South, the Midwest had very substantial numbers of European immigrants settled in its cities and on its farmlands. Linguistic, religious, and ethnic diversity heightened the appeal of an assimilationist common-school system.

The South, by contrast, though part of the same republican, Protestant tradition, was alienated both economically and culturally from the Northeast and its institutions. There was little manufacturing and little processing of the region's main cash crop. Southerners were engaged in economic growth and westward expansion, but not in economic development. Slavery and cotton remained the keys to regional production. There were few European immigrants, and education was widely deemed inappropriate and dangerous for slaves. In this environment a conservative ideology was asserted by influential plantation owners and their intellectual allies. It did not garner allegiance from all southerners, but when added to the region's cyclical economic problems and the curse of slavery, it contributed to the failure of common-school legislation. Because the aristocratic defense of slavery was at odds with the interests of the South's small farmers and others of middling status, and because the politics of education partook of this class-related, sectional tension within the southern states, the drama of school reform was different in the South and the North. The differences centered on the slave-labor system.

Still, it is also important to remember that there were many similar characteristics of the common-school reform movement and its opponents in all three regions. The early state superintendents, Calvin Wiley of North Carolina, Samuel Lewis of Ohio, William Perry of Alabama, Horace Eaton of Vermont, and others, shared many goals and sounded very much alike. Nor were their opponents regionally unique. Rural people who resisted new taxes and urban dwellers who preferred the old charity-school system were found throughout the nation. In no region was there overwhelming consensus on state intervention in common schooling. There were close votes and seesaw battles in the North and the South. Geography, class structure, economic development, and cultural heritage combined to tip the scales in favor of state systems in the North and against them in the South. Everywhere, however, time was on the side of the common-school reformers.

9

Epilogue: The Legacy of Common Schooling

IN his sermon praising railroads, the Reverend Thomas King envisioned God's providential express dropping off churches and schools along its westward path. In Vermont, Horace Eaton linked the creation of a state school system to the development of railroads and to the commercialization of agriculture. A businessman in Connecticut complained that eliminating the state school superintendent's job showed that the state was taking "steps backward in the cause of education whilst her sister states and the Nations of the whole earth are going forward." Images of progress pervaded the school reformers' arguments. That made it hard for their opponents. It is difficult to be against progress. Many people opposed the reforms anyway, progress or no progress, but the reformers eventually won. Was it certain in the long run that if we were to have universal white male suffrage, a semiofficial native Protestant culture, and industrial capitalism, we would also have state-regulated, free common-school systems? State education policies could have gone in several directions, and there is no formula for predicting the details of such developments. But there is a rough congruence between a nation's political economy, its dominant culture, and its educational policies.

The common-school reformers of the antebellum period were on the forward edge of an evolving relationship between social belief, social change, and educational change in their day. What made their eventual success inevitable was not some abstract or universal logic of modernization but the growing popular acceptance of the reformers' version of modernization in their own day. Dissenters had some impact upon the way state systems evolved, and the Roman Catholic Church erected a sizable alternative system, but the solutions of many other dissenters, ranging from radical socialists to urbane pluralists to reluctant rural taxpayers, were rejected. Their solutions did not fit the needs of the republic as expressed by a majority of leaders, backed by the influential native Protestant ideology, and sweetened with the language of progress. When a majority of voters came to associate common-school systems with modernity and equality, the reformers' success in the North was assured.

This had occurred by 1860. Connecticut restored its state superintendent's position in 1845 and, under a strongly nativist government in the 1850s, passed laws to strengthen consolidation and central supervision. In New York the highly charged opposition to full tax support almost vanished by 1867, and rate bills were legally abolished without a fight. There are several reasons why common-school reform became less controversial after 1860 and why there was an expanding consensus around its ideology. People became accustomed to a state role that was initially disturbing. Common-school supporters worked the bugs out of some reforms, like formulas for tax support. Other issues, especially slavery and sectionalism, came to preoccupy the nation. To some degree, localities stopped resisting the state's bureaucratic role in education as they discovered that it did not affect local schooling as much as they had feared, nor as much as the reformers wished. In Massachusetts many towns ignored laws for compulsory school attendance by factory children and for the mandatory establishment of high schools in sizable towns; midwestern state officials often complained that most people didn't know what the education laws said. Nineteenth-century legislation was sometimes only exhortatory; enforcement provisions were weak.

Was the systematization of common schooling largely completed by 1860 or only beginning? If by that question we mean: had state and county superintendents established effective supervision over local schools, and did most teachers receive professional training and read education journals, and did corporal punishment end?—the answer is no. In a still largely rural America, many communities hired untrained, transient teachers to work in crude buildings, teaching an ungraded crowd of students who showed up with their family schoolbooks. There was in many communities little daily evidence of the schools' connection with state or county regulation.

Yet almost all communities were devoting more time and money to schooling. State reports reveal longer sessions and more regular attendance from year to year; required inspection visits by town-wide committee members subjected the teachers' practices to scrutiny. The annual reports, published by many towns, provided a forum for school committees' reform ideas. The prominent common-school crusaders had provided the arguments and the institutional outlines for consolidated districts, shared state-local authority, and professionalized teachers. Town school committees spread the gospel.

Women were crucial to the reform program. We should not forget their role as workers in common schools just because men dominated policy discussions and the most visible decision-making roles. The wage differentials that exploited women teachers allowed communities to devote the savings to other costly reforms like a longer school year and better facilities. The practice of grouping female assistants under male principal teachers in graded schools established for the first time an enduring gender-oriented hierarchy in elementary schooling. Finally, reformers relied chiefly upon women to implement the new pedagogy of "moral suasion" and to soften the abrupt transition from the protective Victorian home to the bureaucratic Victorian school. Women teachers for the early school years would be more motherly.

By 1860, urban schools were more highly structured than they had been in 1830, and consolidated rural schools in the North were more like their urban neighbors. School sessions and attendance patterns were more similar from town to town. Private schools had become more rare and more elite. Children who earlier might have gone to the less expensive pay schools now went to public schools. Rate bills and fees for public school sessions had been reduced or abolished in many areas of the North. There was a great deal more tuition-free education in 1860 than in 1830. Reformers at the state level accomplished these changes through persuasion and through local allies but also through the beginnings of centralized control and standardization, which have negative as well as positive consequences. More decisions were made farther away from neighborhoods, often by strangers—town committeemen, state superintendents, or legislators. As equity increased, conformity necessarily increased. As commonality emerged as a goal, diversity was muted or denigrated. Although public debate on the initial issues concerning systematization subsided somewhat after 1860, dissent did not end. Rural districts still fought encroachments on local control, and many Catholics went their own educational way. Various other outgroups did what they could to fight for their distinctive views and to protest a common-school system that had left major problems of equity and pluralism unsolved.

The story, then, does not end with 1860—only my portion of the story. While the germ of many later changes can be found in the antebellum cosmopolitan reform values of increased schooling, professionalization, standardization, and cultural assimilation, the unfolding of those values in practice revealed profoundly new aspects of American public-school systems during the years after 1860. Increased schooling extended to the secondary-school years, and as high-school attendance became more widespread, educators devised different curricula for different groups of children. Schools became the arbiters between family and economy in a much more programmatic way than they had been in 1860. Professionalization fostered the development of school administration as a field and of state-regulated training for all teachers. Standardization and demands for equality finally prompted the substantial racial desegregation of southern schools. The shift in the schools' basis for moral education, from doctrinal religion to generalized Christianity, continued its evolution in an ever more secular direction.

Although the years since the Civil War have witnessed these and other important changes, they can also be seen as variations and trends within a process established during the new republic's first eighty years, a period in which education underwent a profound shift toward common schools that were publicly funded, centrally regulated, and professionally managed. Two enduring legacies of the common-school reform movement are the American faith in education and the cosmopolitan ideal of inclusive public schools. School reformers believed that common schools could solve the problems of diversity, instability, and equal opportunity. That faith has been resilient in American history. Despite the periodic rediscovery that schools have not in fact solved our problems, and despite occasional periods of disillusionment with the education profession, the American common-school system has always revived, buoyed by Americans' faith that education is the best approach to most social problems. That faith is best redeemed, American leaders say, in schools that are common to all, respectful of all, and equal in their treatment of all children. Despite the cultural cost involved in having a common public-school system, and despite the public schools' manifest failure to treat children equally, Americans widely share a belief in fairness and cohesion through common schools, a belief that is the core of the cosmopolitan solution.

In the twentieth century, faith in the efficiency, the equity, and the necessity of centralized decision making has been manifested in many ways. It has meant a statewide biology curriculum for New York State, approved textbook lists in Texas, and a decree that all Wisconsin schools must teach the comparative nutritive value of dairy products and dairy substitutes. The cosmopolitan cause has enlisted Ellwood Cubberley to urge rural district consolidation in the 1920s, James Conant to praise big high schools in the 1950s, Albert Shanker to oppose urban decentralization in the 1960s, and Judge Garraty to order crosstown busing in the 1970s. Federal courts and agencies have recently asserted a version of cosmopolitanism that centers on integration, sexual equality, and secularism. At the state level, cosmopolitanism has meant financial equalization, development of standard curricula, statewide competency testing programs, and other regulatory devices aimed at standardizing and upgrading local common schooling.

What I have called the cosmopolitan solution is based on the conviction that decisions have to be more centrally directed and more standard in their application across communities in order to insure quality, progress, equity, and cultural cohesion. This impulse does not dictate the *content* of such decisions. There are probably very few people who would sympathize with all of the examples I have given of federal and state involvement in local schooling. Most people appreciate the sanction of state or federal authority for values they share and resent it for values they reject. Cosmopolitanism, then, is not a simple issue. Few people are for local control on all issues, and few favor a radical dismantling of the common public-school system in order to serve diversity.

The fifteen years during which I have been studying the history of American education have been characterized by much criticism of public schooling, from all sides. Public schools, it seems, are too permissive, too strict, too open, too bureaucratic, offensively monolithic and bland in their message, offensively pluralistic and sinful in their message, and have many other failings. I am sure that my perception of these present-day concerns has shaped my understanding of the nineteenth-century creation of common-school systems, although I have tried to render the story in the terms of the past as best I can understand them. The relationship between present-day issues and historical scholarship is problematic in both directions. Not only can current concerns shape our understanding of the past, but historians' interpretations of the past can influence policy decisions. I do not believe, however, that we can draw specific policies from historical judgments. Many paths may follow from historical developments, no matter how accurately we have drawn them.

Historians are usually reluctant to make explicit connections between their work and present policy matters, because we think that such commentary abandons the stance of detachment that helps us to treat the past on its own terms. Moreover, to leap from the 1860s to the 1980s is quite a flight. Still, when historians refuse to speculate about the policy implications of their work, others sometimes do it for them. My work portrays nineteenth-century opponents of common-school systems sympathetically, and it is critical in retrospect of the narrowness of the common-school reformers' ideology. Some readers have suggested that my interpretation supports the position of present-day critics who advocate more public aid to nonpublic schools and who maintain that the public schools' failure to teach cognitive skills effectively while grappling with ideals of equality and diversity justifies a rejection of the idea of a common-school system. For what it is worth, that is not my own view.

I believe that we need a unified, tax-supported, common-school system. I believe that the public school systems of our states and localities need to be more common in some respects, that is, more equal and more integrated. But they also need to be much more diverse in other respects—more open to different teaching and learning styles, different cultural content, different parental preferences, and different community needs. Like most people, I agree with some aspects of cosmopolitan school reform and central control while I disagree with others. My personal inclination is to support cosmopolitan solutions on constitutional issues like separation of church and state, equal rights, and free expression, which require staunch central protection whatever the views of local majorities. I am more skeptical and selective about supporting the standardization of curriculum, program organization, or learning style, which is often argued on grounds of efficiency, upgrading standards, or the superior abilities of central decision makers. The apportioning of authority among federal, state, and local levels is a delicate matter, one which will continue to be debated in the decades ahead. But that is good. Centralization should not be mindless drift or merely a matter of who is more powerful. We need not be trapped by history, nor by the language of modernization and efficiency. We must be imaginative about the control of schools.

When the American colonies asked England to give their legislatures independent authority on some matters, Parliament replied that there was no such thing as absolute authority within an absolute authority. "*Imperium in imperio*," they said, was an impossibility. For that lack of imagination they lost the American colonies. The history of American federalism is one of constantly evolving relationships between local, state, and national governments, conditioned but not mechanically determined by technological, economic, political, constitutional, and cultural changes. The debates between cosmopolitans, locals, and independents over the control and content of elementary schooling in the new republic are just one part of that larger story. The adjustment of the claims and powers of the different levels of government is an imperfect, a continual, and a bruising process. It is one of the central dynamics of American educational history, and of American political life. Local control is not virtuous merely by being closer to home, but neither is central authority superior just because it is bigger and lays claim to a cosmopolitan ideal.

Notes

CHAPTER 1

1. Lawrence Cremin, *American Education: The Colonial Experience* (New York, 1971); Kenneth Lockridge, *Literacy in Colonial New England* (New York, 1974); Carl F. Kaestle, *The Evolution of an Urban School System: New York 1750–1850* (Cambridge, Mass., 1973), ch. 1.
2. Bernard Bailyn, *The Ideological Origins of the American Revolution* (Cambridge, Mass., 1967); Gary B. Nash, *The Urban Crucible: Social Change, Political Consciousness, and the Origins of the American Revolution* (Cambridge, Mass., 1979); Gordon Wood, *The Creation of the American Republic* (Chapel Hill, 1969).
3. Noah Webster, "On the Education of Youth in America," 1790, reprinted in Frederick Rudolph, ed., *Essays on Education in the Early Republic* (Cambridge, Mass., 1965), p. 66.
4. Lyman Butterfield, ed., *Letters of Benjamin Rush* (Princeton, 1951), vol. 1, p. 388; Webster, "On the Education of Youth," p. 66.
5. Thomas Jefferson, "Bill for the More General Diffusion of Knowledge," 1779, quoted in Roy Honeywell, *The Educational Work of Thomas Jefferson* (Cambridge, Mass., 1931), p. 199.
6. Noah Webster, quoted in Jonathan Messerli, "The Columbian Complex: The Impulse to National Consolidation," *History of Education Quarterly* 7 (Winter 1967), 420, 421; Webster, "Education of Youth," p. 45; Benjamin Rush, quoted in David B. Tyack, "Forming the National Character: Paradox in the Educational Thought of the Revolutionary Generation," *Harvard Educational Review* 36 (Winter 1966), 37.
7. Benjamin Rush, "A Plan for the Establishment of Public Schools and the Diffusion of Knowledge in Pennsylvania; to Which Are Added, Thoughts Upon the Mode of Education, Proper in a Republic," in Rudolph, *Essays on Education*, pp. 16, 17.
8. Samuel Harrison Smith, "Remarks on Education," in Rudolph, *Essays on Education*, pp. 188–189.
9. Webster, "Education of Youth," p. 67.

227

10. George Clinton, speech to the New York legislature, July 1782, in Charles Z. Lincoln, ed., *State of New York, Messages from the Governors* (Albany, 1909), vol. 2, p. 183; Robert Coram, "Political Inquiries: to Which Is Added, a Plan for the General Establishment of Schools throughout the United States," in Rudolph, *Essays on Education*, p. 136.

11. On Jefferson's plan, see Gordon C. Lee, ed., *Crusade Against Ignorance: Thomas Jefferson on Education* (New York, 1961), pp. 83–92; the Rush quotation is from his "Plan for the Establishment of Public Schools," in Rudolph, *Essays on Education*, p. 5; Joseph Cabell to Thomas Jefferson, December 29, 1817, in Honeywell, *Educational Work of Jefferson*, p. 244; Thomas Jefferson to Albert Gallatin, February 15, 1817, in *ibid.*, p. 20.

12. George Clinton, speech to the New York legislature, January 1795, in Lincoln, *Messages from the Governors*, vol. 2, p. 350.

13. The New York State figures for 1800 are presented in Carl F. Kaestle and Maris A. Vinovskis, *Education and Social Change in Nineteenth-Century Massachusetts* (New York, 1980), p. 15.

CHAPTER 2

1. Heman Humphrey to Henry Barnard, Pittsfield, December 12, 1860, in Barnard, *First Century of National Existence: Educational Development* (n.p., n.d., republished from L. Stebbins, ed., *One Hundred Years' Progress of the United States*, Hartford, 1873), p. 369; Sarah Josepha Hale, *Sketches of American Character*, 6th ed. (Philadelphia, 1838), p. 121; Ira Mayhew, *A Compilation from the Annual Reports of the Superintendent of Public Instruction of the State of Michigan for the Years 1845 and 1846, with Important Additions, Embracing the Report for the Year 1847* (Detroit, 1848), p. 110.

2. A. H. Nelson, "The Little Red Schoolhouse," *Educational Review* 23 (January–May 1902), 305.

3. Warren Burton, *The District School As It Was By One Who Went To It* [1833], ed. Clifton Johnson (New York, 1928), p. 6; Horace Greeley, *Recollections of a Busy Life* (New York, 1868), p. 42; Elizabeth Buffum Chace and Lucy Buffum Lovell, *Two Quaker Sisters* (New York, 1937), p. 18; William A. Mowry, *Recollections of A New England Educator 1838–1908* (New York, 1908), pp. 16–17.

4. Hiram Orcutt, *Reminiscences of School Life; An Autobiography*

(Cambridge, Mass., 1898), pp. 14–15; Burton, *District School*, p. 48; Mowry, *Recollections*, p. 16.

5. Orcutt, *Reminiscences*, p. 15; Barnard, *First Century*, p. 369; John Burroughs, *My Boyhood* (Garden City, New York, 1922), p. 80.

6. Lloyd J. Jorgenson, *The Founding of Public Education in Wisconsin* (Madison, Wisconsin, 1956), p. 140; Theodore Dwight, *Things as They Are: or, Notes of a Traveller Through Some of the Middle and Northern States* (New York, 1834), p. 123.

7. "Recollection of Peter Parley [Samuel Goodrich]," in Barnard, *First Century*, p. 379; Chace, *Quaker Sisters*, p. 23.

8. William A. Alcott, *Confessions of a School Master* (Andover, 1839), p. 69; Burton, *District School*, pp. 25–26.

9. Alcott, *Confessions*, pp. 98, 100; Eliphalet Nott to Henry Barnard, January 1861, in Barnard, *First Century*, p. 374; James M. Sims, *The Story of My Life* (New York, 1884), p. 56.

10. Barnard, *First Century*, p. 374; *New York Teacher* 6 (January 1857), pp. 164–165.

11. Sims, *Story of My Life*, p. 66; *Report of the Superintendent of Public Instruction of the Commonwealth of Pennsylvania for the Year Ending June 1, 1877* (Harrisburg, 1878), pp. 16–19.

12. Benjamin H. Matteson, "New York Schools 100 Years Ago," *New York History* 17 (1936), 156; *First Annual Report of the State Superintendent of Common Schools* (Montpelier, Vermont, 1846), p. 7; *Second Annual Report . . .* (St. Albans, Vermont, 1847), p. 13; Robert G. Bone, "Education in Illinois Before 1857," *Journal of the Illinois Historical Society* 50 (1957), 131.

13. Humphrey to Barnard, in Barnard, *First Century*, p. 371; Orcutt, *Reminiscences*, pp. 49–50.

14. Humphrey to Barnard, in Barnard, *First Century*, p. 370; Mowry, *Recollections*, p. 47.

15. On this process in the Rochester area see Paul Johnson, *A Shopkeeper's Millennium: Society and Revivals in Rochester, New York 1815–1837* (New York, 1978). See also Alan A. Dawley, *Class and Community: The Industrial Revolution in Lynn* (Cambridge, Mass., 1976), and Rolla Tryon, *Household Manufactures in the United States, 1640–1860* (Chicago, 1917).

16. Kaestle and Vinovskis, *Education and Social Change*, pp. 14–15; *New York Enquirer*, quoted in Paulson's *American Daily Advisor* (Philadelphia), March 6, 1829.

17. Thomas B. Stockwell, ed., *A History of Public Education in*

Rhode Island, from 1636 to 1876 (Providence, 1876), pp. 19, 34, 282–283, 384–385; Wickersham, *Education in Pennsylvania,* pp. 182–183.

18. Frederick Rudolph, ed., *Essays on Education in the Early Republic* (Cambridge, Mass., 1965), p. 28.

19. Thomas Woody, *A History of Women's Education in the United States,* 2 vols. (New York, 1929), vol. 1, pp. 145–146; *Salem Register,* May 21, 1827; on literacy, see Kenneth A. Lockridge, *Literacy in Colonial New England* (New York, 1974), p. 39, Maris A. Vinovskis and Richard Bernard, "Beyond Catharine Beecher: Female Education in the Antebellum Period," *Signs* 3 (Summer 1978), 856–869, Nancy F. Cott, *The Bonds of Womanhood: "Woman's Sphere" in New England, 1780–1835* (New Haven, 1977), p. 101, and Lee Soltow and Edward Stevens, *The Rise of Literacy and the Common School in the United States: A Socioeconomic Analysis to 1870* (Chicago, 1981), pp. 156–158. On female academies, see Woody, *Women's Education,* pp. 216, 195–196.

20. Fletcher H. Swift, *A History of Public Permanent Common School Funds in the United States, 1795–1905* (New York, 1911), pp. 98–99, 235, 239, 352.

CHAPTER 3

1. Carl F. Kaestle, *The Evolution of an Urban School System: New York City, 1750–1850* (Cambridge, Mass., 1973), pp. 41–55; Stanley K. Schultz, *The Culture Factory: Boston Public Schools, 1789–1860* (New York, 1973), p. 24.

2. Stephen Allen to [?], May 14, 1826, Stephen Allen Letters, typescript, New York Historical Society, p. 45.

3. Patrick Colquhoun to Thomas Eddy, London, February 16, 1803, in Samuel L. Knapp, *Life of Thomas Eddy* (London, 1836), p. 149; *New York Daily Advertiser,* January 27, 1791. On urban problems of the Revolutionary and early national periods see Carl Bridenbaugh, *Cities in Revolt: Urban Life in America, 1743–1776* (New York, 1955); Gary B. Nash, *The Urban Crucible: Social Change, Political Consciousness and the Origins of the American Revolution* (Cambridge, Mass., 1979); and Raymond A. Mohl, *Poverty in New York, 1783–1825* (New York, 1971).

4. The Eddy quotation is found in Knapp, *Thomas Eddy,* p. 62. A more fully documented version of the following section appeared

in Carl F. Kaestle, " 'Between the Scylla of Brutal Ignorance and the Charybdis of a Literary Education': Elite Attitudes toward Mass Schooling in Early Industrial England and America," in Lawrence Stone, ed., *Schooling and Society* (Baltimore, 1976), ch. 7.

5. John Weyland, *A letter to a country gentleman on the education of the lower orders . . .* (London, 1808), p. 5.

6. Benjamin Shaw in the British and Foreign School Society, *Report* (London, 1817), p. 58.

7. E. E. Hale, ed., *Joseph Tuckerman on the elevation of the poor; a selection from his reports as minister at large in Boston* (Boston, 1874), p. 116.

8. On the Quakers' activities, see James B. Stewart, *Holy Warriors: The Abolitionists and American Slavery* (New York, 1976), pp. 16–17; Sydney V. James, *People Among Peoples: Quaker Benevolence in Eighteenth-Century America* (Cambridge, Mass., 1963); and James P. Wickersham, *A History of Education in Pennsylvania* (Lancaster, 1886), pp. 150–151 and 281–295. On black education in the early national period, see John L. Rury, Education and Black Community Development in Ante-Bellum New York City (unpublished M.A. thesis, City College, City University of New York, 1975); Claudia Christie Foster, Motives, Means and Ends in Gradual Abolitionist Education, 1785 to 1830 (unpublished Ph.D. thesis, Columbia University, 1977), pp. 124–130; Arthur O. White, Blacks and Education in Antebellum Massachusetts: Strategies for Social Mobility (unpublished Ed.D. thesis, State University of New York at Buffalo, 1971), p. 101; and Charles C. Andrews, *History of the New York African Free School* (New York, 1830). The Shaw quotation is found in the *Report of the British and Foreign School Society to the General Meeting, May, 1817* (London, 1817), pp. 56–57.

9. Andrews, *African Free School*, pp. 132, 117; Rury, Education and Black Community, p. 12.

10. William O. Bourne, *History of the Public School Society of the City of New York* (New York, 1870), p. 3.

11. See Carl F. Kaestle, ed., *Joseph Lancaster and the Monitorial School System: A Documentary History* (New York, 1973). For a recent argument in favor of older students teaching younger students see Alan Gartner, Mary Kohler, and Frank Riessman, *Children Teach Children* (New York, 1971).

12. Charles C. Ellis, *Lancasterian Schools in Philadelphia* (Philadel-

phia, 1907), pp. 5–10; Bernard C. Steiner, *The History of Education in Connecticut* (Washington, Bureau of Education, 1893), p. 36; Charles Coon, *Public Education in North Carolina, A Documentary History, 1790–1840*, 2 vols. (Raleigh, 1908), vol. 1, pp. 140–141; William H. Shannon, Public Education in Maryland (1825–1868) with Special Emphasis upon the 1860's (unpublished Ed.D. dissertation, University of Maryland, 1964), p. 50; Edgar W. Knight, "Interest in the South in Lancasterian Methods," *North Carolina Historical Review* 25 (July 1948), 382.

13.   The *American Register* comment is quoted in the British and Foreign School Society, *Annual Report* (1817); Detroit *Gazette*, January 25, 1822, quoted in Mary Rosalita, *Education in Detroit Prior to 1850* (Lansing, 1928), p. 185; B. O. Williams, "My Recollections of the Early Schools of Detroit That I attended From the Year 1816 to 1819," in Kaestle, *Joseph Lancaster*, p. 169.

14.   Anon., "My School Days in New York City Forty Years Ago," *The New York Teacher and American Educational Monthly* 6 (March 1869) 94–96.

15.   Joseph Stratford, *Robert Raikes and others; the Founders of Sunday Schools* (London, 1880); Philadelphia First Day or Sunday School Society, Constitution, quoted in Lewis G. Pray, *The History of Sunday Schools and of Religious Education, from the Earliest Times* (Boston, 1847), pp. 205–206. See also Theodore F. Savage, *The Presbyterian Church in New York City* (New York, 1949), p. 58; and Vera Butler, *Education as Revealed by New England Newspapers Prior to 1850* (Philadelphia, 1935), p. 246.

16.   Henry Anstice, *History of St. George's Church* (New York, 1911), p. 89; Anne M. Boylan, "The Nursery of the Church": Evangelical Protestant Sunday Schools, 1820–1880 (unpublished Ph.D. dissertation, University of Wisconsin, 1973), Ch. 1; Butler, *Education as Revealed by New England Newspapers*, p. 251. On Sunday schools in rural areas see David Tyack and Elisabeth Hansot, *Managers of Virtue: School Leadership in America, 1820–1980* (New York, 1982), pp. 34–39.

17.   Ella Gilbert Ives, *The Evolution of a Teacher* (Boston, 1915), p. 36.

18.   John F. C. Harrison, ed., *Utopianism and Education: Robert Owen and the Owenites* (New York, 1968), pp. 173–174.

19. See John Jenkins, Infant Schools and the Development of Public Primary Schooling in Selected American Cities Before the Civil War (unpublished Ph.D. dissertation, University of Wisconsin; 1978); Dean May and Maris A. Vinovskis, "A Ray of Millennial Light: Early Education and Social Reform in the Infant School Movement in Massachusetts, 1826–1840," in Tamara K. Hareven, ed., *Family and Kin in Urban Communities*, 1700–1930 (New York, 1977), and Butler, *Education as Revealed by New England Educators*, ch. 10.

20. George Washington Bethune, *Memoirs of Joanna Bethune* (New York, 1864), p. 215; Sylvester Graham, *Thy Kingdom Come: A Discourse on the Importance of Infant and Sunday Schools* (Philadelphia, 1831), pp. 4–16, 13; May and Vinovskis, "Millennial Light," p. 62.

21. William Russell, *A Lecture on the Infant School System of Education and the Extent to Which It May Be Advantageously Applied to All Primary Schools* (Boston: Hilliard, Gray, Little, and Wilkins, 1830); *Ladies' Magazine* 2 (February 1829), 89–90.

22. Mathew Carey, *Miscellaneous Essays* (Philadelphia, 1830), pp. 284–287.

23. Theodore Dwight, *Things As They Are: or, Notes of a Traveller Through some of the Middle and Northern States* (New York, 1834), p. 120.

24. Edward Everett Hale, *A New England Boyhood*, in *The Works of Edward Everett Hale* (Boston, 1900), vol. 6, pp. 17–18, 21, 29, 40–42.

25. Joseph Cogswell to Robert L. Livingston, Northampton, Massachusetts, March 29, 1828, and March 31, 1829, MS, New York Historical Society.

26. Maria Turnbull to Governor Jonathan Turnbull, December 14, 1800, and Maria Turnbull to Mrs. Jonathan Turnbull, March 5, 1801, in Helen M. Morgan, ed., *A Season in New York, 1801: Letters of Harriet and Maria Turnbull* (Pittsburgh, 1969), pp. 63, 133–134.

27. Thomas Earle and Charles Congdon, eds., *Annals of the General Society of Mechanics and Tradesmen of the City of New York from 1785 to 1880* (New York, 1882), p. 69.

28. John S. Hopkins, Schenectady: A Case-Study in the Development of Education in New York State from 1800 to 1854 (unpublished honors thesis, Union College, Schenectady, 1965); Jeanette Neisular, *The History of Education in Schenectady,*

1661–62—1961–62 (Schenectady, 1964); Reports of the Commissioners of Common Schools, Glenville, New York, 1821–1841, MS in possession of Mr. Donald Kieffer, Glenville historian.

29. New York Free School Society, *Annual Report* (New York, 1825), p. 7; and Kaestle, *The Evolution of an Urban School System*, ch. 6.

30. Wickersham, *A History of Education in Pennsylvania*, p. 287.

31. William Bentley, *The Diary of William Bentley*, 4 vols. (Salem, Essex Institute, 1905–1914), vol. 3, p. 365 (June 13, 1808); Carl F. Kaestle and Maris A. Vinovskis, *Education and Social Change in Nineteenth-Century Massachusetts* (New York, 1979), ch. 2; Salem, Mass., Mayor, *Annual Report . . . 1841–42* (Salem, 1843), p. 7.

32. The New York City and Salem enrollment estimates are given in Kaestle and Vinovskis, *Education and Social Change*, p. 19.

CHAPTER 4

1. Douglas C. North, *The Economic Growth of the United States, 1790–1860* (New York, 1966); Jeffrey G. Williamson, "Antebellum Urbanization in the American Northeast," *Journal of Economic History* 25 (December 1965), 592–608; *Historical Statistics of the United States: Colonial Times to 1970*, 2 vols. (Washington, 1975).

2. The estimate of workers in establishments numbering over twenty employees is from Robert B. Zevin, *The Growth of Manufacturing in Early Nineteenth-Century New England* (New York, 1975), pp. 10–11; Richard Cobden, *England, Ireland and America*, in *Political Writings of Richard Cobden*, 2 vols. (London, 1867), vol. 1, p. 54; Per Adam Siljeström, *The Educational Institutions of the United States* (London, 1853), p. 200; Carl Bode, *Antebellum Culture*, rev. ed. (Carbondale, Illinois, 1970), p. 116; Alfred M. Lee, *The Daily Newspaper in America* (New York, 1947), p. 718.

3. For the work discipline thesis see Sidney Pollard, "Factory Discipline in the Industrial Revolution," *Economic History Review*, 16 (1963), 254–271; E. P. Thompson, "Time, Work, Discipline and Industrial Capitalism," *Past & Present*, 38 (1967), 84; Paul Faler, "Cultural Aspects of the Industrial Revolution: Lynn, Mass., Shoemakers and Industrial Morality, 1826–1860," *Labor*

History, 15 (1974), 367–394; Alexander J. Field, Educational Reform and Manufacturing Development in Mid-Nineteenth Century Massachusetts (unpublished Ph.D. dissertation, Univ. of California, Berkeley, 1974), pp. ii–iii; Samuel Bowles and Herbert Gintis, *Schooling in Capitalist America: Educational Reform and the Contradictions of Economic Life* (New York, 1976), pp. 174–175. See also Daniel T. Rodgers, *The Work Ethic in Industrial America, 1850–1920* (Chicago, 1978).

4. See Horace Mann, *Seventh Annual Report of the Board of Education* (Boston, 1844); Calvin E. Stowe, *Report on Elementary Public Instruction in Europe* (Columbus, 1837); Henry Barnard, *National Education in Europe*, 2nd ed. (Hartford, 1854).

5. Oscar and Mary Flug Handlin, *Commonwealth: A Study of the Role of Government in the American Economy: Massachusetts, 1774–1861*, rev. ed. (Cambridge, Mass., 1969); Louis Hartz, *Economic Policy and Democratic Thought: Pennsylvania, 1776–1860* (Cambridge, Mass., 1948); the Seward quotation is found in Rush Welter, *Popular Education and Democratic Thought in America* (New York, 1962), pp. 82–83.

CHAPTER 5

1. John Plamenatz, *Ideology* (London, 1970), p. 72. For a more extended discussion of the concept of ideology and its use, see Carl F. Kaestle, "Ideology and American Educational History," *History of Education Quarterly* 22 (Summer 1982), and the references cited there.

2. Marvin Meyers, *The Jacksonian Persuasion: Politics and Belief* (New York, 1960), p. 206. Excellent analyses of the social beliefs of antebellum political and educational leaders are found in Daniel W. Howe, *The Political Culture of the American Whigs* (Chicago, 1979); Eric Foner, *Free Soil, Free Labor, Free Men: The Ideology of the Republican Party Before the Civil War* (New York, 1970); John Higham, "Hanging Together: Divergent Unities in American History," *Journal of American History* 61 (June 1974); Merle Curti, *The Social Ideas of American Educators* (New York, 1935); and Anthony F. C. Wallace, *Rockdale: The Growth of an American Village in the Early Industrial Revolution* (New York, 1978).

3. Paul E. Johnson, *A Shopkeeper's Millennium: Society and Revivals in Rochester, New York, 1815–1837* (New York, 1978);

Mary Ryan, *Cradle of the Middle Class: The Family in Oneida County, New York, 1790–1865* (New York, 1981).

4. On republican ideology, see Bernard Bailyn, *The Ideological Origins of the American Revolution* (Cambridge, Mass., 1967); Gordon S. Wood, *The Creation of the American Republic, 1776–1787* (Chapel Hill, 1969); and J. G. A. Pocock, "Virtue and Commerce in the Eighteenth Century," *Journal of Interdisciplinary History* 3 (Summer 1972), 119–134.

5. John Pierce, Superintendent of Common Schools, *Annual Report* (Ann Arbor, 1837), p. 5; Elia Cornelius, *Sermon . . . Salem Society for the Moral and Religious Instruction of the Poor* (Salem, 1824), pp. 5–6; New York Association for Improving the Condition of the Poor, *Fourth Annual Report* (New York, 1847), p. 13.

6. Superintendent of Common Schools, *First Annual Report* (Montpelier, 1846), p. 58; J. Orville Taylor, *The District School* (Philadelphia, 1835), p. 281; Frederick Packard, *Thoughts on the Condition and Prospects of Popular Education in the United States* (Philadelphia, 1836), Preface.

7. Lyman Cobb, *Cobb's Juvenile Reader No. 2* (Oxford, New York, 1833), pp. 65, 68; Gould Brown, *The Institutes of English Grammar* (New York, 1853), pp. 23–24; Marcius Wilson, *The Third Reader of the School and Family Series* (New York, 1860); Joseph Burleigh, *The Thinker* (1855), quoted in Ruth Miller Elson, *Guardians of Tradition: American Schoolbooks of the Nineteenth Century* (Lincoln, Nebraska, 1964), pp. 253–254.

8. Jacob Abbott, *Rollo at Work; or, the Way to be Industrious* (New York, 1855), pp. 51–52, 57.

9. Oliver Angell, *The Select Reader* (Philadelphia, 1833), Washington Irving, "The Wife," in Richard Parker and J. Madison Watson, *The National Fourth Reader* (New York, 1863).

10. Horace Mann, *A Few Thoughts on the Powers and Duties of Woman* (Syracuse, 1853), p. 79; Catharine Beecher, *A Treatise on Domestic Economy* (New York, 1841).

11. Mann, *Powers of Woman*, pp. 57, 70; Beecher, *Domestic Economy*, p. 49; Stephen Simpson, *The Workingman's Manual: A New Theory of Political Economy* (Philadelphia, 1831), p. 206–207; Salem School Committee, *Annual Report* (Salem, 1848).

12. See Peter Slater, Views of Children and Child-Rearing During the Early National Period (unpublished Ph.D. dissertation, University of California at Berkeley, 1971); and Philip Greven, *The*

Protestant Temperament: Patterns of Child-Rearing, Religious Experience and the Self in Early America (New York, 1977).

13. Henry Ward Beecher, *Seven Lectures to Young Men*, rev. ed. (Boston, 1858), p. 54; William G. McLaughlin, *The Meaning of Henry Ward Beecher* (New York, 1970), p. 160.

14. Jesse Olney, *Practical System of Modern Geography*, 21st ed. (New York, 1836), pp. 167, 183, 187; Elson, *Guardians of Tradition*, pp. 87–88, 157; William Stanton, *The Leopard's Spots: Scientific Attitudes Toward Race in America, 1815–59* (Chicago, 1960); Stanley Schultz, *The Culture Factory: Boston Public Schools, 1789–1860* (New York, 1973), p. 196; Arthur O. White, Blacks and Education in Antebellum Massachusetts (unpublished Ph.D. dissertation, State University of New York at Buffalo, 1971), p. 222.

15. See David J. Rothman, *The Discovery of the Asylum: Social Order and Disorder in the New Republic* (New York, 1971).

16. Taylor, *District School*, pp. 270–271; Timothy Dwight, *Travels in New England and New York* (London, 1823), vol. 4, p. 462; John McVickar, *First Lessons in Political Economy*; Francis Wayland, *Elements of Political Economy* (New York, 1837), p. 113; Theodore Sedgwick, *Private and Public Economy* (New York, 1836), p. 23. On the political economy of early America, see Joseph Dorfman, *The Economic Mind in American Civilization, 1606–1865* (New York, 1946); Drew R. McCoy, *The Elusive Republic: Political Economy in Jeffersonian America* (Chapel Hill, 1980); Paul Conkin, *Self-Evident Truths* (Bloomington, Indiana, 1974); and John F. Kasson, *Civilizing the Machine: Technology and Republican Values in America, 1776–1900* (New York, 1976).

17. Superintendent of Common Schools, *Report* (Detroit, 1837), p. 33.

18. Superintendent of Common Schools, *Annual Report* (Montpelier, Vermont, 1946), p. 33.

19. Samuel G. Goodrich, *The Young American* (New York, 1845), p. 41; Anon., *The Progressive Reader* (Montpelier, 1834), pp. 144–145; Ira Mayhew, *A Compilation from the Annual Reports of the Superintendent of Public Instruction* (Detroit, 1848), p. 6.

20. Beecher, *Domestic Economy*, p. 25; Elson, *Guardians of Tradition*, pp. 58, 46, 47; Thomas King, *The Railroad Jubilee: Two Discourses Delivered in Hollis Street Meeting House* (Boston,

1851), p. 32. See Ray A. Billington, *The Protestant Crusade: 1800–1860* (New York, 1938).

21. Jesse Olney, *History of the United States*, quoted in Merton England, "The Democratic Faith in American Schoolbooks, 1783–1860," *American Quarterly* 15 (1963), 197.

22. King, *Railroad Jubilee*, pp. 17–18. On millennial beliefs in this period see Ira V. Brown, "Watchers for the Second Coming: The Millenarian Tradition in America," *Mississippi Valley Historical Review* 39 (December 1952), 441–458; Whitney Cross, *The Burned Over District: The Social and Intellectual History of Enthusiastic Religion in Western New York, 1800–1850* (Ithaca, New York, 1950); and Lois Banner, "Religious Benevolence as Social Control: A Critique of an Interpretation," *Journal of American History* 60 (June 1973).

23. J. Orville Taylor, *The District School*, 3rd ed. (Philadelphia, 1835), pp. 105, 110; Alonzo Potter, *The School and the Schoolmaster* (New York, 1844), part I, pp. 67, 73–74; Horace Mann, *Eighth Annual Report* (Boston, 1845), pp. 122–129.

24. Charles Northend, *The Teacher and the Parent: A Treatise on Common School Education* (Boston, 1853), pp. 106–107; Superintendent of Public Instruction, *Annual Report* (Springfield, 1855), p. 5.

25. Superintendent of Schools, *Annual Report* (Brooklyn, 1851), pp. 117–118; Superintendent of Public Instruction, *Annual Report* (Springfield, 1862), p. 120. On religion in the common schools see Robert Michaelsen, *Piety in the Public School* (New York, 1970); and David B. Tyack, "Onward Christian Soldiers: Religion in the American Common School" in Paul Nash, ed., *History and Education* (New York, 1970).

26. Henry Steele Commager, ed., *Noah Webster's American Spelling Book* (New York, 1962), p. 4; New York Public School Society, Executive Committee Minutes, July 6, 1843, cited in Carl F. Kaestle, *The Evolution of an Urban School System: New York, 1750–1850* (Cambridge, Mass., 1973), p. 144.

27. George S. Hillard, quoted in Edward Twisleton, *Evidence as to the Religious Working of the Common Schools in the State of Massachusetts* (London, 1854), p. 59.

28. Henry Barnard, Introduction, in Philobiblius [Linus P. Brockett], *History and Progress of Education* (New York, 1859), p. 17.

CHAPTER 6

1. Thaddeus Stevens, in the *Gettysburg Compiler*, July 29, 1826, quoted in Donald J. Smith, Thaddeus Stevens and the Politics of Educational Reform, 1825–1868 (unpublished Ed.D. dissertation, Rutgers University, 1968), p. 22; Calvin Stowe, *Report on Elementary Public Instruction in Europe* (Columbus, Ohio, 1837), p. 7; William Seward, Annual Message, 1839, in George E. Baker, ed., *The Life of William H. Seward, with Selections from his Works* (New York, 1855), p. 212. On the common-school reform movement see Lawrence A. Cremin, *American Education: The National Experience, 1783–1876* (New York, 1980); David Tyack and Elisabeth Hansot, *Managers of Virtue: Public School Leadership in America, 1820–1980* (New York, 1982); and Frederick M. Binder, *The Age of the Common School, 1830–1865* (New York, 1974).

2. On enrollment in New York and Massachusetts see Carl F. Kaestle and Maris A. Vinovskis, *Education and Social Change in Nineteenth-Century Massachusetts* (New York, 1980); estimates for the other states were calculated from annual state school reports and U.S. Census figures. See also Albert Fishlow, "The American Common School Revival: Fact or Fancy?" in Henry Rosovsky, ed., *Industrialization in Two Systems* (New York, 1966). The detailed community studies are: Carl F. Kaestle and Maris A. Vinovskis, "From Fireside to Factory: School Entry and School Leaving in Nineteenth-Century Massachusetts," in Tamara K. Hareven, ed., *Transitions: The Family and the Life Course in Historical Perspective* (New York, 1978); Charles Barquist, Common Schooling in the Nineteenth Century: A Quantitative Study of the Determinants of School Attendance in a Michigan County in 1850 (unpublished senior honors thesis, University of Michigan, 1975); Lage Anderson, School Attendance in Chicago: 1860 (unpublished seminar paper, University of Wisconsin, 1973).

3. Charles Andrews, *History of the New York African Free School* (New York, 1830), p. 113; Matthew H. Smith, *Sunshine and Shadow in New York* (Hartford, 1869) p. 206.

4. George E. McNeill, *Factory Children* (Boston, 1875), p. 29; Peltz report, Pennsylvania, *Journal of the Senate* 1 (December, 1937), 323.

5. Massachusetts, *House Documents* (Boston, 1866), document 98, p. 8.
6. Carl F. Kaestle and Maris A. Vinovskis, "From Apron Strings to ABC's: Parents, Children and Schooling in Nineteenth-Century Massachusetts," in John Demos and Sarane Boocock, eds., *Turning Points: Historical and Sociological Essays on the Family* (Chicago, *American Journal of Sociology* supplement 84, 1978–79).
7. Superintendent of Common Schools, *Eleventh Annual Report* (Harrisburg, 1845), p. 7; Superintendent of Common Schools, *Annual Report* (Albany, 1856), p. 49; Superintendent of Schools, *Fourth Report* (Chicago, 1858), p. 42, and *Fifth Report* (Chicago, 1859), p. 4.
8. George H. Martin, *The Evolution of the Massachusetts Public School System* (New York, 1894), pp. 158, 184.
9. Horace Mann, in *Common School Journal* 3 (1841), 285; J. Orville Taylor, in *Common School Assistant* 2 (1837), 41; Superintendent of Common Schools, *Seventh Annual Report* (Hartford, 1852), pp. 50–51; Superintendent of Common Schools, *Report* (Detroit, 1837), p. 40.
10. Carl F. Kaestle, *The Evolution of an Urban School System, 1750–1850* (Cambridge, Mass., 1973), p. 89; Kaestle and Vinovskis, *Education and Social Change in Nineteenth-Century Massachusetts*, pp. 19, 35; Lloyd P. Jorgenson, *The Founding of Public Education in Wisconsin* (Madison, 1956), p. 47; John W. Stearns, ed., *The Columbian History of Education in Wisconsin* (Milwaukee, 1893), p. 21.
11. Hiram Orcutt, *Reminiscences of School Life* (Cambridge, Mass., 1898), p. 26; George F. Miller, *The Academy System of the State of New York* (Albany, 1922), pp. 40, 42; John Wurts, report on education, *Journal of the Senate* (Harrisburg, 1822), p. 493.
12. Edward Hitchcock, *The American Academic System Defended* (1845), excerpted in Theodore R. Sizer, ed., *The Age of the Academies* (New York, 1964), pp. 99, 100, 111.
13. Kaestle, *Evolution of an Urban School System*, p. 175–176; Superintendent of Common Schools, *Third Annual Report* (Hartford, 1848), pp. 15–16; Hiram H. Barney, *Report on the American System of Graded Free Schools* (Cincinnati, 1851), pp. 9, 10.
14. Alexander Inglis, *The Rise of the High School in Massachusetts* (New York, 1911), p. 48 and *passim*; Miller, *Academy System*.

15. Barney, *Graded Free Schools*, pp. 26–27; Anderson, School Attendance in Chicago; Kaestle, *Evolution of an Urban School System*, pp. 107–108; the Salem study by Kaestle is unpublished.
16. On Trempeleau County see Merle Curti, *The Making of an American Community* (Stanford, 1959), pp. 384–387; on Mann's lists, see Kaestle and Vinovskis, *Education and Social Change in Nineteenth-Century Massachusetts*, p. 196.
17. Samuel Lewis, cited in Keith Melder, "Woman's High Calling: The Teaching Profession in America, 1830–1860," *American Studies* 13 (Fall 1972), 22; Michigan wages are given in Ann Weingarten, Women Common School Teachers in Michigan, 1836–1860 (unpublished senior honors thesis, University of Michigan, 1976), for Wisconsin in Martha E. Coons, The Feminization of the Wisconsin Teaching Force, 1850–1880 (unpublished seminar paper, University of Wisconsin, 1976), and for Massachusetts in Richard M. Barnard and Maris A. Vinovskis, "The Female School Teacher in Antebellum Massachusetts," *Journal of Social History* 10 (Spring 1977).
18. Superintendent of Public Instruction, *Annual Report* (Madison, 1867), p. 13; Philip L. White, *Beekmantown, New York: Forest Frontier to Farm Community* (Austin, 1979), p. 233.
19. Bernard and Vinovskis, "Female Teacher"; Coons, Feminization of the Wisconsin Teaching Force; Weingarten, Women Teachers in Michigan. See also Myra Strober and David Tyack, "Why Do Women Teach and Men Manage? A Report on Research on Schools," *Signs* 5 (Spring 1980), 494–503, which makes a more complex argument about the rural-urban dimension of the feminization of teaching.
20. Ella Gilbert Ives, *The Evolution of a Teacher* (Boston, 1915), p. 99; the Emma Willard quote is from a report of a teachers' institute at Oneida, New York, reprinted in Ira Mayhew, *A Compilation from the Annual Reports of the Superintendent of Public Instruction of the State of Michigan* (Detroit, 1848), p. 40.
21. Thomas Woody, *A History of Women's Education in the United States* (New York, 1929), p. 465.
22. J. Orville Taylor, *The District School,* 3rd ed. (Philadelphia, 1835), p. 85.
23. Sheldon E. Davis, *Educational Journals in the Nineteenth Century* (Washington, 1917), pp. 76–82; *Ohio Journal of Education* 5 (1856); Richard Thursfield, *Henry Barnard's American Journal of Education* (Baltimore, 1945), pp. 37–38.

24. David N. Camp, *Recollections of a Long and Active Life* (New Britain, Connecticut, 1917), p. 27; William A. Mowry, *Recollections of a New England Educator 1838–1908* (New York, 1908), p. 55; the Barnard quote is found in Paul H. Mattingly, *The Classless Profession: American Schoolmen in the Nineteenth Century* (New York, 1975), p. 67; the Wisconsin estimate is from Albert Salisbury, *Historical Sketch of Normal Instruction in Wisconsin 1846–1876* (Madison, 1876), pp. 80–82; the Michigan estimates are in Weingarten, Women Teachers in Michigan, p. 61.

25. Arthur O. Norton, ed., *The First State Normal School in America: The Journals of Cyrus Peirce and Mary Swift*, (Cambridge, Mass., 1926), pp. xiv, xlvii.

26. Spencer's views are cited in William French, "How We Began to Train Teachers in New York," *New York History* 17 (1936) 187; on the Albany normal school see *An Historical Sketch of the State Normal College at Albany* (Albany, 1895); on Canandaigua see Miller, *Academy System*, p. 167.

27. White makes the contrast between the number of academy-trained teachers and the number of school districts in New York in his *Beekmantown*, p. 240; the Michigan estimates are from Weingarten, p. 56; Superintendent of Public Instruction, *Second Biennial Report* (Springfield, 1858), p. 63; the development of normal schools in Massachusetts is analyzed in David A. Gould, Policy and Pedagogues: School Reform and Teacher Professionalization in Massachusetts, 1840–1920 (unpublished Ph.D. dissertation, Brandeis University, 1977).

28. Curti, *Making of an American Community*, pp. 387–388; White, *Beekmantown*, pp. 237–238.

29. Superintendent of Common Schools, *Seventh Annual Report* (Hartford, 1852), p. 33; Superintendent of Public Instruction, *Report* (Albany, 1854), p. 120.

30. Superintendent of Common Schools, *Seventh Annual Report* (Hartford, 1852), p. 34; George B. Emerson, in the *Common School Journal* 2 (1840), 53.

31. Barney, *Graded Free Schools*, pp. 10, 17.

32. Superintendent of Common Schools, *Second Annual Report* (Montpelier, 1847), p. 39, and *Sixth Annual Report* (Montpelier, 1851), p. 41; S. S. Randall, *The Common School System of the State of New York* (Troy, 1851), p. 163; Herman K. Kuehner, A History of the Development of the Common Ele-

mentary Free School from 1850 to 1860 in Massachusetts, Indiana, and Wisconsin (unpublished Ph.D. dissertation, University of Wisconsin, 1926), p. 87; Superintendent of Common Schools, *Annual Report* (Harrisburg, 1855), p. 12.

CHAPTER 7

1. Horace Mann's manuscript Journal for January 5, 1840, quoted in Carl F. Kaestle and Maris A. Vinovskis, *Education and Social Change in Nineteenth-Century Massachusetts* (New York, 1980), p. 214; George H. Martin, *The Evolution of the Massachusetts Public School System* (New York, 1894), p. 184.

2. For the imposition argument see Michael B. Katz, *The Irony of Early School Reform: Educational Innovation in Mid-Nineteenth Century Massachusetts* (Cambridge, Massachusetts, 1968), and his *Class, Bureaucracy and Schools: The Illusion of Educational Change in America*, 2nd ed. (New York, 1975). For the conflict theme see Samuel Bowles and Herbert Gintis, *Schooling in Capitalist America* (New York, 1976).

3. On organized labor and educational reform in antebellum America see Frank Tracy Carleton, *Economic Influences upon Educational Progress in the United States, 1820–1850* (Madison, 1908); R. V. Curoe, *Educational Attitudes and Policies of Organized Labor in the United States* (New York, 1926); Joan L. Stachiw, The Contributions of the American Working Man's Movement to the Establishment of Common Schools in New York and Pennsylvania between 1828 and 1842 (unpublished Ed.D. dissertation, Pennsylvania State University, 1963); and Jay Pawa, The Attitudes of Labor Organizations in New York State toward Public Education, 1829–1890 (unpublished Ed.D. dissertation, Columbia University, 1964).

4. *Mechanics' Free Press* (Philadelphia), September 20, 1828, and September 26, 1829, quoted in Stachiw, Working Man's Movement, p. 150; John R. Commons, *Documentary History of American Industrial Society*, 11 vols. (Cleveland, 1911), vol. 5, p. 158; (Albany) *Workingman's Advocate*, October 30, 1830, quoted in Stachiw, Working Man's Movement, p. 142; the Delaware quotation is in Ellwood P. Cubberley, *Public Education in the United States* (Boston, rev. ed., 1934), p. 174; the National Trades Union statement is reprinted in Commons, *Documentary History*, vol. 6, p. 207.

5. *Mechanics' Magazine* 4 (September 20, 1834), 180; Daniel Appleton White, *An Address Delivered at Ipswich, Before the Essex County Lyceum* (Salem, 1830), pp. 27–29.

6. Timothy Claxton, *Memoir of a Mechanic, Being a Sketch of the Life of Timothy Claxton, Written by Himself, Together with Miscellaneous Papers* (Boston, 1839); see also Marie L. Ahearn, The Rhetoric of Work and Vocation in Some Popular Northern Writings Before 1860 (unpublished Ph.D. dissertation, Brown University, 1965).

7. On England see Brian Simon, *Studies in the History of Education, 1780–1870* (London, 1960) and Harold Silver, *The Concept of Popular Education* (London, 1965). On the social class composition of early workingmen's parties see Walter Hugins, *Jacksonian Democracy and the Working Class: A Study of the New York Workingman's Movement, 1829–1837* (Stanford, 1960); William G. Shade, "The 'Working-Class' and Educational Reform in Early America: The Case of Providence, Rhode Island," *The Historian* 39 (November 1976), 1–23; and Donald S. McPherson, "The Mechanics' Institute and the Pittsburgh Workingman, 1830–1840," *Western Pennsylvania Historical Magazine* 56 (April 1973), 155–169.

8. On New Harmony and the Owenite movement see John F. C. Harrison, *Quest for the New Moral World: Robert Owen and the Owenites in Britain and America* (London, 1968); Harrison, ed., *Utopianism and Education: Robert Owen and the Owenites* (New York, 1968); Arthur E. Bestor, *Backwoods Utopias: The Sectarian and Owenite Phases of Communitarian Socialism in America, 1663–1829* (Philadelphia, 1950); and Bestor, ed., *Education and Reform at New Harmony: Correspondence of William Maclure and Marie Duclos Fretageot, 1820–1833* (Indianapolis, 1948). The Maclure quotation is given in Bestor, *Backwoods Utopias*, p. 157.

9. Maclure, *Opinions on Various Subjects* (1838) in Harrison, ed., *Utopianism and Education*, pp. 232–252.

10. New Harmony *Gazette*, May 17, 1826. See R. W. Leopold, *Robert Dale Owen* (Cambridge, Mass., 1940); Elinor Pancoast and Anne E. Lincoln, *The Incorrigible Idealist: Robert Dale Owen in America* (Bloomington, Indiana, 1940), and William R. Waterman, *Frances Wright* (New York, 1924).

11. *The Free Enquirer* (New York), April 22, 1829; on the New York Workingmen's Party see Hugins, *Jacksonian Democracy and the Working Class*.

12. See *The Free Enquirer*, November 14, 1829; Beecher's sermon is quoted in Waterman, *Frances Wright*, p. 185.
13. Katz, *Irony of Early School Reform*, part I; Maris A. Vinovskis, The Politics of Educational Reform in Nineteenth-Century Massachusetts: The Controversy Over the Beverly High School in 1860 (Final Report, National Institute of Education, 1980).
14. On Pennsylvania see the state's reports of 1844, 1845, and 1847, as well as James P. Wickersham, *A History of Education in Pennsylvania* (Lancaster, 1885); on Connecticut see Cubberley, *Public Education*, pp. 203–204, and Hendrik D. Gideonse, Common School Reform: Connecticut, 1838–1854 (unpublished Ed.D. dissertation, Harvard University, 1963).
15. For the Rhode Island and Connecticut calculations see Fletcher Swift, *A History of Public School Permanent Common School Funds in the United States, 1795–1905* (New York, 1911), pp. 27–28; for Michigan, Charles Barquist, Common Schooling in the Nineteenth Century: A Quantitative Study of the Determinants of School Attendance in a Michigan County in 1850 (unpublished senior thesis, University of Michigan, 1975), p. 16; for New York, S. S. Randall, *The Common School System of the State of New York* (Tray, 1851), p. 91; Leon Rostker, Michael Frank: The Rise of Free Schools in Wisconsin (unpublished M.A. thesis, University of Wisconsin, 1933), pp. 15–16; Philip White, *Beekmantown, New York: Forest Frontier to Farm Community* (Austin, Texas, 1979), p. 250; the remaining New York State quotations are found in Thomas Finegan, *Free Schools: A Documentary History of the Free School Movement in New York State* (Albany, 1921), pp. 256–262. See also James C. Mohr, "New York State's Free School Law of 1867," *New York Historical Quarterly* 53 (July, 1969); Edwin R. Van Vleeck, The Development of Free Common Schools in New York State: The Campaign to Eliminate the Rate-Bill and to Divert Funds From Sectarian Schools (unpublished Ph.D. dissertation, Yale University, 1937); and Arthur R. Mead, *The Development of Free Schools in the United States as Illustrated by Connecticut and Michigan* (New York, 1918).
16. *Report of the Proceedings and Debates in the Convention to Revise the Constitution of the State of Michigan, 1850* (Lansing, 1850), pp. 263–276, 541–557, 785–791.
17. Kaestle and Vinovskis, *Education and Social Change*, ch. 8.
18. On Whigs and Democrats see Marvin Meyers, *The Jacksonian Persuasion: Politics and Belief* (Stanford, 1960); Daniel Walker

Howe, *The Political Culture of the American Whigs* (Chicago, 1979); Rush Welter, *The Mind of America, 1820–1860* (New York, 1975); Robert Kelley, *The Cultural Pattern in American Politics: The First Century* (New York, 1979), chs. 5 and 6; and Ronald Formisano, *The Birth of Mass Political Parties: Michigan, 1827–1861* (Princeton, 1971).

19. The Rantoul quotations are cited in Meyers, *Jacksonian Persuasion* pp. 218, 224; Bigelow's views are reported in Lee Benson, *The Concept of Jacksonian Democracy: New York as a Test Case* (Princeton, 1961), p. 107.

20. On the politics of education in Connecticut see Gideonse, Common School Reform; for New York see Roscoe Dale LeCount, Jr., The Politics of Public Education: New York State, 1795–1851 (unpublished Ed.D. dissertation, Columbia University, 1971), ch. 2; on Vermont, David M. Ludlum, *Social Ferment in Vermont, 1791–1850* (New York, 1939), p. 231; on Ohio, Eugene Roseboom and Francis Weisenburger, *A History of Ohio* (New York, 1934), ch. 7.

21. Kaestle and Vinovskis, *Education and Social Change*, p. 218; Gideonse, Common School Reform, p. 324.

22. William G. Lewis, *Biography of Samuel Lewis* (Cincinnati, 1887), pp. 174–180.

23. Packard's criticisms of Mann are quoted in Raymond Culver, *Horace Mann and Religion in Massachusetts Public Schools* (New Haven, 1927), pp. 270, 79–80, 56.

24. Wisconsin Teachers' Association, Minutes, MS, box 1, 1853–1870, Wisconsin State Historical Society.

25. The Allen County report is found in the Superintendent of Common Schools, *Annual Report* (1854), p. 154. Ohio education reports are in *Ohio Legislative Documents*. Some of the Massachusetts town reports were published, some were not; they are all found in the vault of the State Library Annex, Boston.

26. Edwin Jocelyn, *The Parents and the Teacher; the Home and the School* (Salem, 1845), p. 12.

27. This argument is made at greater length in Carl F. Kaestle, "Social Change, Discipline, and the Common School in Early Nineteenth-Century America," *Journal of Interdisciplinary History* 9 (Summer 1978), 1–17, upon which the preceding section is based.

28. Constance M. Green, *Holyoke, Massachusetts: A Case History of the Industrial Revolution in America* (New Haven, 1939).

29. Donald B. Cole, *Immigrant City: Lawrence, Massachusetts, 1845–1921* (Chapel Hill, North Carolina, 1963), pp. 23–29; Katherine O'Keefe, *Sketch of Catholicity in Lawrence and Vicinity* (Lawrence, 1882), pp. 9–21; Lawrence annual school reports of 1855 and 1856.

30. Carl F. Kaestle, *The Evolution of an Urban School System: New York City, 1750–1850* (Cambridge, Mass., 1973) pp. 141, 144, 154; Arthur J. Heffernan, *A History of Catholic Education in Connecticut* (Washington, 1937), p. 15; *Western Tablet*, April 3, 1852, quoted in James W. Saunders, *The Education of an Urban Minority: Catholics in Chicago, 1833–1965* (New York, 1977), p. 21.

31. Howard K. Macauley, Jr., A Social and Intellectual History of Elementary Education in Pennsylvania to 1850 (unpublished Ph.D. dissertation, University of Pennsylvania, 1972), p. 312.

32. The Kenosha district school is described in Mary D. Bradford, *Memoirs* (Evansville, Wisconsin, 1932), p. 35; the Pierce County schools in Nils P. Haugen, "Pioneer and Political Reminiscences," *Wisconsin Magazine of History* 11 (December, 1927). See also Susan J. Kuyper, the Americanization of German Immigrants: Language, Religion, and Schools in Nineteenth-Century Rural Wisconsin (unpublished Ph.D. dissertation, University of Wisconsin, 1980); Lloyd P. Jorgenson, *The Founding of Public Education in Wisconsin* (Madison, 1956), pp. 143–149; Ruth Sanding, The Norwegian Element in the Early History of Wisconsin (unpublished M.A. thesis, University of Wisconsin, 1936). I have especially benefited from Jacqueline Jones, Cultural Conflict in Rural Public School Districts: The Case of Wisconsin, 1848–1890 (unpublished seminar paper, University of Wisconsin, 1973).

33. Jones, Cultural Conflict.

34. Ray A. Billington, *The Protestant Crusade, 1800–1860* (New York, 1952).

35. Kaestle, *Evolution of an Urban School System*. See also Diane Ravitch, *The Great School Wars: New York City 1805–1973* (New York, 1974), and Vincent P. Lannie, *Public Money and Parochial Education: Bishop Hughes, Governor Seward, and the New York School Controversy* (Cleveland, 1968).

36. Hughes's remark is in Lawrence Kehoe, ed., *Complete Works of . . . John Hughes* (New York, 1866), vol. 1, pp. 41–43, Brownson's in *Boston Quarterly Review* (October 1839), pp. 406, 413.

37. Pastoral, First Plenary Council (1852) in Neil G. McCluskey, ed., *Catholic Education in America: A Documentary History* (New York, 1964), pp. 78–80; for the Baptists see Charles J. Mahoney, *The Relation of the State to Religious Education in Early New York, 1633–1825* (Washington, 1941); for Hughes's "monopoly" charge, "Address of the Roman Catholics," New York City, *Documents* (1840), no. 20, p. 315; for Spencer's views, Kaestle, *Evolution of an Urban School System*, pp. 149–150.

38. Theodore Sedgwick, in William O. Bourne, *History of the Public School Society of the City of New York* (New York, 1870), pp. 228–229; *Hartford Courant*, April 14, 1853; Horace Bushnell, "Common Schools" (1853), reprinted in his *Building Eras in Religion* (New York, 1881), p. 73.

39. Billington, *Protestant Crusade*, ch. 9; Nancy R. Hamant, "Religion in the Cincinnati Schools, 1830–1900," *Bulletin of the Historical and Philosophical Society of Ohio* 21 (October 1963), 240–241; Horace Bushnell, *Discourse on the Modifications Demanded by the Roman Catholics* (Hartford, 1853), p. 1.

40. *Truth Teller*, e.g., February 15, 1840, cited in Lannie, *Public Money and Parochial Education*, p. 41; on Catholic children in Boston's schools see Per Adam Siljeström, *The Educational Institutions of the United States* (London, 1853), p. 9, for Chicago, Saunders, *Education of an Urban Minority*, p. 12. On the Oswego case see Billington, *Protestant Crusade*, pp. 293, 315n; for the Boston case and the Maine case, Daniel F. Reilly, *The School Controversy, 1891–1893* (Washington, 1944), pp. 18–21. For the establishment of Catholic schools in Massachusetts see Richard J. Quinlan, "Growth and Development of Catholic Education in the Archdiocese of Boston," *The Catholic Historical Review* 22 (1936), 35; in Connecticut, Heffernan, *Catholic Education in Connecticut*, pp. 23–24; for Wisconsin, Harry H. Heming, *The Catholic Church in Wisconsin* (Milwaukee, 1898), pp. 925–927; for Chicago, Saunders, *Education of an Urban Minority*, p. 4; for Pennsylvania, Macauley, Elementary Education in Pennsylvania, p. 514; for Cincinnati, Roseboom, *History of Ohio*, p. 421; for St. Louis and Baltimore, James A. Burns and Bernard J. Kohlbrenner, *A History of Catholic Education in the United States* (New York, 1937), pp. 117–118; the quotation is in *ibid.*, p. 119.

41. Marion M. Wright, *The Education of Negroes in New Jersey*

(New York, 1941), p. 106; the Smith quotation appeared in Tocqueville's *Democracy in America* (1835), cited in Harry C. Silcox, "Delay and Neglect; Negro Public Education in Antebellum Philadelphia," *Pennsylvania Magazine of History and Biography* 97 (October 1973), 444. Arthur O. White, Blacks and Education in Antebellum Massachusetts (unpublished Ed.D. dissertation, State University of New York at Buffalo, 1971), ch. 5.

42. *Northern Star and Freeman's Advocate*, March 17, 1842, quoted in Jane H. and William H. Pease, *They Who Would Be Free: Blacks' Search for Freedom, 1831–1861* (New York, 1974), p. 142. On independent black schools see Carleton Mabee, *Black Education in New York State: From Colonial to Modern Times* (Syracuse, 1979), ch. 4; Frederick McGinnis, *The Education of Negroes in Ohio* (Wilberforce, Ohio, 1962), ch. 6; Wickersham, *History of Education in Pennsylvania*, pp. 253f; Wright, *Education of Negroes in New Jersey*, pp. 114–115.

43. Stanley K. Schultz, *The Culture Factory: Boston Public Schools, 1789–1860* (New York, 1973), ch. 7. The New York teacher's comment is in *The Liberator*, January 4, 1850, cited in Leon F. Litwack, *North of Slavery: The Negro in the Free States, 1790–1860* (Chicago, 1961), p. 136; William Stephenson, "Integration of the Detroit Public School System During the Period 1839–1869," *The Negro History Bulletin* 26 (October 1962); Mabee, *Black Education in New York State*, p. 75.

44. John L. Rury, Education and Black Community Development in Ante-Bellum New York City (unpublished M.A. thesis, City University of New York, 1975).

45. Silcox, "Delay and Neglect," pp. 452, 461.

46. Brown's president is quoted in White, Blacks and Education in Antebellum Massachusetts, p. 280.

47. The details and quotations from the Boston battle are found in White, Blacks and Education in Antebellum Massachusetts; see also Schultz, *Culture Factory*, chs. 7 and 8. The original Fletcher opinion is in Salem School Committee, Minutes, MS, vol. 2, pp. 115f., Salem Public Schools.

48. *The New York Herald* editorial was reprinted in *The Liberator*, May 4, 1855; Superintendent of Public Instruction, *Annual Report* (Harrisburg 1854), p. 17; Superintendent of Common Schools, *Annual Report* (Columbus, 1851), p. 30.

CHAPTER 8

1. Amory D. Mayo, "Education in the Northwest During the First Half Century of the Republic, 1790–1840," *Report of the Commissioner of Education* (Washington, 1896), vol. 2, p. 1543.
2. The Ohio auditor's remark is quoted in Howard C. Taylor, *The Educational Significance of the Early Federal Land Ordinances* (New York, 1922), p. 95; George W. Knight, *History and Management of Land Grants for Education in the Northwestern Territory* (New York, 1885); see also Fletcher H. Swift, *A History of Public Permanent Common School Funds in the United States, 1795–1905* (New York, 1911).
3. Edward Ehlert, *The History of 'Learnin' in Manitowoc County* (Manitowoc, Wisconsin, 1971), p. 1; Mary D. Bradford, *Memoirs* (Evansville, Wisconsin, 1932), p. 26; J. G. Adams, *Sawyer County, Wisconsin* (McIntyre, Iowa, 1902), pp. 31–33; Belle C. Bohn, "Early Wisconsin School Teachers," *Wisconsin Magazine of History* 23 (September 1939), 60; Theodore Boerner, "A Pioneer Educator of Ozaukee County," *Wisconsin Magazine of History* 11 (December 1927), 196; Merle Curti, *The Making of an American Community: A Case Study of Democracy in a Frontier County* (Stanford, 1959), p. 382; Truman O. Douglass, "Platteville in Its First Quarter Century," *Wisconsin Magazine of History* 6 (September 1922), 51–54.
4. Albert Fishlow, "The American Common School Revival: Fact or Fancy?" in Henry Rosovsky, ed., *Industrialization in Two Systems* (New York, 1966), pp. 50–51; Steven L. Schlossman, "Education and Society on the Central Illinois Frontier," unpublished essay prepared in 1976 as part of the research for ch. 2 of Lawrence A. Cremin, *American Education: The National Experience, 1783–1876* (New York, 1980), pp. 13–18.
5. On Ohio's educational history from 1780 to 1860 see James B. Tyler, *A Manual of the Ohio School System* (Cincinnati, 1857); Mayo, "Education in the Midwest . . . 1790–1840," as well as his continuation of the story, which appeared as Amory D. Mayo, "The Development of the Common School in the Western States From 1830 to 1865," in the *Report of the Commissioner of Education* (Washington, 1900), vol. 1, pp. 357–373. See also, of course, the annual reports of the state's Superintendent of Common Schools, beginning in 1838, printed in the *Ohio Legislative*

Documents; and Ohio Teachers' Association, *A History of Education in the State of Ohio* (Columbus, 1876).

6. On Illinois see the Mayo articles cited above, plus John Pulliam, "Changing Attitudes Toward Free Public Schools in Illinois, 1825–1860," *History of Education Quarterly* (Summer 1967), 191–208; Robert G. Bone, "Education in Illinois Before 1857," *Journal of the Illinois State Historical Society* 40 (1957), 119–140; Lawrence A. Cremin, *American Education: The National Experience, 1783–1876* (New York, 1980), pp. 432–440; and the biennial reports of the state's Superintendent of Public Instruction beginning in 1855. On Michigan see the Mayo articles cited above, plus Daniel Putnam, *The Development of Primary and Secondary Education in Michigan* (Ann Arbor, 1904); Charles O. Hoyt and R. C. Ford, *John D. Pierce* (Ypsilanti, 1905); Arthur R. Mead, *The Development of Free Schools in the United States as Illustrated by Connecticut and Michigan* (New York, 1918); Floyd R. Dain, *Education in the Wilderness* (Lansing, 1968); and the annual reports of the Superintendent of Public Instruction beginning in 1837.

7. There is a huge literature on New England and New York influence on the Midwest, examples of which are: Kenneth V. Lottich, "New England Leadership in Ohio Educational Legislation," *Social Science* 31 (1961), 98–106; J. Harold Stevens, "The Influence of New England in Michigan," *Michigan History Magazine* 19 (Autumn 1935), 321–353; and Edward P. Alexander, "Wisconsin, New York's Daughter State," *Wisconsin Magazine of History* 30 (September 1946), 11–30.

8. For Guilford's remark see Emilius O. Randall, *History of Ohio* (New York, 1915), pp. 379–380; for Lewis's see his first annual report (1838) as state superintendent of Ohio.

9. James J. Burns, *Educational History of Ohio* (Columbus, 1905).

10. For Prussian influence in Michigan see James B. Edmonson, *The Legal and Constitutional Basis of a State School System* (Bloomington, Illinois, 1926), ch. 1; Barney's remark is in his 1855 report as state superintendent; the Belleville judge is quoted in Bone, "Education in Illinois," p. 126; and Ira Mayhew's qualms are in his *Compilation from the Annual Reports of the Superintendent of Public Instruction* (Detroit, 1848), p. 148.

11. Edwards's remarks are in his 1855 report as state superintendent; Mayhew's are in his *Compilation*, p. 109.

12. On Grant County see Lloyd J. Jorgenson, *The Founding of Pub-*

lic Education in Wisconsin (Madison, 1956), pp. 41–42; on Macoupin County, Schlossman, "Education and Society on the Central Frontier." The argument that wealth and commerce help account for the North-South bias in Illinois educational development is in Don R. Leet, The Development of a Common School System: A Comparative Analysis: Mississippi and Illinois (unpublished paper, California State University at Fresno, Economics Department, n.d.).

13. The academy estimates are given in Clement Eaton, *The Growth of Southern Civilization, 1790–1860* (New York, 1961), p. 115; see also Edgar W. Knight, *The Academy Movement in the South* (Chapel Hill, 1919). The description of Talladega is in Minnie C. Boyd, *Alabama in the Fifties: A Social Study* (New York, 1931), p. 124. On schools established by religious denominations, see Kimball Templeton, "The Establishment of Church Schools in West Virginia," *West Virginia History* 9 (July 1948), 369–387; Sadie Bell, *The Church, The State, and Education in Virginia* (Philadelphia, 1930); M.C.S. Noble, *A History of the Public Schools of North Carolina* (Chapel Hill, 1930), ch. 3; and Elbert Boogher, *Secondary Education in Georgia, 1732–1858* (Philadelphia, 1933). On the religious content in academies in general, see Bell, *Church, State and Education*, and Charles L. Coon, *North Carolina Schools and Academies, 1790–1840* (Raleigh, 1915), pp. xxxvi–xxxvii.

14. The Goosepond memoir is from Richard M. Johnston, "Early Educational Life in Middle Georgia," in the *Report of the Commissioner of Education* (Washington, 1896) vol. 2, p. 1702; Gilmer's recollections are quoted in Dorothy Orr, *A History of Education in Georgia* (Chapel Hill, 1950), pp. 54–55.

15. On old-field schools that received funds for poor students in Virginia see Roy C. Woods, "A Short History of Education in West Virginia," *West Virginia History* 17 (July 1956), 304–328. The Lunenburg report is in "Second Auditor's Report on the State of the Literary Fund," *Virginia Documents, 1849–50,* document 4 (Richmond, 1850), pp. 65–68. The Greenbriar quote is from "Governor's Letter Transmitting A Statement of the Accounts of the Literary Fund," *Journal of the House of Delegates, 1825–26* (Richmond, 1826), p. 26.

16. Robert W. Eaves, "A History of the Educational Developments of Alexandria, Virginia, Prior to 1860," *William and Mary Quarterly* 16 (April 1936), 122–230; Minerva Turnbull, "Early

Public Schools in Norfolk and its Vicinity," *William and Mary Quarterly* 12 (January 1932), 4–9; "Governor's Letter . . ." *Journal of the House of Delegates* (Richmond, 1824), p. 5; Coon, *North Carolina Schools and Academies*, pp. 441–444, 516; Charles W. Dabney, *Universal Education in the South* (Chapel Hill, 1936), p. 227; Frederick E. Salzillo, Jr., The Economic and Political Foundations of Educational Reform Activity in Georgia, 1830–1840 (unpublished M.A. thesis, Georgia State University, 1973); the antebellum poor-school records of Georgia localities are found in the Georgia State Archives, County Files.

17. See Carter G. Woodson, *The Education of the Negro Prior to 1861*, 2nd ed. (Washington, 1919).

18. On the S.P.G. see John Calam, *Parsons and Pedagogues: The S.P.G. Adventure in American Education* (New York, 1971).

19. Levi Coffin, *Reminiscences of Levi Coffin*, 2nd ed. (Cincinnati, 1880), pp. 69–71.

20. Frederick Douglass, *Narrative of the Life of Frederick Douglass*, (1845, reprinted Cambridge, Mass., 1967), pp. 58–59; Norman R. Yetman, *Life Under the "Peculiar Institution": Selections from the Slave Narrative Collection* (New York, 1970), pp. 140, 259.

21. J. B. O'Neill, "Slave Laws of the South," in J.D.B. DeBow, ed., *Industrial Resources of the Southern and Western States* (Boston, 1852), p. 279; Anne Loveland, *Southern Evangelicals and the Social Order, 1800–1860* (Baton Rouge, 1980), pp. 232–233; Yetman, *Life Under the "Peculiar Institution,"* p. 189.

22. Thomas Webber, *Deep Like the Rivers: Education in the Slave Quarter Community, 1831–1865* (New York, 1978), p. 152 and *passim*. See also John W. Blassingame, *The Slave Community* (New York, rev. ed., 1979).

23. Jefferson's remark was in a letter to Joel Barlow, December 10, 1807, quoted in Henry E. May, *The Enlightenment in America* (New York, 1976), p. 312. On Jefferson's opposition to the Mercer bill, see Dabney, *Universal Education*, pp. 37–40, and David E. Swift, "Thomas Jefferson, John Holt Rice and Education in Virginia, 1815–1825," *Journal of Presbyterian History* 49 (Spring 1971), 32–58.

24. Tyler's remarks are in the "Governor's Message," *Journal of the House Delegates* (Richmond, 1826) and the committee's in "Report of the Committee of Schools and Colleges," in *ibid*. In

Benjamin Smith's "Report on the Prussian School System," document 26 in *Journal of the House of Delegates* (Richmond, 1839), see especially pp. 3–5, 22–23. The house of delegate's lukewarm position on reform in 1841 is found in "Report of the Committee of Schools and Colleges," document 34, *Journal of the House of Delegates* (Richmond, 1842), and the second auditor's negative response is in his "Report," document 4, *Journal of the House of Delegates* (Richmond, 1843).

25. The reformers' cries are quoted from the Secretary of State's 1845 report, cited in Turnbull, "Early Public Schools in Norfolk," p. 4; and the "Report of the Committee" of 1841–42 cited above. On the implementation of the laws of the late 1840s, see William A. Maddox, *The Free School Idea in Virginia Before the Civil War* (New York, 1918), pp. 163–166 and B. S. Morgan and J. F. Cork, *History of Education in West Virginia* (Charleston, 1893), pp. 12–16. The Harrison County commissioners are quoted in the "Second Auditor's Report," document 4, *Journal of the House of Delegates* (Richmond, 1846), pp. 31–32.

26. On Georgia's early educational legislation see Amory D. Mayo, "The American Common School in the Southern States During the First Half Century of the Republic, 1790–1840," *Report of the Commissioner of Education for the Year 1895–1896* (Washington, 1897), pp. 295–307; and Swift, *Common School Funds*. For Georgia's subsequent educational history to 1860 see Salzillo, Educational Reform Activity in Georgia; Orr, *History of Education in Georgia*; Forest David Matthews, The Politics of Education in the Deep South: Georgia and Alabama, 1820–1860 (unpublished Ph.D. thesis, Teachers College, 1965); and Milton Heath, *Constructive Liberalism: The Role of the State in Economic Development in Georgia to 1860* (Cambridge, Mass., 1954), pp. 338–350. See also *Report on Public Education, by Mr. Lewis of Hancock* (Milledgeville, 1860).

27. The description of Lincolnton is quoted in Guion G. Johnson, *Antebellum North Carolina: A Social History* (Chapel Hill, 1937), p. 273. On North Carolina's educational history from 1780 to 1860 see M.C.S. Noble, *A History of Public Schools in North Carolina* (Chapel Hill, 1930); Charles L. Coon, ed., *The Beginnings of Public Education in North Carolina: A Documentary History* (Raleigh, 1908); Charles L. Coon, ed., *North*

Carolina Schools and Academies, 1790–1840 (Raleigh, 1915); and Edgar G. Knight, *Public School Education in North Carolina* (Boston, 1916).

28. On charity schools in Charleston see Colyer Meriwether, *Higher Education in South Carolina* (Washington, 1888), pp. 116–117; for Nashville, Francis G. Davenport, *Cultural Life in Nashville on the Eve of the Civil War* (Chapel Hill, 1941), ch. 2.

29. Elliott and Thornwall's advice is cited in Meriwether, *Higher Education in South Carolina*, p. 113; the Ruffner quotation is in his "Proposed Plan for the Organization and Support of Common Schools in Virginia," document 35, *Journal of the House of Delegates* (Richmond, 1842), pp. 1–2; the Nansemond County comment is in the "Second Auditor's Report," document 4, *Virginia Documents* (Richmond, 1853), p. 54.

30. The human capital argument is made in Douglass C. North, *The Economic Growth of the United States 1790–1860* (New York, 1961), p. 133.

31. Harry Hughes, *A Treatise on Sociology* (1854), excerpted in Eric L. McKitrick, ed., *Slavery Defended: The Views of the Old South* (Englewood Cliffs, New Jersey, 1963), p. 54; Edmund Ruffin, *The Political Economy of Slavery* (1853), in *ibid.*, p. 80. On the complexities of pro-slavery arguments see Drew Gilpin Faust, ed., *The Ideology of Slavery: Proslavery Thought in the Antebellum South, 1830–1860* (Baton Rouge, 1981) and James Oakes, *The Ruling Race: A History of American Slaveholders* (New York, 1982).

32. The Hamlet metaphor is quoted from "Memorial of the Trustees of the Southern Female Institute at Fredericksburg," document 29, *Virginia Documents* (Richmond, 1851), pp. 6–7.

33. Frederick Law Olmstead, *A Journey to the Back Country* (New York, 1860), pp. 116–117; William Harper, "Memoir on Slavery," in DeBow, *Industrial Resources*, pp. 217–221; "Agrarian Education Systems," *Southern Review* 6 (1828), 16; *DeBow's Review*, vol. 20 (February 1856), 149.

34. *Southern Recorder*, December 18, 1860, cited in Donald A. DeBats, Elites and Masses: Political Structure, Communication and Behavior in Ante-Bellum Georgia (unpublished Ph.D. thesis, University of Wisconsin, 1973), p. 307; George M. Frederickson, *The Black Image in the White Mind* (New York, 1971), p. 69.

256 / Notes

35. The Tennessee quotation is found in Charles S. Sydnor, *The Development of Southern Sectionalism, 1819–1848* (Baton Rouge, 1948), pp. 62–63; see also *ibid.*, pp. 276–279.

36. Charles H. Ambler, *Sectionalism in Virginia from 1776 to 1861* (Chicago, 1910), pp. 170–171; David Campbell, "Governor's Message," *Journal of the House of Delegates* (Richmond, 1839), p. 3; for the complaints from county officials see the "Second Auditor's Report" in the *Journal of the House of Delegates* for both 1840 and 1841. Alexander Campbell's speech is found in the records of the "Education Convention of Northwestern Virginia," document 7, *Journal of the House of Delegates* (Richmond, 1842), p. 40; *Wheeling Intelligencer*, May 3, 1860, cited in Ambler, *Sectionalism in Virginia*, p. 282.

37. Salzillo, Educational Reform Activity in Georgia, pp. 107–112; DeBats, Elites and Masses, pp. 297–299.

38. The *Western Carolinian* quotation is from Guion G. Johnson, *Ante-Bellum North Carolina: A Social History* (Chapel Hill, 1937), p. 35.

39. Calvin Wiley, "History of the Common Schools of North Carolina," quoted in Edgar Knight, *Public School Education in North Carolina* (Boston, 1916), p. 147.

40. [Dr. S. Cartwright], "The Education, Labor and Wealth of the South," *DeBow's Review* 7 (September 1859), 263–279. James Mason's speech of February 1, 1859 is quoted in John S. Ezell, "A Southern Education for Southrons," *Journal of Southern History* 17 (August 1951), 324.

41. Superintendent of Public Instruction, *Report* for 1857, quoted in Robert C. Reinders, "New England Influences on the Formation of Public Schools in New Orleans," *Journal of Southern History* 30 (May 1964), 193; the Memphis quotation is given in Avery O. Craven, *The Growth of Southern Nationalism, 1848–1861* (Baton Rouge, 1953), p. 255; *Kanawha Valley Star*, July 12, 1859, in Ambler, *Sectionalism*, p. 281; the Knoxville and Georgia quotations are from *DeBow's Review* and are reprinted, along with other complaints about Northern textbooks, in Edgar Knight, ed., *A Documentary History of Education in the South Before 1860* (Chapel Hill, 1950), ch. 3. The DeBow quote is cited in Ezell, "Southrons," p. 309. See also William R. Taylor, "Toward a Definition of Orthodoxy: The Patrician South and the Common School," *Harvard Educational Review* 36 (Fall 1966), 412–426.

42. C. K. Marshall, in Ezell, "Southrons," p. 313; "An Alumnus," in the *North Carolina Standard*, September 29, 1856, reprinted in Knight, *Documentary History*, p. 299.

43. Davis's remark is found in Henry S. Commager, *Noah Webster's American Spelling Book* (New York, 1962), p. 5; Gilmer's is in Clement Eaton, *The Freedom-of-Thought Struggle in the Old South*, rev. ed. (New York, 1964), p. 231, and the Davidson College address in Noble, *Public Schools of North Carolina*, p. 241.

44. On Rice see Dabney, *Universal Education*, pp. 68, 443–444. Henry Ruffner to Horace Mann, August 13, 1848, in Knight, *Documentary History*, p. 349; and Edmund Jackson in *The Liberator*, May 6, 1853, quoted in Arthur O. White, Blacks and Education in Antebellum Massachusetts (unpublished Ed.D. dissertation, State University of New York at Buffalo, 1971), p. 252.

Index

End-notes included in the index contain references to basic secondary readings on particular topics.